CyberCities

Visual Perception in the Age of Electronic Communication

M. Christine Boyer

Princeton Architectural Press

Published by
Princeton Architectural Press
37 East 7th Street
New York, New York 10003
(212) 995-9620

99 98 97 96   4 3 2 1

Printed and bound in the United States
Editing by Caroline Green
Design by Allison Saltzman

Library of Congress Cataloging-in-Publication Data
Boyer, M. Christine.
CyberCities: visual perception in the age of
electronic communication / by M. Christine Boyer.
p. cm.
Includes bibliographical references.
ISBN 1-56898-048-5
1. Computers and civilization.
2. Telecommunication.
3. Virtual reality.
I. Title.
QA76.9.C66B69   1995
720' .1'05--dc20
95-25746 CIP

For a free catalog of other books
published by Princeton Architectural Press,
call (212) 995-9620

Visit Princeton Architectural Press on the Web
http://www.designsys.com/pap.

Contents

5 Introduction

13 The Imaginary Real World of CyberCities

45 Labyrinths of the Mind and the City—Real and Virtual

73 Disenchantment of the City: An Improbable Dialogue between Bodies, Machines, and Urban Form

137 Imaging the City in the Age of Electronic Communication

183 Electronic Disruptions and Black Holes of the City: The Issues of Gender and Urbanism in the Age of Electronic Communication

241 Conclusion

INTRODUCTION

Οταν πιγαινεζ, εγω ερχομονα

Loosely translated: on your way there, you met me returning

O nce upon a time there were two modest IBM offices in Technology Square, one containing a systems support team, and the other a software group. On the top floor of the building in which they were located—a structure that resembled an IBM punch card—the guru Marvin Minsky and Project MAC (Man-Assisted Computer) were trying to build models of thought out of symbolic processes embedded within computer programs. Nicholas Negroponte was located in the IBM support office (or, at least, visited often) and would eventually spend years of "inventing new systems for computer graphics, human communication, and interactive multimedia."[1] On the lowest floor, George Lakoff was part of an IBM team exploring the possibility of language-like software based on generative grammars and recursive rules. Perhaps it should be mentioned that across from this office, Roman Jakobson was writing his memoirs. Although today it is necessary to make distinctions, in those early days of mainframe computer history there was constant trafficking between the floors that produced a heady mixture of cognitive science, structural linguistics, symbolic logic, metamathematics, and pattern languages. This is a strange story, one that if told in detail would involve the last thirty years' development of software languages, operating systems, and artificial intelligence, not to mention technological advances in microprocessors. Today, if we take a bird's eye view over the terrain, we find Marvin Minsky exploring how computers might eventually be manipulated by thought, if a small cerebral interface could be tapped, thus allowing the contents of a person's mind to be downloaded into the computer.[2] And we find Negroponte, the director of the Massachusetts Institute of Technology Media Lab, exploring the futuristic world of what "being digital means to your life," arguing that "computing is not about computers anymore. It is about living."[3] Lakoff, the author of such wondrous books as *Women, Fire, and Dangerous Things: What Categories Reveal about the Mind*, now belongs to a group of cognitive linguists who advocate a conceptualist analysis of language stressing that both metaphor and analogy, plus the mental models that speakers build, hold a role in shaping language and determining meaning.[4]

Perhaps this series of essays is an attempt to rejoin this gang of three by the same door through which I exited many years ago. At that time, the spectre of war seemed to be swirling around this vortex of computational theories. Whether it was the funding that inevitably stemmed from the Defense Department's Advanced Research Projects Agency (DARPA)—or the brutal fact that American urban ghettos in cities such as Detroit, Los Angeles, and Newark were erupting in flames of anger and rage, while the Vietnam War heated up and urban renewal and I-95 highway projects kept plundering their way through viable communities—something seemed to be missing from the cool abstractions and symbolic processes of computational theory.

Today there are different issues to be raised, but both the inheritance of violence that technology breeds and the decline of reality as a serious referent still have to be addressed.[5] As mainframes have been transformed into personal computers and personal computers transform into laptops that dramatically reduce in size and weight with each year's new model, computers have in fact become a way of life for some of the world, a life that has bred its own form of transcendental utopianism. Indeed, it is now being argued that being released from reality and all of its messy and uncontrollable chaos enables the virtual to recover reality, even while, paradoxically, it implicates a withdrawal from it.[6]

In his essay "The Author as Producer,"[7] Walter Benjamin noted that the information technologies of his day—the newspaper, the periodical, and the illustrated magazine—no longer allowed a contemplative reception of information. The format of their pages, with texts laid out in columns of disparate narrations and juxtaposed to illustrations, required the reader to develop a new set of interpretative processes for selecting, connecting subordinating, and comparing items taken from a set of fragmented data. Thus the newspaper represented a matrix of knowledge, the recombination of which determined the amount and kind of information a given reader would receive.[8] With electronic data-processing technology, the rapid dispersions and regroupings of textual fragments can be made on demand from a prescribed set of keywords with which readers define their interests. As Negroponte describes, we can now use computers to "filter, sort, prioritize, and manage multimedia on our behalf—computers that read newspapers, and look at television for us, and act as editors when we ask them to do so."[9] Obviously we have to develop new modes of perception that enable us to navigate between, to explore and question, the framework of pre-digested and pre-selected nodes of data that represent highly mediated forms of communication delivered over centerless, network-like electronic structures often called the space of flows.[10]

Negroponte argues that we have achieved the benefits of being digital because "over the past fifteen years, we have learned how to compress the raw digital form of sound and picture by looking at the bits over time, space, or both and removing the intrinsic redundancies and repetitions."[11] It is the reduction, the removal of the bits—the data compressions and error corrections—that we must perceive and question. Most of these indirect forms of communication involve images, not language; in fact, images seem to have eclipsed the need for language in our digital machines, for images are a speedier and more efficient means of imparting information. When all media becomes digital, Negroponte claims, bits get mixed up and turn into multimedia. This produces a new bit about bits which is called a header, and it allows information to be delivered on demand. A few examples of headers are the well-known openers at the top of newspaper columns, key words, tables of contents, and the notational marks that enable us to choose between songs on a music compact disc.[12] But here again we have to learn what it means to receive and digest, as a constant diet, images and information that have been constructed by headers or that have not been mediated by us, yet that provide a predigested or configured world view. How do we explore this digital box of fragments that pastes together disjunctive arrays of images and sets of data into a seemingly continuous display?

This series of essays begins to question the issue of willful agency—the matter of choice and control—over the construction and content of electronic communications. It recognizes the need to develop new modes of perception with which to receive, absorb, criticize, and produce new combinations of information. It examines the implications that the disappearance of reality as a referent and that the rise of the virtual entail. Negroponte claims that "…the world, as we experience it, is a very analog place. From a macroscopic point of view, it is not digital at all but continuous. Nothing goes suddenly on or off, turns from black to white, or changes from one state to another without going through a transition."[13] The essays included here take issue with this assumption of a space of transition, for more and more we seem to experience the world as if framed by a digital box with binary on/off choices and disjunctions, with combinatorial lists and arrays, with encoded video games and program languages. If we draw an analogy between the computer matrix of data management and the city, then it is precisely the spaces of disjunction between the rows and columns of the data entries that represent the forgotten spaces, the disavowed places, and the bits eradicated because of the noise and redundancy they generate. The form of the matrix brings to the city a systemic order that hides its heterogeneous nature and the disjunctive positions we hold within it. Paradoxically, while the analogy allows for the discussion of the disappearance of the city from our postmodern social and cultural agendas, the very immateriality of this electronic matrix and the world of virtual reality that it projects defies the grounding of that analogy. And it is exactly this crossroads that I shall explore: both the analogy between the computer matrix and the space of the city, and the moment of withdrawal or disappearance from the excesses of reality into the cybernetic representations of the virtual world of computers.[14]

Finally, these essays are themselves examples of associative thinking: they are disjunctive assemblages utilizing strategies of analogy, metaphorical associations, and circumlocutions that juxtapose unexpected subjects in an attempt to make suggestive connections. There is a logic of displacement and delay at play—from computers to the city and back— that is not a progressive, cause-and-effect, rational argumentation arriving at a final conclusion. Instead—as electronic communication allows—we dance with data, enjoying recursive reflexivity, strange loops, and nonlinear inconclusive structures.

There are also a few basic assumptions that run through this collection of essays. First of all, it is assumed that the machine is to modernism what the computer is to postmodernism. But while we can draw connections between the machine and art, architecture, or the city, the computer has immaterial effects—after all, its memory bank is a matrix of electronic pulses. Yet both the machine and the computer affect the way we think, imagine, and organize information. From the Futurists' use of the machine metaphor as a dynamic model for integrative totalization and functional harmonization to the Boolean search logic of the computer age with its binary logic of and/or command structures, scanning techniques, information stacks, and data interfaces, machines and now computers guide the way we model the world and grasp reality—and by analogy, the way we form or pattern the city.

At least, the city was the major focus of modernism, although now—and this is the second assumption—it appears to be disappearing from critical debate. It is hard to imagine any discussion of the modern movement that is not grounded in some aspect of metropolitan existence: from Otto Wagner, who helped to plan and build the new railway system for metropolitan Vienna at the beginning of the twentieth century, to Le Corbusier and his plans for Paris, Rio de Janeiro, Algiers, or Chandigarh, to the 1950s and 1960s problems of urban renewal and revitalization, the city was the underlying force or deep structural issue behind the discourse on modernism. But here I tend to agree with William Gibson, who decided even before writing *Neuromancer* that what was happening in the space behind the video screen was more interesting than what was happening in the space in front of it—in other words, that cyberspace pulls the user into the receding space of the electronic matrix in total withdrawal from the world. Thus our critical engagement with the city is, at best, action at a distance.

The third assumption is that the specifics of time, space, and architecture that Sigfried Giedion discussed in the early 1940s have been condensed or eradicated by our instantaneous modes of telecommunications, telemarketing, telepresence, and telesurveillance. Here all our bodily senses seem to get transferred to, plugged into, or downloaded into machines, as our body parts become simple emitters and receivers of information stimuli in a sensorial feedback loop that links our senses of sight, touch, smell, and hearing to information flowing through computer data banks and simulation programs. Reality is increasingly immaterial, and our modes of travel become static terminal transmissions. Meanwhile, the contemporary city stands with all of its gaping wounds as crime escalates, megacities erupt, blood continues to spill, disease accelerates, and unemployment and undereducation continue. We experience this global urban disruption instantaneously and continuously with every telecasted news report, yet we remain incapable of immediate action, frozen in front of our computer terminals. This is a critical issue that city planning and architecture must question—although we may not have the means to solve it, for our postmodern era appears to be decadent and devoid of social responsibility.

1   Nicholas Negroponte, *Being Digital* (New York: Alfred A. Knopf, 1995), 7.

2   Klaus Bartels, "The Box of Digital Images: The World as Computer Theater," *Diogenes* 41, no. 3 (1993): 45–70.

3   Negroponte, *Being Digital*, 6–7.

4   George Lakoff, *Women, Fire, and Dangerous Things: What Categories Reveal about the Mind* (Chicago: The University of Chicago Press, 1987).

5   Michael Heim, *The Metaphysics of Virtual Reality* (New York: Oxford University Press, 1993), 117–118, 131.

6   These are claims that virtual world advocates such as Benjamin Wolley and Brenda Laurel make. See Akira Mizuta Lippit, "Virtual Annihilation: Optics, VR, and the Discourse of Subjectivity," *Criticism* 36, no. 4 (1994): 595–596.

7   Walter Benjamin, *Reflections*, trans. Edmund Jephcott (New York: Schocken Books, 1978), 224–225.

8   David Herman, "Postmodernism as Secondary Grammar," *Boundary* 2/20, no. 2 (1993): unpaginated.

9   Negroponte, *Being Digital*, 20.

10   Manuel Castells, "The Space of Flows," Chap. 7 in *The Net and the Self: Economy, Society, and Culture in the Information Age* (Oxford: Basil Blackwell, forthcoming 1997).

11   Negroponte, *Being Digital*, 16.

12   Ibid., 19.

13   Ibid., 15.

14   Albert Moreiras, "The Leap and the Lapse: Hacking a Private Site in Cyberspace," in *Rethinking Technologies*, ed. Verena Adnermatt Conley (Minneapolis: University of Michigan Press, 1993), 196.

The human mind works by association.

THE IMAGINARY REAL WORLD
OF CYBERCITIES

So why don't computers?

F rom the moment William Gibson announced in his dystopian science-fiction account *Neuromancer* (1984) that the new informational network or computer matrix called cyberspace looks like Los Angeles seen from five thousand feet up in the air,[1] there has been a predilection for drawing a parallel between the virtual space of computer networks and post-urban places of disorder and decay. Cyberspace has also been called a huge megalopolis without a center, both a city of sprawl and an urban jungle.[2] What do these comparisons and analogies really express? This unwieldy mixture of urban dystopia and cyberspace—here called CyberCities—turns the reality of time and place into an imaginary matrix of computer nets electronically linking together distant places around the globe and communicating multilinearly and nonsequentially with vast assemblages of information stored as electronic codes. What does it mean that this electronic imagery generates a unique mental ordering that seems to parallel, not represent, reality? What significant effects result from the fact that textual universes of postmodern accounts conjure up fictional worlds that disavow any link with material reality, any connectivity with a shared community? It is as an attempt to answer these questions of the imaginary real world of information, to search for the meaning of CyberCities affected by the logic of computers and cyberspace, that this account is offered.

In the mental geography of architectural theorists, an affinity between science-fiction narratives and contemporary cities is often expressed,[3] and it involves speculating on how the possible worlds of artificial intelligence and cyberspace might affect the material reality of design, conceptual models of space, and architectural or urban intuitions. Much of this theory either assumes implicitly or states explicitly that a profound mutation has taken place, one that effects a transformation from the machine city of modernism to the informational city of postmodernism. This transformation, it is said, replaces the traditional western space of geometry, work, the road, the building, and the machine with new forms of diagramming, bar graphs, spreadsheets, matrices, and networks expressive of "a new etherealization of geography" in which the principles of ordinary space and time are altered beyond recognition.[4] This matrix is a metaspace or hyperspace superimposed above the level of reality—a space in which reality is transferred from the screen to the memory bank, to the video disk, to imaginary networks. Or perhaps a better analogy of the computer matrix of disrupted space and time is the audio-visual jumps and leaps that are achieved by viewers of cable television when, remote control in hand, they flip through an array of television programs to experience disparate blank spaces, arbitrary sound bites, and fragmented images that never coalesce into a single knowable order.

If a transformation from the machine to the computer has taken place, even if it affects only the imaginary, then we need to question what has been transformed and what these changes rearrange with respect to architecture in the city, for the imaginary and the artistic are closely aligned. As one cyberspace advocate reminds us, technological and artistic fascination are linked: "With an electronic infrastructure, the dream of perfect FORMS becomes the dream of inFORMation....Filtered through the computer matrix, all reality becomes patterns of information....Further, the erotic-generative source of formal idealism becomes subject to the laws of information management."[5] Consequently, the absorption of architectural theory and architectural fascination into the language of computers (and I am not referring to CAD systems here, but rather to the theory of information science and all the science fiction it seems to conjure up) may be founded on a categorical paradox: one side of the equation in CyberCity is immaterial, while the other remains material; one side of the analogy is about the construction of information networks, the other about the construction of space. Perhaps this confusion undermines many of our postmodern architectural theories as they apply themselves to architecture in the city.

THE MACHINE CITY

Both the machine of the Machine City and the computer of
CyberCity are metaphors that become ingrained in the way we represent and imagine (or have represented and imagined) the modern
and postmodern city. It is easy to see the metaphors of the Machine
City as being linked to representations of and reflecting attitudes
towards modernity and the metropolis at the turn of the twentieth
century. Calvin Coolidge seemed to encapsulate the idolatry of the
machine age when he proclaimed, "The man who builds a factory
builds a temple. The man who works there worships there."[6]

   The metropolis in the early twentieth century was believed to
be an inorganic and fabricated environment, produced by mathematics and created by the engineer. Thus we find, for example,
Ludwig Meidner in "Directions for Painting Images of the
Metropolis" advising the artist to pay attention to "tumultuous
streets, the elegance of iron suspension bridges, the gasometers…
the howling colors of the autobuses and express locomotives, the
rolling telephone wires, the harlequinade of the advertisement pil-
lars…"[7] And it would not be long before the dynamics of motion
in the big city, and the ability to create picture-poems by visually
juxtaposing an array of disparate items such as graphics, musical
rhythms, typography, and photography, were captured by one of
the machines of the twentieth century: the movie camera. László
Moholy-Nagy explained in his fourteen-page film script of
Dynamics of the Metropolis (1921–1922) that there were to be shots of
the city's construction sites from below, from above, and from
revolving cranes, as well as shots that set up the dynamic tempo of
the city by filming from racing automobiles and moving trains and
by capturing the flashing letters of electric advertisements.
Although Moholy-Nagy's script was never produced, it seems to
have reached fruition in William Ruttmann's film *Berlin: A
Symphony of the City* (1927). Ruttmann's film chronologically documents one day in Berlin, focusing on the area around Potsdamer
Platz. This space has been fragmented into many images, and

orchestrated like a musical score by utilizing the different rhythms and tempos of machines and men. Views of construction sites, playing fields, restaurants, kitchens, streets, and street facades are clustered into sets and organized by the repetition of images of clocks. The camera's eye is able to capture the time and space of ordinary vision and transform it into the abstract patterns of graphically- and temporally-related objects and processes.[8]

The machine city of modernism also embodied a darker side: the mechanisms of discipline and the architectural spaces of enclosure, such as the asylum, the prison, the factory, the school, and the family—spaces which Michel Foucault has so brilliantly described.[9] Discipline, or the self-construction of the individual, became an efficacious instrument of power deployed by these spaces of enclosure. Here the acts of comparing, contrasting, and categorizing were organizational relations supporting new disciplinary procedures, for the individual was constantly forced to compare himself to the established norm, and these acts of contrast and comparison determined the range of deviations and diversions to be brought under control. Thus the machine-like norm established control over an individual without any overt reference to a sovereign's might.[10]

We can certainly extend the analogy of disciplinary control to the Machine City, for disciplinary control proceeds by distributing bodies/uses in space, allocating each individual/function to a cellular partition, creating an efficient machine out of its analytical spatial arrangement. In becoming a target of disciplinary control, the city offered up new forms of knowledge: its disciplinary methodologies came to describe an anatomy of detail. An ideal architectural model was conceived to house this disciplinary system, not simply for ceremonial purposes from which the power of the sovereign state could be deduced, but one which would allow disciplinary surveillance to operate continuously. A network of urban observatories bent the space of the city to a set of norms that both established the line of horizontal and comparative vision and surveyed the movement of each individual and every cellular space. Thus the process of city planning arose at the end of the nineteenth century.[11]

CyberCities

Gilles Deleuze has recently suggested that Michel Foucault's spaces of enclosure are increasingly strained.[12] Thus the family, the factory, the school, the de-industrialized city, and certainly the process of city planning are in various stages of dissolution, reflective of the disciplinary breakdown that CyberCities entail. So, Deleuze maintains, disciplinary societies that molded behavior are being replaced by numerical societies of modulating control facilitated by computer technology. We have evolved from using machines of production that require a disciplined labor force and an efficiently planned and organized city to inhabiting what is known as a space of flows defined by global networks of computers—a free-floating membrane of connectivity and control encircling the globe in ultra-rapid fashion and enabling a new economic order of multinational corporations to arise. In this new order, control acts like a sieve (a computer matrix) whose mesh transmutes from point to point, undulating and constantly at work. The code, not the norm, becomes the important device; now it is the password, not the watchword, that provides or inhibits access.

In addition, the emergence of the multinational corporation brings into play a marketplace mentality of competition, conquering through colonization, specialization, and the deformable and transformable decisions that computer tracking allows. A market mentality of short-term advantages and high turnover rates overtakes any long-range or continuous planning endeavors. In computer-led societies, jamming, viruses, piracy, and corruption replace the machine-age dangers of entropy and sabotage. If we accept Deleuze's description, we are at the beginning of the socio-technological revolutions and dispersed systems of domination that accompany societies of control.

It is curious that while CyberCities narrate the dematerialization of physical space and chronological time, space has become a dominant issue within postmodern criticism. Edward Soja in *Postmodern Geographies* argues that the nineteenth century's affair with progress valued time over space, allowing the latter to hide things from us, to be used as a veil drawn over the surface.[13] And David Harvey in *The Condition of Postmodernity* talks about space-time compressions creating crises of representation: he allows that each revolution in communication technology caused an annihilation of space by time, and produced a crisis of representation in its wake.[14] Fredric Jameson notes in *Postmodernism, or, the Cultural Logic of Late Capitalism* that the cultural conditions of postmodernity have created the need for cognitive maps to link our ideological positions with our imaginations, and hence they enable social transformations to take place.[15]

In all three accounts, the postmodern body is surrounded and bombarded with incoherent fragments of space and time, for in CyberCity we seem to be continuously in motion—be it driving the freeways, shopping at the mall, or pushing carts through supermarket aisles. It has been argued that electronic telecommunications have reformulated our perception of space and time, so that we experience a loss of spatial boundaries or distinctions, so that all spaces begin to look alike and implode into a continuum, while time has been reduced to obsessive and compulsive repetitions. The result is an inability to map our contemporary terrain, to envision space and representational forms, and thus to weave things together, to conclude, to be able to act.

As controlled and disciplined spaces of modernist enclosure seem to be increasingly in crisis, there has occurred in tandem a massive restructuring of our perception of space and time, so that we now espouse the nonlinear vision of a computer matrix full of ruptures, breaks, and discontinuities. Might our postmodern fixation on shifting positions in space and time and our common pronouncements of the invisible or disappearing city hide deeper anxieties and ambivalent negations within the metropolitan core? At the same moment when computational connectivity holds out the promise of non-hierarchical, multi-centered, open-ended forms defining a "new community," voices from other times and different spaces are beginning to emerge and disturb the supposed unity. Is the gesture of electronic connectivity more than simply an attempt to contain contested terrains and to absorb excluded parts, thus allowing the whole to reorganize without challenging its fundamental assumptions?

There are other issues to be raised in relation to the computer matrix as unifier. As Michael Hein claims in "The Erotic Ontology of Cyberspace," the matrix or computer network holds out a promise of connectivity that reality denies, since the technologies of networking though on-line communication, e-mail, or newsgroups offer each unit at his terminal a way to counter urban isolation and alienation. Even though "new communities" are formed, Hein does acknowledge that there is a dark side to networking: it operates through stand-ins of ourselves, representations in which we can lose our humanity or hide our identity, and it may inspire an amoral indifference to human relations. "As on-line culture grows geometrically, the sense of community diminishes."[16] Of course, human unity and community are totalizations lying along the major conceptual fault lines that CyberCities display.

Lag-Time Places

In the late twentieth century, unknown and threatening territories lie inside the boundaries of the metropolis, where there are many lag-times, temporal breaks in the imaginary matrix, and areas of forced delay put on hold in the process of postmodernization.[17] These partitions, cuts, and interruptions in the urban imaginary allow us to deny our complicity in the making of distinctions between the well-designed nodes of the matrix and the blank, in-between places of nobody's concern. Disavowed, overlooked, marginalized, left out of our accounts, these are the center's truly invisible spaces—the inexpressible, the incomplete, the unattended—that have been rendered absent and forgotten.[18]

To attest to these lag-times and spatial gaps within our metropolitan narrations, we have only to turn to the *New York Times*:

To visit Mott Haven [a neighborhood of some fifty thousand people in the area of East 138th Street]—and there are Mott Havens in most large American cities these days—is to discover a world apart. Here, poverty cuts deeper than the lack of money, the lack of health care, the abundance of drugs. This gray place is largely bereft of many of the threads that knit other very poor neighborhoods together: strong tenant organization, powerful community groups, charismatic leadership, even a safe playground. The strongest neighborhood bind is its struggle with hardship. "We're like the forgotten city."[19]

Jose Delgado lingered at the doorstep of a decaying South Bronx apartment building last week watching Mayor David N. Dinkins promise millions of dollars in development projects. After a while the politicians dispersed. The television cameras were packed up. The onlookers dribbled away. But Mr. Delgado remains, as he always does…."Every time they want to be elected they come here," said the forty-one-year-old building superintendent. "They say they are going to do things to fix the neighborhood, but it's been like this since 1972."[20]

These narrations—and there are numerous others—reveal how the imaginary matrix performs spatial and temporal disjunctions that enable us to think of city centers as if they were naturally bipolar places of uneven development, rather than effects of a willful dismemberment that place certain lives and locations outside of, and only sometimes beside, the main events of contemporary cities.[21] It is this splitting that the binary logic of the computer matrix allows us to achieve with relative ease. Such an arrangement, for example, provides Paul Virilio with his images of the disappearing city where constructed geographical space has been replaced by chronological topographies, where immaterial electronic broadcast emissions decompose and eradicate a sense of place. Virilio's city has lost its form except as a connector point or airport, or as a membrane or computer terminal; it has become a two-dimensional flatland in which the city can disappear. Virilio's position is overdetermined by the binary coding and switching logic of computer technology: the logical +/-, 0/1, on/off of electronic pulses, and hence the appearance/disappearance of the city. But this architectural theory ignores our involvement in the shaping of space, in the production of lag-time places and temporal disjunction.

Smart Computers and Agoric Systems

The logic of computers engenders more than just binary modes of thought, for within connectionist systems or network models there is also an interest in the capacity of machines to learn. Computer learning consists of the shifting of internal connections or linkages (that is, the production of new representations) between units distributed throughout the network as they interact with the world or context and adapt to patterns that the world or context presents.[22] Moreover, "the goal is to develop computer-implemented rule systems that can replicate aspects of the reasoning of humans who perform the function in an expert fashion." Such rules, usually obtained through interviews, are then encoded in a computer program.[23]

Returning to the agoristics of Deleuze's societies of control, Manuel De Landa explains in *War in the Age of Intelligent Machines* that the decentralization of intelligent computer networks around the globe introduces a problematic paradox, since these networks spawn "independent software objects" known as "demons" which may lie beyond the network's control. De Landa proclaims that these demons operating within the membrane of global networks are already displaying a tendency to form societies that resemble insect communities or economic markets:

> Independent software objects [or demons] will soon begin to constitute even more complex computational societies in which demons trade with one another, bid and compete for resources, seed and

spawn processes spontaneously, and so on. The biosphere…is preg-
nant with singularities that spontaneously give rise to processes of
self-organization. Similarly, the portion of the "mechanosphere" constituted by computer networks, once it has crossed a certain critical
point of connectivity, begins to be inhabited by symmetry-breaking
singularities, which give rise to emergent properties in the system.
These systems can "encourage the development of intelligent (software) objects, but there is a sense in which these systems themselves
will be intelligent."[24]

In this scenario, the agoric market-like computer system takes
on a life of its own, trapping us within a giant machine from which
we cannot escape—a fear exploited by the best and worst of science
fiction. Or, expressive of yet another postmodern narrative, we
find ourselves in the nihilistic and deterministic terrain of Jean
Baudrillard, where the computer "code is the unseen, 'ob-scene'
vehicle by which that power [the power of corporations] moves
towards global control, toward the profitable creation and regimen-
tation of ever more sign-oriented, media-bound, simulated and
simulationist cultures."[25] But even a cursory look at computer literature shows that way back in 1959, Oliver Selfridge, who was
searching for a means of pattern recognition for handwritten letters
of the alphabet, came up with a theoretical model he called
"Pandemonium" composed of "cognitive demons" that acted in
parallel without attention to each other, and each eventually
"shouted out" its judgment of what letter had been presented to it.
The "decision demon" then made the identification of the letter, on
the basis of which demon shouted the loudest; that is, each cognitive demon was responding to lower-order "feature demons," and
the greater the number of features represented by the letter, the
louder the demon could shout. In other words, the computer field
is alive with attempts to develop network models of parallel processors attempting to simulate cognitive processes.[26]

Now, what does this development of "smart computers"—able
to learn from their environment, plan problem-solving strategies

at increasingly difficult levels of complexity, and even eliminate irrelevant details from consideration as they become endowed with a relentless common sense—have to do with the city and with architecture?

MINI-MAX STRATEGIES

From its inception, the history of computers has been deeply affected by military needs and funding, and this has tainted its logic and its modes of operations. The paradigm for decision-making is the "prisoner's dilemma," a model that guided our military policy during the Cold War years and still influences corporate decision processes. Every graduate business school offers a course in game theory; the purpose is to teach competitors how to minimize their maximum losses.[27] Consequently, there is a pro-conflict, anti-cooperation bias worked into this model. Need we be reminded that during the Cold War neither the Soviet Union nor the United States ever made a gesture of unilateral disarmament? Instead, potential losses were supposedly minimized by supporting nuclear build-up. We can apply this Cold War rhetoric of chance and risk to the city, for corporate adversarial politics, the agoristics of the market, fundamentally affect the space of the city.

Look at New York City today and you will see John von Neumann's mini-max logic[28] at work, as maximizing one's unilateral private gains at the expense of the collective good appears to be the rational solution. As an example, I have only to mention the twenty or so "business improvement districts" (BIDs) that have pockmarked the city with privatized, protected zones in the last decade. These are commercial and business areas of the city where property owners have agreed to assess themselves at a rate higher than the city's, in order to generate funds to improve their local environment despite the disintegration of the whole. BIDs usually disperse their collective funds to private security forces, private sanitation collection, and street and sign beautification programs.[29] No matter how lucrative their assessments may be, the problems of drugs, homelessness, or security are wrongly treated as boundary maintenance issues, when in fact they permeate the entire city; minimizing the maximum risks of doing business in one area simply pushes the problems elsewhere.

Another example of these struggles can be found in the recent complaints from some builders that New York City has a faulted economic development policy. Since 1976 the city has tried to form incentive packages for developers through tax breaks and credits, to lure them to the outer boroughs or above 96th Street in Manhattan. As a consequence, downtown Brooklyn has seen a surge of new development. However, during the present economic recession this policy is thought to be misguided, for it was pursued to the detriment of Manhattan—the borough that must remain the epicenter of commerce if maximum losses are to be minimized.[30]

THE CITY OF ARTIFICE

Another aspect of the logic of computer mathematics applied to the city is the application of the art of spatial and temporal ordering—what can be called the creation of the city of artifice. In her book *Radical Artifice*, Margorie Perloff points out that our word processors and electronic devices have taught us to snip, sort, cut, edit, and rearrange our data, word-processing texts, and VCR tapes until they become constructed artifices. She finds that in poetry, language has given way to a medium that, to quote Charles Bernstein, is "constructed, rule governed, everywhere circumscribed by grammar & syntax, chosen vocabulary: designed, manipulated, picked, programmed, organized, & so an artifice, artifact— monadic, solipsistic, homemade, manufactured, mechanized, formulaic, willful."[31]

Perloff finds that artifices have leaped off the page and moved into the public realm in the poetics of greeting cards, in ingenious advertisements, in the sign inflection of billboards.[32] Such powerful images challenge the artist to move beyond mere duplication. Since images are now sold by corporations, Perloff argues, the poetic image has become problematic—as has the architectural image. "Given the sophisticated print media, computer graphics, signpost, and advertising formats of our culture, all writing—and certainly all poetic writing—is inevitably 'seen' as well as 'seen through' or heard."[33] To see the latter not as phonemic but as ink on the page is to contest the status of language as a bearer of uncontaminated meaning.[34]

We might say the same of the spaces of the city. In spite of all we may have learned from the semiotics of Las Vegas, pop architecture of the late 1960s and 1970s merely duplicated commercial artifice, raising it to the level of high art. If we turn to our cities of the 1980s and 1990s, is it surprising that we find their public spaces structured as if there were a labyrinthian network thrown over their surfaces? These urban matrices become aggregates of atomistic detail, for the urban artifice valorizes the local, the regional, the particular—it becomes an array of historical and stylistic details.

Turning back to the city, and to New York in particular, I would recommend a walk through South Street Seaport, Battery Park City, Times Square, and the large historic districts of the Upper East Side, the Upper West Side, Greenwich Village, and Ladies' Mile to examine the artifice at work; for the nodes of the urban matrix have become cut-outs of local details controlled by design codes, historic district regulations, and contextual zoning ordinances. In between there are, of course, plenty of spaces—those numerous lag-time spaces explored above—that have been ignored, left unimproved, or dropped out of the transforming grid. For, as Sigmund Freud proclaimed, detail owes its privileged status to the primary process of displacement.[35]

WARRING AGAINST TOTALITIES

The matrix of urban space, which is clearly an artifice with all of its contrived and manipulated details, sets itself up in opposition to the reality of the city; it imposes itself as a gesture against totalities, a recognition that harmony of life can never be achieved. Its commitment is to the struggle, to the resistance, to opposition, to us-versus-them, and in this sense it is radically anti-urban and highly postmodern. Modernism, on the other hand, held its enemy to be artifice, and searched for what Ezra Pound called "good art…that bears true witness…the art that is most precise.…Bad art is inaccurate art. It is art that makes false reports."[36] The modernist intended images—both visual and verbal—to be precise and clear analogies of reality, while postmodernists discredit the use of imagery because contemporary culture is saturated with manipulated, commercialized signs designed and fabricated by product advertisers.[37] When confronted with these powerful and complex images, Perloff recounts, poetic discourse is challenged "to deconstruct rather than to duplicate them. They prompt what has become an ongoing, indeed a necessary dialectic between the simulacrum and its other, a dialectic no longer between the image and the real, as early modernists construed it, but between the word and the image."[38]

So we find that on the eve of the twenty-first century, our technological fascination with computers merges with our artistic conceptualizations of multivalent assemblages in which the individual, the collectivity, and the data set play separate parts. Yet how does the outside, the material world, penetrate and infuse the images and representations of this imaginary assemblage? How is the community, the *polis*, the center allowed to inform our position? And why is our contemporary era so fearful of centering devices, evident from the fact that we refer so frequently to the invisible, the disappearing, the de-industrialized, the disfigured, and the decentered city? What is this center but a point of concentration or gravity, one that holds together verbal sequences and gives meaning to utterances? Centering is both recursive and precursive—helping to give order to what precedes and what follows.[39] It is the sign unerringly pointing the way to "the center" that we read as we enter the outskirts of every European metropolis. In the Western world, centering events or images are understood symbolically; they demand to be interpreted and deciphered, for they often mask the very powers that center a discourse, and they are feared for their potential enslavements.

Postmodern critics, in particular, think that the notion of unity, totality, or a "center" is an artifice, an arbitrarily constructed narrative, and that its implicit relationships can no longer be accepted as true, nor can they retain a stable significance. Jean-François Lyotard tells us that "we have paid a high enough price for the nostalgia of the whole and one, for the reconciliation of the concept and the sensible, of transparent and communicable experience....Let us [instead] wage war on totality, let us be witness of the unpresentable, let us activate the difference."[40] Eventually, however, we have to come full circle in this de-centering game of postmodernism, and ask, in our war against all totalities, in our contemporary discontent, just what is it that we are affirming? We have in turn deconstructed the promise of the Enlightenment, the logocentrisms of Western discourse, the purposive rational action systems of science and technology, the process of city planning, Marxism, and so forth. And of course architecture and the city are among postmodernism's major structures of ambivalence. The *polis*—the Greek city—was the center of Western communal life, based on the now-faulty assumptions of a common purpose, a common consensus, and an unmediated harmony and unity of all human life. Through our postmodern deconstruction of totalizations, we think we have reinstated freedom of choice and enabled the voice of alterity to rise, but we have clearly done so at the cost of community.[41]

When Karl Scheffler, a member of the Deutscher Werkbund, confronted the reality of the metropolis in the early 1900s, he realized that the city was no longer a closed organism held together by small-scale patriarchal groups in which "every man could recognize the whole, and [thus]...each took part in the prosperity of a whole on which one's own prosperity depended." The metropolis was devoid of a "spirit of community," being merely an accidental place of residence.[42] The move to the city was a voyage away from home and toward the unknown, and once this voyage began there was no promise of a safe return; the urge to travel was also a gesture that abandoned the security and safety of home.[43]

For example, Franz Kafka used the motif of travel in his first novel, *Der Verschollen* (the missing ones; for example, passengers missing at sea), dating from 1912, which was written about New York, even though he had never been there. "Traffic" is Kafka's metaphor for the transitory nature of things experienced in the metropolis—not just the comings and goings of subways and cars and the ebb and flow of crowds as they followed their daily rhythms, but also changes in fashions and architectural styles, as well as the fragmentary, illusory quality of perception itself. Each chapter is organized around a different mode of travel that propels the hero into an endless succession of new circumstances. The complex traffic patterns of the New York streets give way to pedestrians and automobiles along the highway, which are in turn supplanted by the vertical movements of elevators, leading finally into the subway and towards the endless expanse of the American continent. America and New York are landscapes without beginning or end, labyrinths of accident, disorder, and uncertainty in which the images of the city are continually destabilized, dematerialized, and erased; they are landscapes from which the protagonist is constantly expelled.[44]

Here, too, we find the theme of the stability of home versus the open-ended, rootless metropolis that defies connectivity and belonging. At the start of the narrative, the protagonist is forced to move from his family home for fathering an illegitimate child; he is banished to a world without a past and without a center, "a world of changing appearances, unstable impressions, accident, and death: a world of 'traffic' " that will not stand still and is oblivious to his presence.[45] Modernism set itself the task of describing these fragmented experiences of the metropolis, trying to close the gap between the individual and his environment and to re-center and re-construct the city until it formed an organic whole. The city was a place of immigration and estrangement, yet it was simultaneously a register through which passed a dynamic array of local styles, cultures, and languages. Modernist artistic expression arose out of and through this metropolitan experience.[46]

To take up a postmodern traveling narrative we need only turn to Italo Calvino's *Invisible Cities*. Calvino's character Marco Polo reveals, "Traveling, you realize that differences are lost: each city takes to resembling all cities, places exchange their form, order, distances, a shapeless dust could invade the continents."[47] The type of city is uniform, the detailed variations endless. Hence every city must be read in quotation marks, its representation excessive and privileged; we have to learn what is not present in "the city" and what that absence might mean. *Invisible Cities* is structured as a numerical set: five cities are allocated to each of eleven different categories, so there are fifty-five cities in all. The idea of the city is fractured by this systematic artifice, and influenced by the definition of each element in the set. As Marco Polo claimed, "I will put together, piece by piece, the perfect city, made of fragments mixed with the rest, of instants separated by intervals discontinuous in space and time, now scattered, now more condensed, you must not believe the search for it can stop."[48]

Calvino's *Invisible Cities* bears a similarity to travel within the informational matrix of CyberCity, where borders are crossed by a hypermedia navigator who guides travelers in riding, traversing, browsing, playing the links between different texts, images, words, and graphs as they move across the grid of the electronic screen establishing new relationships in unpredictable ways. Marcos Novak describes traveling through this hypertext in the following manner:

> Every paragraph an idea, every idea an image, every image an index,
> indices strung together along dimensions of my choosing, and I
> travel through them, sometimes with them, sometimes across them.
> I produce new sense, nonsense, and nuisance by combination and
> variation, and I follow the scent of a quality through sand dunes
> of information. Hints of an attribute attach themselves to my sensors and guide me past the irrelevant, into the company of the

important; or I choose to browse the unfamiliar and tumble through volumes and volumes of knowledge still in the making.[49]

Can this thrill of constant travel in the unknown network of information without a centered focus or bounded domain make us critically aware of how abstract the matrix of CyberCity is, and how far from reality it lies? The relays of references, the inversion of orders of precedence, the endless lists of texts all present the chaotic effects of randomness and indeterminacy, generating neither options nor choices. Being constantly on the move in order to escape the repressive machines of disciplinary societies or to fully exploit the uncertain voyages of complexities in societies of control offers us no foundation on which to stand, to criticize, to remember the past, or to plan the future.

THE RHETORIC OF INDETERMINACY

So let us finally analyze the text that prompted this entire discussion: "Manual for 5 Appliances in the Alphabetical City: A Pedagogical Text" by Brian Boigon and Sanford Kwinter, and ask what these appliances can do.[50] Apparently, the Alphabetical City was a studio room located in an architectural school and open twenty-four hours a day. To quote the authors, "Every action and intervention in the Alphabetical City must be recorded in a logbook that will be present at all times."[51] This studio was a "form of publishing, social life, billboard, historical inscription, archive"—it was a happening, a situation, a drift and derive, both a collective memory and a diagram of every fleeting moment.[52] The "Manual" is, of course, the familiar tool kit, the "ABC" instructional book for constructing the Alphabetical City. But far from being radically disruptive, as was the intention, this manual actually replicates disciplinary control: a set of commands prescribed in military tones such as "You are required…" and "We will be ruthless in our pedagogical approach…"[53] reveals how close the concepts of CyberCity can be to military logic. The mere reference to "pedagogy" as opposed to "performance" is sufficient to implicate these authors in continuing the hierarchical teacher/student relation, even though they disavow the power of authority.[54]

Boigon and Kwinter borrow from Le Corbusier, transforming his five points of architecture into five appliances: time, screen, sleep, information, and site/domain. Quite clearly, these appliances reflect a shift from the machine city of modernism to the CyberCity of postmodernism where theoretical architecture, the authors note, becomes a set of "diagrammatical acts"—radical machines that internalize an abstract mechanism (a computer code or program) for producing (in unspecified ways) political and social change. Memories of Le Corbusier's claim of "architecture or revolution" simply bounce off their text, albeit in highly indeterminate ways. Out of these five radical appliances, however, it is sleep that will most probably turn on itself, allowing the blank spaces of the contemporary city, the unknown lag-time sites outside of the computer mesh, or the dream spaces of nightmares and repressed fantasies to make their appearance as slips of meaning and translation.

Boigon and Kwinter claim, "If the contemporary city has undergone a partial dismantling of its (traditional) spatial unity as well as a radical deployment of what used to be called 'time,' this does not necessarily imply that it 'expresses' any less coherently the regime silently working within it....The Alphabetical City corresponds less to a formed and distinct object than to a specific regime (of power, of effects) that currently, or increasingly, inhabits the social field."[55] If we understand the mutations that coincide with the shift to CyberCity, these statements about regimes of disciplinary control appear to be misplaced, or exceedingly nihilistic, when their social fields are left indeterminate, never discussed, never presented with any specificity. The open-ended networks of the Alphabetical City allow for nomadic thought to skid across the computer matrix, reversing hierarchical order and closed representations wherever it may range. But Boigon and Kwinter never question who might control the programming, with what values, or to what ends, nor how monads could be manipulated at their isolated computer terminals. And they do not ask what is being represented in the imaginary space of the network removed from the public sphere. Instead they use indeterminacy and repetition as a means of avoiding criticism and commitment.

This manual desires to place itself within the avant-garde of architecture, for what does this Alphabetical City do but mimic the role of avant-garde texts by generating more discourse around it? Look at the epitaph of the demolished Alphabetical City: it lasted 1008 hours, its analysis filled sixty-one pages of a logbook and a ninety-two-page document, and it generated a case of arson, several acts of vandalism, an article in *Assemblage* (which itself may have brought about more studio jobs for the two writers), this paper, and some gossip. In other words, like a good avant-garde work of art, it caused discourse to be distributed, bought, and consumed.

The point is that in the last two decades, architecture has become an important discursive event, with weekly if not daily coverage in the printed media, documentary films on television, and a consistent presence as background in advertisements for style-of-life consumer items. The value of an architectural work seems to be its ability to generate a discussion around itself, for at that point it has been inserted into the endless circulation of cultural signs. Confusion over whether a theoretical discourse is productive or constraining, liberating or controlling, is the mechanism by which that discourse sustains itself. Paul Mann has written in *The Theory-Death of the Avant-Garde* that

> discourse thrives on negations, revisions, resyntheses, and resublimations: more texts can be produced, more claims and counterclaims, more theses and antitheses; vast researches and polemics sponsored by just such confusions as these. But not forever: this indeterminate movement of alignments and misalignments, the uncertainty of both left and right about the proper and plausible role of art, is acted out in the avant-garde until it is only theater, only a representation, and hence absorbed by the problematics of representation as such.[56]

The avant-garde's position is an anti-position, a theoretical discourse constrained to relate to a dominant discourse that it rejects but cannot transcend. Its role is to articulate polarities: innovation/tradition, destruction/creation, movement/stability.[57] Futurist manifestos were the prototypical anti-gesture, as they were both for and against the metropolis, both breaking the frame and being enframed. Returning to the text of "The Alphabetical City," we note in Boigon and Kwinter's manifesto the following:

> Hypothesis: architecture is the name of the universal system of oppression (of what Foucault called the "human multiplicity," the undifferentiated mass of human flesh, thought, and desire). In this sense, its domain is the social and psychological control of the environment, including images, odors, weather, sexual practices, fantasies, documents, collective representations (but this also suggests a guerrilla architecture of subversion and resistance).[58]

Here we are in the worst of science fictions, battling against the closed world of the architectural studios, the purisms of high art, and the regimes of domination within the disciplinary spaces of the architectural school. As the authors tell us, we must abandon the architectural jury that is the "squadlike spectacle of the review" with its "fascist-style adjudication techniques."[59] Or, in another anti-gesture of radical inversion, "drawing becomes an editing, selecting, or sampling process, a wreaking havoc with the preexisting, overcoded, collective, social drawing."[60] And of course underslept and cynical design students accept that there is no returning home, no private internal space of retreat, for they are forced out into the world to engage with forces that are always drawing up a social diagram or messing up ours. They have become "itinerant warriors continually on the move," "punk-guerrillas" armed with computer viruses and jamming mechanisms admitted "through back channels" to subvert and eliminate.[61]

Architecture, we are told, "must be seen as a collector, servomechanism, or sensitive screen, monitoring the results of endless and still-unnamed experiments."[62] "A piece of architecture…may be defined not by how it appears but by practices: those that it partakes of and those that take place within it."[63] These are some examples of the rhetoric of indeterminacy plaguing Boigon and Kwinter's text, for it is the intent of their studio to open architecture to adjacencies, pollutants, and impure practices, to effect transformations within the institutions of architecture and the city.

This idea of encounters and co-adaptations of various forms resemble the maps and diagrams suggested by Michel Foucault, or the machine phylum of Gilles Deleuze, and is far from being radically new: here disconnected elements, upon reaching a critical threshold, are expected to cooperate to produce order out of chaos. It is reminiscent of El Lissitzky's Proun Room, which he believed would have a profound effect on architecture." The Proun [Lissitzky defined] is the station where one changes from painting to architecture."[64] In Lissitzky's view, the *prounen* were experiments in architectural design: documents, indices of the world to come, and theoretical models for the revolutionary reality which needed to be built.[65] Or, to cite a more recent example, these assemblages resemble the exhibitions proposed by members of the Independent Group in England during the 1950s, such as "Parallel of Life and Art" of 1953 (organized by Peter and Alison Smithson, Eduardo Paolozzi, and Nigel Henderson) and Richard Hamilton's "Man, Machine and Motion" of 1955. These shows displayed a non-hierarchical approach to imagery (mostly photographs), attempting to wring a new way of seeing things out of unusual juxtapositions.[66] As Laszlo Moholy-Nagy noted in *Vision in Motion*, in the 1920s the technique of photomontage wanted to set up a "concentrated gymnastic of the eye and brain to speed up the visual digestion and increase the range of associative relationships."[67]

These loose arrangements of associative materials, based on the notion that contiguities breed connections, are also prevalent in computer networks that model cognitive processes.[68] Since computers have been the most important instrument in creating a new system of cartography for weather, in studying DNA, in mapping atomic surfaces and subatomic particles, and especially in enabling the visual maps that explore chaos theory, then why not hope this juxtaposition of masses of visual information and high-tech appliances will produce a new map for the city and for architecture, a map that will describe nonrandom order suddenly appearing in the midst of seeming disorder? Yet here the analogies wear thin, since arrays of information are not the same as knowledge. Information is merely data, devoid of an abstract processing framework that can make comparisons, draw connections, recognize exemplars, and set and accomplish goals. The science-fiction world of smart computers usurping executive control has yet to arrive at the architectural school.

This is why in the end I question the meaning of "The Alphabetical City"—its open-ended rhetoric masks what it literally means. Does the title itself refer to Jean-Luc Godard's 1965 movie *Alphaville*, in which a megalomaniacal computer named Alpha 60 embodied the triumph of instrumental reasoning and dehumanized control systems? But this is hardly reality today, since the guerrilla tactics of PC hackers can easily subvert such mainframe controls. Might it refer instead to "alphabyte cities," imagistic video elements that are recombined and rearticulated electronically as if they were letters in the alphabet? Or does it refer to the finite and fixed alphabetical ordering of words in a dictionary or of entries in an encyclopedia, an arrangement that eliminates hierarchy and significance? Clearly the use of the title "The Alphabetical City" presents a paradox, for has not Jacques Derrida argued that "alphabetic writing... is a restrictive definition that ties the broad range of marks, spatial articulations, gestures, and other inscriptions at work in human cultures too closely to the representation of speech, the oral/aural word"?[69] Therefore haven't Boigon and Kwinter, far from liberating us to achieve new levels of perception and new orders for the city, put us back into the imposed discourse and analysis implied by alphabetical writing?

Returning to the analogies that computer matrices imply, I am reminded of Stephen Tyler's remark that "the matrix makes the shape that has shaped Western thought since the beginning of writing."[70] Be it in the trace of the cultivator, in the grid of the city, or in the matrix that alphabetical language implies, Western culture has been imposed on the land. Here we might also note, albeit briefly, another paradox Boigon and Kwinter's text interjects: they have transformed the primary generative device of modern urbanism—the plan marked upon the land—into the body characterized "as a manifold endlessly generating structure (that is, desire) on the run...where nothing is given and everything yet to be produced, where control depends on outputs yet to come."[71] Indeed, postmodernism has seen a complete restructuring of the body/machine relationship with the advent of the cyborg citizen who dwells in a post-gendered "technological polis where machinic-desires drive cybernetic systems by artificial instincts and recursive feedback loops."[72]

We also need to read Boigon and Kwinter's essay and the entire postmodern discourse and cultivation of the "clean body" as it relates to Foucault's *History of Sexuality*, in which he cleverly warned us that

> the emphasis on the body should undoubtedly be linked to the process of growth and establishment of bourgeois hegemony: not, however, because of the market value assumed by labor capacity, but because of what the "cultivation" of its own body would represent politically, economically, and historically for the present and the future of the bourgeoisie....One understands why [the bourgeoisie] took such a long time and was so unwilling to acknowledge that other classes had a body and a sex—precisely those classes it was exploiting.[73]

Perhaps therein lies our real fascination with the computer, with the binary logic of computer codes, with the cyber-networks that hold out the hallucinatory promise of virtual connectivity. The computer seems to be our age's clean, innocent machine, promising a synthetic world born from mathematics in a pure state, not yet tainted by the dark disciplinary devices of our all-too-human making.[74] And once again we might note that as issues of race and gender begin to emerge in the lag-time spaces of the city, we can transcend these anxieties and therein refuse their corporeal demands thanks to the hyper-materialistic synthetic connections of computer networks in which the body, technology, and community are reduced to the hallucinatory metaphors of cyberspace.

Finally, we must note an odd juxtaposition: Louis Aragon's poem entitled "Suicide"—which reads "A b c d e f/g h i j k l/m n o p q r/s t u v w/x y z"[75]—has been inserted into the text of "The Alphabetical City," and it underscores the final rhetorical paradox of our postmodern position. As we war against totalities, afraid of their prescriptions and over-determinations, and believing that winning will liberate us from tyranny and oppression, we are driven on and on by negativity, by standing against, by not being for, until we reach a state of abjection. Abjection, Julia Kristeva describes, is a narcissistic crisis, a revulsion hurling us away from that which limits our being, and it is caused by the breakdown of our objects or appliances of desire.[76] The Abject Machine = The Alphabetical City, a narrative of failure, an architectural enclosure of nonsense signifying nothing at all. Let the *cortège* pass by!

This paper was originally written for a symposium on artificial intelligence and architectural design held at Technical University in Delft, Holland, 15 April 1992.

1   William Gibson, *Neuromancer* (New York: Ace Books, 1984), 51.

2   Michael Hein, "The Erotic Ontology of Cyberspace," in *Cyberspace: First Steps*, ed. Michael Benedikt (Cambridge: MIT Press, 1992), 77.

3   For example, see Michael Benedikt, ed., *Cyberspace: First Steps* (Cambridge: MIT Press, 1992); Brian Boigon and Sanford Kwinter, "Manual for 5 Appliances in the Alphabetical City: A Pedagogical Text," *Assemblage* 15 (1992): 30–42; and Sharon Willis, "Seductive Spaces," in *Seduction and Theory*, ed. Dianne Hunter (Urbana: University of Illinois Press, 1989), 47–70.

4   Michael Benedikt, introduction to *Cyberspace: First Steps*, ed. Michael Benedikt (Cambridge: MIT Press, 1992), 22.

5   Hein, "The Erotic Ontology of Cyberspace," 65.

6   Quoted in Karen Lucic, *Charles Sheeler and the Cult of the Machine* (Cambridge: Harvard University Press, 1991), 16.

7   Quoted in Charles W. Haxthausen, "'A New Beauty': Ernst Ludwig Kirchner's Images of Berlin," in *Berlin Culture and Metropolis*, ed. Charles W. Haxthausen and Heidrun Suhr (Minneapolis: University of Minnesota Press, 1990), 63.

8   William C. Uricchio, "Ruttmann's Berlin and the City Film to 1930" (Ph.D. diss., New York University, 1982), 1–43.

9   Once sovereigns controlled their subjects through dramaturgical displays of might and ceremonies of exaggerated torture (from which the sovereign's power to appropriate wealth, taxes, goods, services and life could be deduced). Beginning at the end of the eighteenth century, this power was transformed into a power to ensure, maintain, and develop the life of a social body, and to this effect it utilized space and architecture as its tools and instruments of normalization. Michel Foucault, *The History of Sexuality*, trans. Robert Hurley (New York: Pantheon Books., 1978), 1: 136.

10   François Ewald, "A Power without an Exterior," in *Michel Foucault Philosopher*, trans. Timothy J. Armstrong (New York: Routledge: 1992), 169–175.

11   M. Christine Boyer, *Dreaming the Rational City* (Cambridge: MIT Press, 1983), 71.

12   Gilles Deleuze, "Postscript on Societies of Control," *October* 59 (1992): 3–7.

13   Edward Soja, *Postmodern Geographies: The Reassertion of Space in Critical Social Theory* (New York: Verso Press, 1989).

14   David Harvey, *The Condition of Postmodernity* (Cambridge: Basil Blackwell, 1989).

15   Fredric Jameson, *Postmodernism, or, the Cultural Logic of Late Capitalism* (Durham: Duke University Press, 1991).

16   Hein, "The Erotic Ontology of Cyberspace," 76.

17   The ideas of lag-times and temporal breaks are taken from Homi K. Bhabha, " 'Race,' Time and the Revision of Modernity," *The Oxford Literary Review* 13, no. 1–2 (1991): 193–219.

18   Alan Liu, "Local Transcendence: Cultural Criticism, Postmodernism, and the Romanticism of Detail," *Representations* 32 (Fall 1990): 75–113.

19   Celia W. Dugger, "A Neighborhood Struggles With Despair," *New York Times*, 5 November 1991.

20   Alison Mitchell, "Euphoria Is Scarce as Dinkins Loosens Fiscal Belt," *New York Times*, 26 April 1992.

21   For an account of a split, cut, or temporal break embedded "in" modernity see Bhabha, " 'Race,' Time and the Revision of Modernity." Bhabha suggests that the non-place is the template for colonial space.

22   William Bechtel and Adele Abrahamsen, *Connectionism and the Mind* (Cambridge: Basil Blackwell, 1991), 70, 127–129.

23   Ibid., 155.

24   Manuel De Landa, *War in the Age of Intelligent Machines* (New York: Zone Books, 1991), 121–122; quoting M. S. Miller and K. E. Drexler, "Markets and Computation: Agoric/Open Systems," in *Ecology of Computation*, ed. B. A. Huberman (Amsterdam: North-Holland, 1988) 137. "Two extreme forms of organization are the command economy and the market economy....The command model has frequently been considered more 'rational,' since it involves the visible application of reason to the economic problem as a whole....In actuality, decentralized planning [of the market] is potentially more rational, since it involves more minds taking into account more total information.... One might try to assign machine resources to tasks through an operating system using fixed, general rules, but in large systems with heterogeneous hardware, this seems doomed to gross inefficiency. Knowledge of tradeoffs and

priorities will be distributed among thousands of programmers, and this knowledge will best be embodied in their programs. Computers are becoming too complex for central planning....It seems that we need to apply 'methods of utilizing more knowledge and resources than any one mind is aware of'....Markets are a form of 'evolutionary ecosystem' and such systems can be powerful generators of spontaneous order..." De Landa, *War in the Age of Intelligent Machines*, 121–122; quoting Miller and Drexler, "Markets and Computation," 190.

25   A. Keith Goshorn, "Jean Baudrillard's Radical Enigma," in *Jean Baudrillard: The Disappearance of Art and Politics*, ed. William Stearns and William Chaloupka (New York: St. Martin's Press, 1992), 218.

26   Bechtel and Abrahamsen, *Connectionism and the Mind*, 3.

27   These games are based on the behavioral expectations of two prisoners who have been jailed for an assumed crime and who are both offered, in isolation from each other, the following deal: if you tell on your partner in crime even though he remains silent, you will be released from jail but your partner will receive a long sentence; if both of you squeal on each other you will both get moderate sentences; and if neither of you talk then your sentences will be short. Obviously the best solution for both of you is for neither person to squeal, but there the problem begins, for you must trust the other person. Therefore the most "rational" decision is to betray the other.

28   Game theory was developed by John von Neumann and Oskar Morgenstern during the 1930s and 1940s. William Poundstone, *The Recursive Universe* (Chicago: Contemporary Books, Inc., 1985), 178–179.

29   Alan Oser, "Banding Together for Local Betterment," *New York Times*, 10 February 1991.

30   Thomas J. Lueck, "Time for a Change in Builder Incentives?" *New York Times*, 8 December 1991.

31   Quoted in Margorie Perloff, *Radical Artifice* (Chicago: The University of Chicago Press, 1991), 47.

32   Walter Benjamin commented on this problem years ago when he saw that "...the letter and the word which have rested for centuries in the flatbed of the book's horizontal pages have been wrenched from this position and have been erected on vertical scaffolds in the streets as advertisement." Quoted in Perloff, *Radical Artifice*, 93.

33   Perloff, *Radical Artifice*, 120.

34   Ibid., 129.

35   Naomi Schor, *Reading in Detail* (New York: Methuen, 1987), 65–78.

36   Quoted in Perloff, *Radical Artifice*, 55.

37   Perloff, *Radical Artifice*, 87.

38   Ibid., 92.

39   Vincent Crapanzano, *Hermes' Dilemma and Hamlet's Desire* (Cambridge: Harvard University Press, 1992), 30–32.

40   Jean-François Lyotard, *The Postmodern Condition* (Minneapolis: The University of Minnesota Press, 1984), 81–82.

41   Richard Terdiman, "On the Dialectics of Postdialectical Thinking," in *Community at Loose Ends*, ed. Miami Theory Collective (Minneapolis: The University of Minnesota Press, 1991), 117.

42   Quoted in Francesco Dal Co, *Figures of Architecture and Thought* (New York: Rizzoli, 1990), 55.

43   Andreas Huyssen and David Bathrick, "Modernism and the Experience of Modernism," in *Modernity and the Text: Revisions of German Modernism*, ed. Andreas Huyssen and David Bathrick (New York: Columbia University Press, 1989), 14.

44   Mark Anderson, "Kafka and New York: Notes on a Traveling Narrative," in *Modernity and the Text: Revisions of German Modernism*, ed. Andreas Huyssen and David Bathrick (New York: Columbia University Press, 1989), 142.

45   Quoted in Mark Anderson, "Kafka and New York," 152.

46   Raymond Williams, "Metropolitan Perceptions and the Emergence of Modernism," in *The Politics of Modernism*, ed. Raymond Williams (New York: Verso Press, 1989), 37–48.

47   Italo Calvino, *Invisible Cities*, trans. William Weaver (New York: Harcourt Brace Jovanovich, 1972), 137.

48   Ibid., 164.

49   Marcos Novak, "Liquid Architectures in Cyberspace," in *Cyberspace: First Steps*, ed. Michael Benedikt (Cambridge: MIT Press, 1992), 230.

50   Boigon and Kwinter, "Manual for 5 Appliances in the Alphabetical City," 30–41.

51   Ibid., 39.

52   Ibid.

53   Ibid., 37, note 14.

54   For a deeper analysis of the tensions between "pedagogy" and "perfor-mance" see Homi Bhabha, "DissemiNation," in *Narration and Nation*, ed. Homi Bhabha (London: Routledge, 1990), 291–321.

55   Boigon and Kwinter, "Manual for 5 Appliances in the Alphabetical City," 40.

56   Paul Mann, *The Theory-Death of the Avant-Garde* (Bloomington: Indiana University Press, 1991), 55. Although Boigon and Kwinter proclaim that pornography is "certainly the radical cultural form of our age" (Boigon and Kwinter, "Manual for 5 Appliances in the Alphabetical City," 35, note 8), it can quickly turn into theater and lose its critical edge. A recent performance piece by Arthur and Marilouise Kroker, the editors of *Body Invaders: Panic Sex in America* (New York: St. Martin's Press, 1987), demonstrates that saying dirty words in public can be its own high when the virtual-pornographic perfor-mance eradicates its oppositional claims. In other words, any critical stance is destroyed as it tends towards the theatrical.

57   Mann, *The Theory-Death of the Avant-Garde*, 80–91.

58   Boigon and Kwinter, "Manual for 5 Appliances in the Alphabetical City," 40.

59   Ibid., 38.

60   Ibid., 37.

61   Ibid., 35.

62   Ibid., 32.

63   Ibid., 40.

64   *El Lissitzky* (Eindhoven, Municipal Van Abbemuseum, 1990), 73–74.

65   Ibid., 33.

66   David Robbins, ed., *The Independent Group: Postwar Britain and the Aesthetics of Plenty* (Cambridge: MIT Press, 1990).

67   Ibid., 57.

68   Bechtel and Abrahamsen, *Connectionism and the Mind*, 101–103.

69   Quoted in James Clifford, "On Ethnographic Allegory," in *Writing Culture*, ed. James Clifford and George E. Marcus (Berkeley: University of California Press, 1986), 117.

70   Stephen Tyler, *The Unspeakable Discourse, Dialogue, and Rhetoric in the Postmodern World* (Madison: The University of Wisconsin Press, 1987), 37.

71   Boigon and Kwinter, "Manual for 5 Appliances in the Alphabetical City," 35.

72   Donna Harawy, *Simians, Cyborgs, and Women* (New York: Routledge, 1991), 149–181.

73   Foucault, *The History of Sexuality* 1: 125, 126.

74   Sean Cubitt, *Timeshift: On Video Culture* (London: Routledge, 1991), 178.

75   Boigon and Kwinter, "Manual for 5 Appliances in the Alphabetical City," 40, illustration 25.

76   Cubitt, *Timeshift: On Video Culture*, 178–179.

LABYRINTHS OF THE MIND AND
THE CITY—REAL AND VIRTUAL

Associative Assemblages

Many believe that new electronic technologies that synthesize images in real time, allow for stereophonic visualization, and provide other sensory experiences represent a Copernican revolution. Not only do these virtual devices offer computer navigators new three-dimensional worlds to explore without end, but when linked to specific computer models they can also engender new ideas and images, and can transform voyagers in tangible ways. In these emerging and highly interactive virtual worlds, navigators are no longer content to simply look at an image; now they ask to be immersed in these representations, penetrating their boundaries and moving around inside of them, becoming intimately involved in their dislocating powers.[1] Thus electronic technologies that contain spatial and temporal paradoxes have arisen at the end of the twentieth century, simultaneously facilitating, as Philippe Quéau claims in his book *Le virtuel*, not only the effective means for three-dimensional pedagogy and enlightenment, but also some "stupefying" play in all senses of the term.[2] Virtual imagery presents a "reality" made of half image and half substance, in which the spectator can take the point of view of a missile, inhabit the body of a gymnast, or play music with the fingers of a pianist. Hence there is a constant challenge to understand both the nature of these new media experiences and the composite reality they create.[3]

There is something almost uncanny in this description of "the virtual," or in any other enthusiastic testimony that alludes to what the new worlds of virtual reality will one day provide. As mentioned above, although it is still in its infancy, this postmodern technology already offers new modes of perception and opens new spaces for the imaginary. While every avant-garde makes the same self-referential claims that unconventional modes of representing reality and new state-of-the-art sensibilities are emerging, it is worthwhile in this particular case to compare these testimonials to some of Walter Benjamin's writings in order to draw a few lessons about the promise of progress that technology inevitably offers yet often destroys or dissimulates. There are, in other words, both progressive and regressive factors in every new technological advance, and while new experiences and new processes may result, each step forward is met with anxieties as well as omissions.

Let us begin to draw analogies between "the virtual" and Walter Benjamin's views on modernism by studying what Benjamin referred to as "immaterial resemblances."[4] Paris, Walter Benjamin noted, is a library crossed by the Seine, as unapproachable as a goddess to whom supplicants pour out their futile adoration in words. He warned that women and works of art, which includes the city of Paris, must be approached with caution, for both are unfathomable. In a review of Marthe Bibesco's novel *Catherine-Paris* (1928), Walter Benjamin wrote the following "bibliographic allegory":

> The Goddess of France's capital city, in her boudoir, resting dreamily. A marble fireplace, molding, swelling cushions, animal skins adorning divan and plaster floor. And knick-knacks everywhere. Models of the Bridge of the Arts and the Eiffel Tower. On the pedestal, to keep alive the memory of so rich a past, the Tuileries, the Temple, and the Chateau d'Eau in miniature. In a vase the ten lilies of the city's coat of arms. Yet all this picturesque bric-a-brac is heightened, trumped, buried by the overwhelming multitude of books in a thousand formats—sextodecimos, duodecimos, octavos, quartos, and folios, of every size and color—presented to her by airborne, illiterate amoretti, poured out by fauns from the cornucopias of the portiers, spread before her by kneeling genies: the homage of the whole planet in literary production.[5]

Bernd Witte explains this passage by referring to yet another Benjaminian metaphor: that of Paris as a city of mirrors. For here, in the intimacy of her boudoir, an infinite number of images have been assembled over the ages from many parts of the world. Paris desires to be read like a book through historical memories, phantas-magorical knick-knacks, or the words written in her honor, yet she resists careful analysis and merely reflects back to the reader one of the infinity of images or forgotten fragments found in her read-ing rooms or in mirrored effects.[6] And so we might begin our com-parison by framing the virtual worlds of electronic technology in similar terms.

Perhaps one approach is something known as "hypertext." The word "hypertext" was coined by Theodor Nelson in the 1960s to refer to a process of non-sequential electronic reading and writing that offers the reader/writer a series of branch points within an interactive computer network from which to choose. It is a vast assemblage that enables the user to shuttle constantly back and forth among words, images, sounds, maps, and diagrams.[7] This sys-tem is based on associative indexing and connectionist modes of thought, rather than traditional methods of categorization such as library card classification schemes and fixed sequential readings (for example, film or videographic techniques). As George Landow has explained, hypertext theory abandons the ideas of the center versus the margin, of hierarchy, and of linearity, replacing them with the concepts of multilinearity, nodes, links, and networks.[8] The con-cept of hypertext seems to owe a debt to the work of Michel Foucault, who noted in *Archaeology of Knowledge* that the "frontiers of a book are never clear-cut"—they reference other books, other texts, other sentences; they are a node within a system of reference.[9] Within an interactive hypertext, links between spatial components —be they texts, photographs, animation, film, or sound—can be made in a random associative manner at a click of a computer mouse. One enthusiastic reviewer claims:

> As one moves through a hypertext, making one's choices, one has the
> sensation that just below the surface of the text there is an almost
> inexhaustible reservoir of half-hidden story material waiting to be
> explored. That is not unlike the feeling one has in dreams that there
> are vast peripheral seas of imagery into which the dream sometimes

slips, sometimes returning to the center, sometimes moving through parallel stories at the same time.[10]

This type of associational thinking, as well as the references to dream experiences, are points of similarity between "the virtual" and Walter Benjamin. The ability to reduce images to a number of pixels, numerically located within the matrix of a computer memory, means that these images can be stored, transmitted, and transformed, and it also allows the viewer to penetrate domains heretofore either invisible or on the other side of a boundary wall (for example, medical scanning devices that probe the internal organs and recesses of the body, or the "virtual cockpit" of a military jet equipped with sensors to scan the back of the "pilot's" retina and thus determine where the eye is looking). As Edmond Couchot has noted in *Images de l'optique au numérique*, numerical images can be assessed directly from a given electronic network and submitted to morphogenetic changes, at which time they quickly become contaminated by different user manipulations and refigurings. Consequently, images no longer constitute a window on the world, they are no longer controlled by linear perspective and seen at a distance; the spectator now penetrates into figural space, gaining access to representations within the electronic network or to image programs that are never stable but are constantly in the process of being made and remade, formed and deformed. Thus a new topology of the image is established, one that offers multiple and paradoxical hybridizations between the mode of generating images and the mode of perception, between figurative thought and logico-numerical codes or languages.[11]

Metaphors abound in the description of "the virtual" or of cyberspace—this non-space completely defined within the matrix of a computer memory. Some refer to it as a fluid countryside with liquefying walls and extending passages, as an infinite interlacing of traces that other voyagers leave behind yet that the traveller as detective chooses to follow, or as a door through which the navigator passes, only to become lost and disoriented.[12] Virtual worlds represent labyrinths that confront our bodies and our experiences of space with paradoxes of a new order. In the past, labyrinths were always spatial in conception, as they were metaphors of disorientation, while in "the virtual" they become meta-labyrinths of strange knots and irrational dizziness.[13] In fact, Quéau notes, these meta-labyrinths are abstract and formal, not material; they are constantly moving and changing into structures that cannot even be imagined. It is not so much a matter of disorientation or of losing one's way as of actually developing entirely new languages with which to move between the formal models and generated images of "the virtual" and the sensual experiences they provide as we walk through, touch, see, and hear synthetic aspects of these virtual worlds.[14] Quéau proclaims that once we are deep within computer-generated cyberspace, we are obliged to pay close attention to the links and nodes that interlace reality and appearances, illusions and symptoms, images and models. Full immersion in "the virtual" means that everything in it relates to the synthetic reality of cyberspace, and not to exterior physical space.

To Make the Invisible Visible— The Progressive Aspects of Technology

Thus meaning—either in Benjamin's "immaterial resemblances" or in "the virtual"—does not appear on the surface, but lies hidden within the surrealistic face of the city or within the ephemeral electronic network's constructions. In keeping with a Surrealist project dating from the 1920s, Walter Benjamin set out to explore the dream images of the nineteenth century, wherever they might dwell, in order to invert all that took cover under a shelter and to fathom out the secret architecture that coverings always veil. For Benjamin believed that it was in a dream, in the form or construction of its images, that the imagination might discover the hidden relations, analogies, and oppositions that made the invisible visible, in order to awaken from both the intoxicating spell of these images and the compulsions their mythic forces engendered. By drawing these images as close as possible to the light, the sleepy dream mood of inaction and obscurity might be dispelled.[15] Benjamin wrote:

> Each knows, through the experience of a dream, the fear of doors that do not close. More precisely, of doors which appear locked but are not. I know this phenomenon in an aggravated form through the following dream: While I find myself in the company of a friend to the left of a house, a phantom appears before me in the window of the ground floor of this house. We continue to walk, and the phantom accompanies us in the interior of all the houses. It crosses the walls and stays constantly at our height. I see all that well even though I am blind. The road that takes us from passage to passage is itself, in the end, such a road of phantoms, on which doors open up and walls retreat.[16]

This dream is a metaphor for the arcades (interior passages through and between buildings in nineteenth-century Paris), which were primeval landscapes of consumption into which the somnambulant *flâneur* was seductively drawn. Yet it also represents the arcade as the allegory of the dream, for a dreamer could become lost within these convoluted interiors that inverted the inside and the outside and shifted about in space and time. At each step the *flâneur* takes, whether in the city of Paris, Berlin, Moscow, or Marseilles, new constellations of images appear that resemble the turns of a kaleidoscope. But as these spectacles of the city are formed, the *flâneur*'s internal thoughts feel devalued and disordered, the result of figures that flow and blend into each other as if they were in a dream. For most decoders, what is interesting about dreams is the opportunity they offer to make associations through their resemblances to other things, to render as clear and rational what appears to be opaque and irrational. But this was not Benjamin's interest in dream interpretation; instead he focused on forgotten objects and outmoded fragments found in the streets of Paris or on walks in other cities, trying to reveal how these things, which appear perfectly utilitarian, are nevertheless surreal residues of a dream world.[17] He said, "In spatial terms, the trick was to exchange distance for nearness," to bring what was far away into closer inspection.[18] Their ability to closely examine the world around him was what Benjamin found emancipatory in the mechanical techniques of reproduction, for they taught spectators to be creators, to be experts; they taught them to understand how images were constructed—that is, to explore their logic of expression—and thus to know the machine in order to produce with it:

> By close-ups of the things around us, by focusing on hidden details
> of familiar objects, by exploring commonplace milieus under the
> ingenious guidance of the camera, the film, on the one hand,
> extends our comprehension of the necessities which rule our lives;
> on the other hand, it manages to assure us of an immense and unex-
> pected field of action....Here the camera intervenes with the
> resources of its lowerings and liftings, its interruptions and isola-
> tions, its extensions and accelerations, its enlargements and reduc-
> tions. The camera introduces us to unconscious optics as does psy-
> choanalysis to unconscious impulses.[19]

Thus Benjamin sought to decipher something that has never been written: an "other" or virtual text, which can only be revealed through a method of constant interruptions, allowing a fleeting glimpse of Benjamin's "immaterial resemblances."[20] The subtitle of his essay "Surrealism: The Last Snapshot of the European Intelligentsia" is therefore prescient of his very methodology. The snapshot represents an instant of pure sensation, capturing the aura of the fleeting and momentary; Roland Barthes referred to this as the "punctum" of a photographic image, and Benjamin called it the "something that cannot be silenced." And the snapshot interrupts the flow of time—it freezes what is always in motion, so that the viewer can analyze what would otherwise appear to be blurred and fleeting.[21]

"To make the invisible visible" was one of the possibilities envisioned for the new technologies of the photograph and the cinema. At the end of the nineteenth century, this was indeed Etienne-Jules Marey's dream: to make what was invisible to the eye, such as heartbeats, bird flights, or the gait of a horse, translatable into a form of writing.[22] Marey, a precursor to the virtual explorers such as Quéau who desire a method and language of explanation, wrote in 1878, "Science has two obstacles that block its advance, first the defective capacity of our sense for discovering truths, and then the insufficiency of language for expressing and transmitting those we have acquired. The aim of scientific methods is to remove these obstacles."[23]

In order to translate the problem of invisible movement into a visible trace, Marey used a combination of the camera's technical ability to capture images in space and a method of graphic inscriptors that expressed the passage of time. If the camera was to see what the eye could not see, then Marey first had to limit the field of visibility, which normally appeared incoherent or blurry due to the abundance of visual information entering the lens. By photographing his model, George Demeny, against a black background, and by clothing him in a black bodysuit to which shiny buttons were affixed that marked each joint, and then stretching metal bands between the buttons to connect these joints, Marey simulated a skeletal structure. Through the artifice of this "moving skeleton" that he photographed, Marey was able to record movement as a continuous passage in time and space by actually decomposing it and then recording its elements on individual readable plates. A machine—the camera—had captured a world that was invisible to the naked eye; surely this was evidence of the nineteenth century's promise of technological progress.

Benjamin also saw the revolutionary potentials of the photograph and the cinema, linking these inventions to changes in modes of perception and reception that made the invisible visible. Film, Benjamin believed, had revolutionary potentials:

Our taverns and our metropolitan streets, our offices and furnished rooms, our railroad stations and our factories appeared to have us locked up hopelessly. Then came the film and burst this prison-world asunder by the dynamite of the tenth of a second, so that now, in the midst of its far-flung ruins and debris, we calmly and adventurously go travelling. With the close-up, space expands; with slow motion, movement is extended. The enlargement of a snapshot does not simply render more precise what in any case was visible, though unclear: it reveals entirely new structural formations of the subject. So, too, slow motion not only presents familiar qualities of movement but reveals in them entirely unknown ones "which, far from looking like retarded rapid movements, give the effect of singularly gliding, floating, supernatural motions." Evidently a different nature opens itself to the camera than opens to the naked eye—if only because an unconsciously penetrated space is substituted for a space consciously explored by man.[24]

The Verbal and the Visual

In Benjamin's theory of language, the power to communicate and to formulate judgments is also the power to deceive. Thus he concentrated on the nonverbal arts, on the silent language of the still image, even though in the end it must be language that enables meaning to be derived from each photographic frame.[25] He wrote:

The Surrealists' Paris, too, is a "little universe"....There, too, are crossroads where ghostly signals flash from the traffic, and inconceivable analogies and connections between events are the order of the day. It is the region from which the lyric poetry of Surrealism reports....And it is as magical experiments with words, not as artistic dabbling, that we must understand the passionate phonetic and graphical transformational games that have run through the whole literature of the avant-garde…whether it is called Futurism, Dadaism, or Surrealism.[26]

In a subversive Surrealist image, verbal and visual distinctions are blurred, enabling spontaneous happenings to emerge and a realm of revolutionary experiences to occur. The crossroad or intersection between the two becomes the site of critical awareness that motivates revolutionary action (that is, political and moral action) in the present; it is the threshold between dreaming and awakening, between the subjectivity of the interior and the objectivity of reality, between the mythical power that images hold and their genuine form of knowledge. It is the crossroad that must be eliminated, so that surrealistic experiences might come forward.[27]

> The city's labyrinth of houses, by the light of day, is like consciousness; the arcades flow out unnoticed into the streets. But at night, beneath the dark masses of houses, their more compact darkness leaps out frighteningly; and the late passer-by hastens past them, unless we have encouraged him to take the journey down the narrow alley.[28]

Comprehension and willing agency, as well as disguise, doubling, and displacement, are at issue here within Surrealism, as they are within "the virtual." For once one is submerged within the technologically contoured hyperspace of "the virtual," Quéau warns, it becomes increasingly difficult to extract oneself and to gain perspective on or acknowledge the mundane reality of the here and now. "The virtual" represents a complete world: it saturates one's consciousness, it surrounds one's imagination, it seizes all one's attention. There is a kind of violence that "the virtual" exercises on the user's sensibility, against which there have to be methods of resistance. Yet most writers treat "the virtual" as a form of the hallucinatory sublime, claiming that its horizons open onto infinity where the ground gives way and spatial and intellectual positions become relative.[29] As Surrealist Luis Buñuel boasted about his film *An Andalusian Dog*, "Nothing symbolizes anything," or, more specifically:

When an image or idea appeared the collaborators discarded it immediately if it was derived from remembrance, or from their cultural pattern, or if, simply, it had a conscious association with another earlier idea. They accepted only those representations as valid which, though they moved them profoundly, had no possible explanation.[30]

However, as Surrealism set forth, what we allow ourselves to understand is a matter of how we fit new information into the frames through which we see, and how we actively question and readjust these frames.[31] Perhaps the most acute problem of "the virtual" for the users lies in their ability to integrate virtual experiences into the real and to fit this new information into their scheme of the world. As the boundary between the true and the false is erased, it becomes possible to confuse what is "virtual" with what is real and vice versa. This was the case in the Gulf War: pilots did not recognize signals on their electronic war screens that identified other unites as friends and not enemies, which caused them to make fatal decisions.[32] And there is the well-known example of "Julie," the computer-generated personality claiming to be a paralyzed and bedridden woman of fifty; "she" became the confidant of many other women belonging to the same usenet newsgroup until "she" was discovered to be a male psychiatrist.[33] Since the border separating truth from falsehood and material "reality" from immaterial "reality" is permeable and unstable within "the virtual," considerable violence can be unleashed in the shadowy environment of electronic communication. Here new modes of discourse are being invented that exaggerate the anonymity of second-order (as opposed to face-to-face) relationships: a few examples of the more intrusive interactions are "flame wars" (vitriolic on-line exchanges), hacker trespassing, electronic e-mail snooping, "spamming," and what has been defined as "unwanted, aggressive, sexual-textual encounter[s] in a multi-user domain" or MUD-rape.[34]

New Technologies and War—
The Destructive Power

Despite his belief in the promises that technology offered, Walter
Benjamin opened and concluded his essay "The Work of Art in the
Age of Mechanical Reproduction" with an account of the violent
misuses of technical devices by both capitalism and fascism for the
purposes of war. Similarly, today one never ventures very far in the
writings on "the virtual" before encountering violence and the war
machine. It is the military that holds responsibility for most developments in this field, and just a quick listing of some of Quéau's
examples of emerging virtual technologies will suffice: the virtual
cockpit, developed at the Wright Patterson airbase in 1977; the
Visually Coupled Airborne Systems Simulation, fully developed in
1982; NASA's telerobotics and DataGlove; simulators of air combat
visualized on something called Head-Up Display; and a telepresence project called Verdex that allows the virtual simulation of hostile environments.[35] Paul Virilio has recently noted that in our present weapons age, "erratic and random weapons…are discreet
weapons whose functioning depends entirely on the definitive split
between real and figurative. Objective lie, unidentified virtual
object, they may be classic carriers, made invisible by radar;…they
may be *kinetic kill vehicles*, using only speed of impact; or *kinetic-
energy weapons*, which are electronic decoys."[36] Because of its
destructive power, Benjamin believed that technology's promise of
progress was a fatal myth that would inevitably bring catastrophe.
And as in the case of "the virtual," the new technologies of the early
twentieth century were primarily developed for war or for increasing the exploitation of man and nature.[37]

Just as the science behind Virtual Reality (VR) was born from
the head of the god Mars, the entertainment industry has been the
first to exploit the experience of immersive videogames with themes
of war and destruction based on "reprogrammable content and
the use of interior (VR) rather than exterior (physical) space."[38]
None other than Walt Disney's grandson, Tim Disney, has turned

Disneyland's Virtual World Entertainment complex into a series of arcade storefronts offering a networked simulation module called "Battletech," a game in which eight different solo players try to annihilate one another by blowing away each other's body parts. Like any good Disneyland experience, the fiction begins the moment a devoted player enters the arcade: uniformed employees offer a pre-game briefing to describe how it should be played, and there is a post-game debriefing to compare notes with other players after they all have tried their luck. Since women tend to turn away from such fight simulations, Virtual World has also embarked on an alternative path of exploration games that depend on cooperative tactics rather than annihilation strategies, thus imitating a distinction already existing in the world of computer games between the female body as a body-in-connection and the male body as a body-in-isolation.[39] Another example of these war games is the incredibly popular "Doom," playable on the Internet. In the role of a trained space marine, an individual player fights demons that have invaded a series of moonbases. There is also a multi-player cooperative version. In these theatricalized games of war, the players identify with the aggressor; they unwittingly accept their own mutilation and annihilation and erroneously recognize their own subjection as a commodity of late capitalism. As Benjamin wrote, speaking of humankind under fascism, "Its self-alienation has reached such a degree that it can experience its own destruction as an aesthetic pleasure of the first order."[40]

THE DEVELOPMENT OF ARTISTIC PERCEPTION, OR THE CRITICAL RECEPTION OF TECHNOLOGICAL EXPERIENCE

Benjamin argued that "technological revolutions are the sites of ruptures in the development of art." They bring forth progressive and reactionary political trends.[41] Thus it was essential for individuals to develop a new questioning and critical mode of artistic reception toward technological or modern experience. He proposed that the radio and the cinema, both recent inventions, could aid in creating this new mode of reception, since they employed the art of montage and interruption, which gave their works a shock effect that could awaken new responses. As he said, film has always been a vital force in the relationship between the masses and art:

> The distracted person, too, can form habits. More, the ability to master certain tasks in a state of distraction proves that their solution has become a matter of habit. Distraction as provided by art presents a covert control of the extent to which new tasks have become soluble by apperception. Since, moreover, individuals are tempted to avoid such tasks, art will tackle the most difficult and most important ones where it is able to mobilize the masses. Today it does so in the film. Reception in a state of distraction, which is increasingly noticeable in all fields of art and is symptomatic of profound changes in apperception, finds in the film its true means of exercise. The film with its shock effect meets this mode of reception halfway. The film makes the cult value recede into the background not only by putting the public in the position of the critic, but also by the fact that at the movies this position requires no attention. The public is an examiner, but an absentminded one.[42]

Benjamin particularly thought that actors' expressive gestures might teach this new mode of questioning and inspection, thus allowing the spectator to draw new correspondences and palpable connections to the world through mimicry.

> The highest capacity for producing similarities…is man's. His gift of seeing resemblances is nothing other than a rudiment of the powerful compulsion in former times to become and behave like something else. Perhaps there is none of his higher functions in which his mimetic faculty does not play a decisive role.[43]

Thus the body because of its mimetic nature became an important emblem in developing a proper non-instrumental relationship—or balance—between man, technology, and nature, a balance that might avert catastrophe and barbarism.

For example, in an essay called "Experience and Poverty," Benjamin claimed that the miraculous metamorphoses and animated machinery found in Mickey Mouse movies offered the spectator a glimpse of a future in which human beings and technology might exist in equilibrium.[44] The Walt Disney animated characters of the 1930s performed miraculous feats that surpassed the capacities of technology of those times, and they did so out of the flexible play of their bodies in a free-for-all exchange between animate and inanimate worlds. Mickey Mouse produced a witty, instructive, even bawdy commentary on what it was like to be caught in a network of machines and events, while trying to escape their consequences.[45] In Mickey Mouse movies, Benjamin argued, the self-alienation and the fragmentation of the characters' own bodies were transformed into an inquiry about the kind of fragmentation that accompanied modern existence and technology. Mickey Mouse ridiculed the power technology might have over the body, and by appearing childishly transcendent over its force, he relieved collective doubts and anxieties produced by the new dichotomies that had arisen, such as organic/mechanical, animate/inanimate, master/slave, and labor/play.[46]

> Nature and technology, primitivism and comfort have completely become one [in these movies], and before the eyes of people who have grown tired of the endless complications of the everyday and to whom the purpose of life appears as nothing more than a distant vanishing point in an endless perspective of means, there appears as a redemption an existence which at every turn is self-sufficient in the most simple and simultaneously most comfortable way, in which a car does not weigh more than a straw hat and the fruit on the tree grows round as fast as a hot-air balloon.[47]

Mickey Mouse addressed both nature and technology through humor and parody, and he prefigured the utopian vision of technology's potential by crossing extreme artificiality with physiological immediacy.[48]

But the mechanical reproduction found in the photograph and film, including animated cartoons, were based on repetition, the omnipresence of the stereotype, and the forgetting of tradition, all of which led directly into the hands of politicians. Even Mickey Mouse with all of his revolutionary potential could be appropriated for other purposes—for example, he became a mascot on German fighter planes during World War II. Politics, Benjamin proclaimed, relies on the control and display of the body and on the readiness of spectators to mimic these gestures.

> Since the innovations of camera and recording equipment make it possible for the orator to become audible and visible to an unlimited number of persons, the presentation of the man of politics before camera and recording equipment becomes paramount. Parliaments, as much as theaters, are deserted. Radio and film not only affect the function of the professional actor but likewise the function of those who also exhibit themselves before this mechanical equipment, those who govern. Though their tasks may be different, the change affects equally the actor and the ruler. The trend is toward establishing controllable and transferable skills under certain social conditions. This results in a new selection, a selection before the equipment from which the star and the dictator emerge victorious.[49]

Thus Benjamin set out to undermine the images that could be distorted by political purposes, working his corrections from within. Yet as Irving Wohlfarth noted, the concept behind Walter Benjamin's "Work of Art in the Age of Mechanical Reproduction" was "a historical gamble" in which things could go terribly wrong after one joined the enemy and began the attack from within its very ranks.[50] Or, as Walter Benjamin himself explained:

The mass is a matrix from which all traditional behavior toward works of art issues today in a new form. Quantity has been transmuted into quality. The greatly increased mass of participation has produced a change in the mode of participation. The fact that the new mode of participation first appeared in a disreputable form must not confuse the spectator.[51]

Wanting to open up a new medium of dialogue as well as to teach new modes of interventionist thinking, Benjamin utilized the latest technical apparatus of entertainment and distraction when between 1929 and 1933 he delivered a series of radio broadcasts to children. He hoped that radio, as well as cinema and photography, would bring about new forms of perception and reception.[52] Perhaps it seems strange that Benjamin—whose writings were seldom understood by his contemporaries and closest associates, and indeed today remain obscure—attempted to deliver a series of talks to children. However, many of Benjamin's writings, such as *One Way Street* (1928) and *A Berlin Chronicle* (1932), contained material from his own childhood. Moreover, he paid special attention to the ability of children to form new intuitive relationships, to make connections between material things—playful correspondences which the disenchanted world of science and technology no longer allowed. He wrote:

In waste products [children] recognize the face that the world of things turns directly and solely to them. In using these things they do not so much imitate the works of adults as bring together, in the artifact produced in play, materials of widely differing kinds in a new, intuitive relationship. Children thus produce their own small world of things within the greater one.[53]

One of Benjamin's radio talks to children spoke of communication failures, and of the fears that technology can bring; he told the story of a railway catastrophe that took place on the bridge across the Firth of Tay in 1879.[54] It took seven years to construct this monumental ironwork bridge, yet the bridge failed twice, once in 1877 and again in 1879, when sudden and violent storms swept away two of its primary supports. In the latter catastrophe the lack of communication as to the bridge's status caused a speeding train to plunge into the icy waters of the Tay, killing all two hundred passengers aboard. No witnesses remained, and it was only after losing telegraph communication that a second train was sent out to verify the condition of the wire cables attached to the bridge. This train nearly plunged into the gap in the central part of the bridge as well, but it managed to slam on its brakes just in time.[55] Benjamin told his young radio audience that he wanted to place this catastrophe within the history of technology—more specifically, within the history of metal construction—since iron was the first artificial material to be used in the history of architecture. Benjamin praised the inventors of the iron bridge, the steam engine, and the railway for being innovators who, in spite of the retrogressive fears of society, valiantly forged ahead, following the progress that technology promised.[56] But Benjamin also recounted the medical fears that trains inspired, such as the threat of cerebral lesions that might be caused by travelling at too great a speed, or the possibility of fainting spells from the sight of these meteors as they rushed through the landscape. And he noted the dehumanizing aspects of early train travel, of "being dispatched to a destination, like a package."[57]

Thus every new technology promises benefits but it also creates anxiety and dissatisfaction, however repressed they might be. As Sigmund Freud noted, by conquering space and time modern technology established a system of new ambivalences:

> If there had been no railway to conquer distance, my child would never have left his native town and I should need no telephone to hear his voice; if travelling across the ocean by ship had not been introduced, my friend would not have embarked on his sea-voyage and I should not need a cable to relieve my anxiety about him.[58]

It is Wolfgang Schivelbush who reminds us in *The Railway Journey* (1986) that although the railway was the emblematic, mythical image of the new technologies that conquered space and time in the nineteenth century, this was offset by the terrifying fears of the railway accident.[59] Indeed, the first medical diagnosis of traumatic neurosis and the acknowledgment that psychic problems could have physical effects were the result of attending to the maladies of train wreck victims who, while not physically hurt, nevertheless suffered from its catastrophic effects.[60] As train travel became more familiar, however, the anxiety it caused was replaced by the knowledge of the possibility of accidents and technological breakdowns. Thus the new systems of communication and transportation gave rise to a new fear of sudden interruption,[61] a fear that exists today in regards to electronic technology.

Benjamin ended this particular radio essay by discussing the building of the Eiffel Tower, a monument to iron construction. As Jeffrey Mehlman has said, quoting Benjamin, " 'At the time of its creation, the Eiffel Tower was not conceived for any use; it was a mere emblem, one of the world's wonders, as the saying goes. But then radio transmission was invented, and all of a sudden the edifice had a meaning. Today the Eiffel Tower is Paris's transmitter.' The broadcaster implies that meaning proper...is very much an aftereffect."[62] Thus in the beginning the Eiffel Tower was merely an empty symbol, devoid of meaning, useful only for obtaining an unobstructed view of the city. Its presence was decried by artists, who protested "the erection in the heart of our capital of the useless and monstrous Eiffel Tower, which the public has scornfully and rightfully dubbed the Tower of Babel," and they also called it an "odious column of bolted metal" with a shadow that covered the city "like a spot of ink."[63] Like the bridge over the Firth of Tay, the Eiffel Tower was a monument to civil engineering and to the minute and exact calculations that determined its form. Nevertheless, this and other glass and iron constructions of the nineteenth century such as arcades, observatories, railway sheds, and exhibition halls were premature developments. These new materials were either received with fear or provisionally accepted yet hidden under-neath the false coverings of elaborate floral ornamentations; while glass and iron ushered in the era of modern architecture, builders in the middle of the nineteenth century did not yet know how to con-struct with them.[64] This new technology—like those that followed —had to wait for the moment when perception and experience changed, when what was once considered to be purely functional or transitional became accepted for its formal attributes.[65]

It may appear that "the virtual," with its cool and detached approach, prohibits any apocalyptic thought or technological anxi-ety. Yet Scott Bukatman writes that cyberspace devotees—often called "cyberpunks"—nevertheless have their own mythology of "terminal culture" that is derived from Surrealism, and that their

> narrations…speak with the voices of repressed desire and repressed
> anxiety about terminal culture. Cyberpunk negotiates a complex
> and delicate trajectory between the forces of instrumental reason
> and the abandon of sacrificial excess. Through their construction of
> cultural politics inscribed by the forces of technological reason, and
> through their resistance to the constraints of that reason, the texts
> promise and even produce a transcendence of the human condition
> which is always a surrender.[66]

With "the virtual" we once again find feelings of awe as well as of terminal terror toward these powerful new communication devices. However, as opposed to the inventions of the nineteenth century, electronic technology operates silently and passively, with hidden capacities involving memory and artificial intelligence that appear to be shrouded in mystery, that are beyond comprehension. Thus rather than borrowing the mechanistic metaphors of energy and force that industrial machinery engendered, narrators of "the virtual" will have to come up with new imagery that adequately characterizes the concealed and fluid processes of computers as well as the centerless and net-like structures they enable.[67] So far, cyber-punks have borrowed worn-out imagery and utilized conventional terms to describe these emergent technologies. They narrate stories of outlaw hackers who single-handedly infiltrate the technological frontier, and who manipulate the labyrinthian passages of codes and passwords to their advantage. Or they tell of cyber-thieves strung out on heady mixes of designer chemicals who rip off the System, performing atrocities as they maneuver the sprawl or the matrix. Corporate power, greed, and manipulative control are still the enemies in synthetically sovereign cyberspace. But these narrators have yet to deal with the fears of interruption or termination of the continuous flow of information, of sensory overload, of excesses of information, and of cybernetic chaos. Nor have they tempered their hallucinatory images of liberation, which is how they envision "the virtual," with the nihilistic manifestations of the precariousness of electronic existence (for example, the devouring of texts by a virus, the crashing of overloaded circuitry, or the failures caused by bugs or miscodings). Finally, they have yet to address the issue of what it means to be human when the subjective self can now be projected onto the computer screen.[68]

This paper was originally written for a collection of essays on computers and contemporary society that was tentatively titled *Digital Anthenaeum* and was to be edited by Timothy Hyde. The collection was never published.

1   Philippe Quéau, *Le virtuel: Vertus et vertiges* (Paris: Champ Vallon, 1993), 9.

2   Ibid., 15.

3   Ibid., 16.

4   Rita Bischof and Elisabeth Lenk, "L'intrication surréelle du rêve et de l'histoire dans les *Passages* de Benjamin," in *Walter Benjamin et Paris*, ed. Heinz Wismann (Paris: Les Editions du Cerf, 1986), 199.

5   Quoted in Bernd Witte, *Walter Benjamin: An Intellectual Biography* (Detroit: Wayne State University Press, 1991), 180.

6   Witte, *Walter Benjamin*, 180–181.

7   George P. Landow, *Hypertext: The Convergence of Contemporary Critical Theory and Technology* (Baltimore: Johns Hopkins Press, 1992), 2–8.

8   Ibid., 2.

9   Quoted in Landow, *Hypertext*, 3–4.

10   Robert Coover, "Hyperfiction: Novels for the Computer," *New York Times Book Review* (29 August 1993): 10.

11   Edmond Couchot, *Images de l'optique au numérique* (Paris: Hermes, 1988), 197.

12   Quéau, *Le virtuel*, 30–44. One example of this virtual architecture that Quéau discusses is a project called "Cyber City," which is being developed in Germany by the association ART+COM (although it is still in a primitive state of development). A virtual museum has been set up as a simulated model of the Berlin National Museum, as it was conceptualized by Ludwig Mies van der Rohe. This "museum" houses four modern thinkers whose philosophies are assumed to be antipodes to each other. It is supposedly a case study on the concepts of adventure, hope, utopia, and catastrophe. A red pyramid, the symbol of fire, represents adventure and is controlled by Vilem Flusser. A green cube symbolizes the house of hope; Joseph Weizenbaum is assigned to it. Marvin Minsky occupies a hexedra of blue water, which is assumed to be a utopian place. And Paul Virilio is housed in a yellow sphere of air—the house of catastrophe. Each house has gaps in its walls, which enable spectators to view the interiors. In order to communicate with the exterior world, the occupants have at their disposal images, colors, music, and words. Quéau recounts

that one user, Monika Fleischmann, has described this virtual architecture as a place where water suddenly turns into a desert or living trees spring up out of the water. The ground has the appearance of a thin paper when the spectator is immersed in the forest. Then trees begin to fall. In order to leave this dangerous place, it is necessary to develop the talents of an experienced player. After considerable water turbulence, four arches appear. Here lies the entry into the labyrinth; here is the forum for discussions. Ibid., 58–59.

13   Ibid., 79–84.

14   Ibid., 101.

15   John McCole, *Walter Benjamin and the Antimonies of Tradition* (Ithaca: Cornell University Press, 1993), 237.

16   "Chacun connaît, [Benjamin wrote in *Passagenwerk*] par le rêve, la peur des portes qui ne ferment pas. Plus précisément, des portes qui paraissent verrouillées et qui ne le sont pas. J'ai connu ce phénomène sous une forme aggravée dans le rêve que voici: Alors que je me trouve en compagnie d'un ami à la gauche d'une maison, un fantôme m'apparaît à la fenêtre du rez-de-chaussée de cette maison. *Nous continuons de marcher, et le fantôme nous accompagne à l'intérieur de toutes les maisons. Il traverse tous les murs et rest constamment à notre hauteur. Je vois tout cela bien que je sois aveugle.* La chemin qui nous mène de passage en passage est en fin de compte, lui aussi, un tel chemin de fantômes, sur lequel les portes cèdent et les murs reculent." Quoted in Bischof and Lenk, "L'intrication surréelle," 180. The italics are Bischof and Lenk's.

17   Bischof and Lenk, "L'intrication surréelle," 179–200.

18   Quoted in McCole, *Walter Benjamin*, 246.

19   Walter Benjamin, "The Work of Art in the Age of Mechanical Reproduction," in *Illuminations*, trans. Harry Zohn (New York: Schocken Books, 1978), 236.

20   Bischof and Lenk, "L'intrication surréelle," 199.

21   McCole, *Walter Benjamin*, 221.

22   For an excellent and extensive analysis of Marey's scientific experiments see Marta Braun, *Picturing Time: The Work of Etienne-Jules Marey (1830–1904)* (Chicago: University of Chicago Press, 1992).

23   Etienne-Jules Marey, "La methode graphique" (1878), quoted in Braun, *Picturing Time*, 12–13.

24   Benjamin, "The Work of Art in the Age of Mechanical Reproduction," 236–237.

25 Jean-Jacques Lecercle, "To Do or Not to Do without the Word Ecstasy and Discourse in the Cinema," *New Formations* 16 (Spring 1992): 80–90.

26 Walter Benjamin, "Surrealism," in *Reflections*, trans. Edmond Jephcott (New York: Shocken Books, 1978), 183–184.

27 For an extended discussion on Benjamin's use of the "threshold" see Winfried Menninghaus, "Walter Benjamin's Theory of Myth," in *On Walter Benjamin*, ed. Gary Smit (Cambridge: MIT Press, 1988), 292–325. For a discussion of Benjamin's use of the crossroads see Max Pensky, *Melancholy Dialectics: Walter Benjamin and the Play of Mourning* (Amherst: The University of Massachusetts, 1993), 184–187.

28 Walter Benjamin, quoted in McCole, *Walter Benjamin*, 243.

29 Quéau, *Le virtuel*, 89–90.

30 Luis Buñuel, *My Last Sign*, trans. Abigail Israel (New York: Alfred A. Knopf, 1983), 108.

31 Mary Ann Caws, "Eye and Film: Buñuel's Act," in *The Art of Interference* (Princeton: Princeton University Press, 1989), 138–139.

32 Quéau, *Le virtuel*, 38–39.

33 Ibid., 74.

34 Anne Balsamo, "Feminism for the Incurably Informed," *The South Atlantic Quarterly* 92, no. 4 (Fall 1993): 695.

35 Quéau, *Le virtuel*, 50–60.

36 Paul Virilio, *The Vision Machine* (Bloomington: Indiana University Press, 1994), 69.

37 Walter Benjamin wrote about World War I: "In the face of the landscape of total mobilization, the German feeling for nature has had an undreamed-of upsurge....The metaphysical abstraction of war professed by the new nationalists is nothing but an attempt to solve the mystery of an idealistically perceived nature through a direct and mystical use of technology, rather than using and illuminating the secrets of nature via the detour of the organization of human affairs." Quoted in McCole, *Walter Benjamin*, 179–180.

38 Michael Krantz, "Dollar a Minute," *Wired* (May 1994): 104–106, 140, 142.

39 Balsamo, "Feminism for the Incurably Informed," 692.

40 Benjamin, "The Work of Art in the Age of Mechanical Reproduction," 242.

41 Quoted in McCole, *Walter Benjamin*, 190.

42   Benjamin, "The Work of Art in the Age of Mechanical Reproduction," 240–241.

43   Walter Benjamin, "On the Mimetic Faculty," in *Reflections*, trans. Edmund Jephcott (New York: Random House, Inc., 1989), 333.

44   This section relies on the work of Miriam Hansen, who has traced Mickey Mouse's appearance in Walter Benjamin's writings during the 1930s, drawing in particular on an earlier version of Benjamin's "The Work of Art in the Age of Technical Reproducibility." See Miriam Hansen, "Of Mice and Ducks: Benjamin and Adorno on Disney," *The South Atlantic Quarterly* 92, no. 1 (Winter 1993): 27–61.

45   McCole, *Walter Benjamin*, 189. See also Miriam Hansen, "Of Mice and Ducks."

46   Hansen, "Of Mice and Ducks," 45–47.

47   Walter Benjamin, translated by Miriam Hansen, quoted in Hansen, "Of Mice and Ducks," 42.

48   Hansen, "Of Mice and Ducks," 43.

49   Benjamin, "The Work of Art in the Age of Mechanical Reproduction," 247, note 12.

50   Irving Wohlfarth, "No-Man's-Land: On Walter Benjamin's 'Destructive Character,'" *Diacritics* 8 (June 1978): 57–58.

51   Benjamin, "The Work of Art in the Age of Mechanical Reproduction," 239.

52   Bernd Whitte, *Walter Benjamin: An Intellectual Biography* (Detroit: Wayne State University Press, 1991), 118–122.

53   Walter Benjamin, "One Way Street," in *Reflections*, trans. Edmund Jephcott (New York: Random House, Inc., 1989), 69.

54   Walter Benjamin, "La catastrophe ferroviaire du Firth of Tay," in *Lumières pour enfants*, trans. Sylvie Muller (Paris: Christian Bourgois Editeur, 1985), 242–249.

55   Jeffrey Mehlman, *Walter Benjamin for Children: An Essay on His Radio Years* (Chicago: The University of Chicago Press, 1993), 11–15.

56   Walter Benjamin, "Eduard Fuchs, Collector and Historian," in *One Way Street*, trans. Edmund Jephcott and Kingsley Shorter (London: New Left Books, 1978), 358.

57 Mehlman, *Walter Benjamin for Children*, 12.

58 Quoted in Tom Gunning, "Heard over the Phone: The Lonely Villa and the de Lorder Tradition of the Terrors of Technology," *Screen* 32, no. 2 (Summer 1991): 185.

59 Wolfgang Schivelbusch, *The Railway Journey: The Industrialization of Time and Space in the Nineteenth Century* (Berkeley: University of California Press, 1986).

60 Gunning, "Heard over the Phone," 186.

61 Ibid., 194.

62 Mehlman, *Walter Benjamin for Children*, 14.

63 *Protestation des artistes*, quoted in Marjorie Perloff, *The Futurist Moment* (Chicago: University of Chicago Press, 1986), 201.

64 Walter Benjamin, *Paris capitale du XIXe siècle*, trans. Jean Lacoste (Paris: Les Editions du Cerf, 1993), 172.

65 Ibid., 176.

66 Scott Bukatman, "Postcards from the Posthuman Solar System," *Science Fiction Studies* 55 (November 1991): 343–357; quoted in Istvan Csicsery-Ronay, "The Sentimental Futurist: Cybernetics and Art in William Gibson's *Neuromancer*," *Critique* 33, no. 3 (Spring 1992): 236.

67 Claudia Springer, "Muscular Circuitry: The Invincible Armored Cyborg in Cinema," *Genders* 18 (Winter 1993): 87–112.

68 David Porush claimed, "You get to cyberspace by killing some obsolete part of your humanity and redeeming another." Quoted in Csicsery-Ronay, "The Sentimental Futurist," 236.

Disenchantment of the City: An Improbable Dialogue between Bodies, Machines, and Urban Form

Our contemporary times have created a veritable cult of the body. From rituals of exercise and dieting to phobias of pollutants and cholesterol, we have developed elaborate purification rites, as if our bodies were under siege and our corporeal boundaries needed to be fortified against all transgressing invaders. Yet this cult of the body with its repetitive and compulsive rituals seems to be nothing short of a cover-up for a deep fear of disembodiment and immateriality. As we constantly undergo changes to annihilate the materiality of the body—cleansing it of pollutants, thinning it of excess weight, emptying it of unwanted foods, and even plastically rearranging its parts at will— we implicitly speak of a body released from its physical restrictions, a body evacuated, devastated, disintegrating, disappearing.[1] Here I want to focus on what this fear of disembodiment may entail, and why it has developed to such fantastic proportions in the last decade or so. By raising these issues, I draw a sharp comparison between the materiality of the modernist body, which incorporated the world with all of its physical senses, and the immateriality of the postmodern body—and thus by analogy between the modernists' engagement with the city and the postmodernists' withdrawal from the city, which has left it emaciated, evacuated, and disappearing. These two separate processes of embodiment and disembodiment involve the fear and promise of quite separate technologies, each acting as a metaphorical device to further illustrate what is at stake in this transformation from the modern to the postmodern city.

BODY METAPHORS

Aesthetics is born as a discourse of the body....The term refers not in the first place to art, but...to the whole region of human perception and sensation, in contrast to the more rarefied domain of conceptual thought....It is as though philosophy suddenly wakes up to the fact that there is a dense, swarming territory beyond its own mental enclave which threatens to fall utterly outside its sway. That territory is nothing less than the whole of our sensate life together.[2]

THE BODY OF HUMANISM

We are all familiar with the Vitruvian drawing of a male body standing upright, inscribed in the space of a circle within a square. In this image, the geometrical and metaphorical centers of all three figures are located at the body's navel. These static forms—the body, the circle, and the square—assume that knowledge is centered, that order, harmony, and proportion are the ruling criteria. They prescribe the classical standard of beauty and the measure of perfection for the entire Western world. Vitruvius also advised that an architect have a knowledge of medicine, in order to fully understand the deep influence the body held over the art of building cities and structures. Subsequently, following Vitruvius, urbanism mimicked this classical ordering: the radially organized city was the ideal design, from the perspective of defense and health of its citizens. And man, a rational thinker, occupied the center of this ordering system, while architecture came to embody the image of this purified and perfectly unified body.[3]

Similarly, Barbara Stafford argues that, in neoclassical theories of art, "reality was geometrical. It did not consist in the fakery of the visual or in the nothingness of the carnal body. Unidirectional straight lines and curves indicated that what was true could not be anamorphically turned to suit the perspective of different beholders."[4] In other words, perfect form was not constituted by nor relative to a spectator's perception. Instead, to quote from Geoffrey Scott in *The Architecture of Humanism*, "arches 'spring,' vistas 'stretch,' domes 'swell,' Greek temples are 'calm,' and baroque facades 'restless.' The whole of architecture is, in fact, unconsciously invested by us with human movement and human moods.... *We transcribe architecture into terms of ourselves....* This is the humanism of architecture. The tendency to project the image of our functions into concrete forms is the basis, for architecture, of creative design."[5] Thus all architecture up to contemporary times has been formed as a mimetic, allegorical, or metaphorical projection of the ideal proportions of man; any deviations from this basis in anthropomorphism have been viewed as provocations of the eccentric, perverse, or monstrous.

Yet Anthony Vidler asserts in "The Building in Pain: The Body and Architecture in Post-Modern Culture" that the classical ideal of architectural embodiment, in which a building drew upon the corporeal body for proportional and figurative authority, was abandoned with the rise of modernism, and that consequently the current return to the body in postmodern architecture is to a different, post-humanist body, constituting an entirely different sensibility.[6] Vidler closely follows the work of Elaine Scarry, who remarked in *The Body in Pain* that there were three different ways that artifacts carry projections of the human body: first, by describing the artifact in terms of specifiable body parts (for example, the classical body/building analogy); second, by identifying bodily capacities and needs within the object (the modernist "machine for living"); and third, by attributing a sense of "aliveness" to inanimate objects. Scarry believes that this third form of projection is the most accurate, "for it calls attention to the fact that it is part of the work of creating *to deprive the external world of the privilege of being inanimate*....To say that the 'inanimateness' of the external world is diminished, is *almost* to say (but is *not* to say) that the external world is made animate."[7]

The fundamental issue, however, remains one of anthropomorphic projection; whether the architecture is based on the classical body of perfection or a body of intense pain is only a matter of different registers. Vidler argues that the post-humanist, fragmented body no longer serves to center or stabilize architecture but demonstrates a perceived loss or lack; it is a morcellated body manifesting psychological symptoms of alienation, schizophrenia, hysteria or nervous collapse. When projected onto architecture, the repressed corporeal body returns in the feeling of the uncanny toward something which has been disavowed or denied, so that the postmodern architectural projects of Bernard Tschumi, Coop Himmelblau, or Daniel Libeskind, for example, carry the haunting traces of this absent body, and they receive the projections of pain, dismemberment, disembodiment, tears, and ruptures. Vidler quotes Coop Himmelblau, who said in 1968, "We want…architecture that bleeds, that exhausts, that whirls and even breaks…a cavernous, burning, sweet hard, angular, brutal, round, delicate, coloured, obscene, voluptuous, dreaming, seductive, repulsive, wet, dry, palpitating architecture. An architecture alive or dead."[8]

This morcellated architecture is figured simply by projecting a dystopian instead of a utopian body onto the realm of architecture. But this dystopia, which both modernists and postmodernists display, has not dispensed with the human body as the model on which architecture is based. In fact, in contradistinction to the position Vidler claims, the modernists were obsessed with the body: they were fearful of its exoticisms, its irrationalities, its way of being controlled by machines, and yet they were simultaneously aware that it and all its senses incorporated the world around it. The bodily senses had a synesthetic effect on perception and consciousness, sucking "reality" in through the fingers and drinking it up with the eyes, and this embodiment could be extended if aided by certain technologies. Once again we must ask what, then, does disembodiment mean, and why does our postmodern stance reject most bodily senses as perceptual devices? Before we answer this question, we have to listen carefully to Susan Buck-Morss's warning—based on the writings of Walter Benjamin—that the alienation of bodily senses that occurred in Germany during the 1920s "numbed" people's consciousness against all feeling, allowing fascism to thrive on the representation of the body as armor. Thus the well-trained, regimented, mechanized body prepared for war offered an illusion of invulnerability as a defense against fragmentation and pain.[9]

Let us return for a moment to morcellated architecture and the building in pain. Drew Leder in *The Absent Body* argues that "the body in pain is often experienced as alien to itself," appearing "in a dys state—*dys* is from the Greek prefix signifying 'bad,' 'hard,' or 'ill.' "[10] It is aware of being in a problematic or "dysfunctional" state, of being apart or asunder.[11] Thus a body disturbed or in pain can appear as "other," as separate from the self, which is in keeping with the Cartesian dualism that disavows the sensuous body and overemphasizes the role of the mind.[12] René Descartes wrote, "I shall now close my eyes, I shall stop my ears, I shall call away all my senses, I shall efface even from my thoughts all the images of corporeal things, or at least (for that is hardly possible) I shall esteem them as vain and false."[13] Since the body is always leading the mind astray, deceiving it or even seducing it through the senses, it can consequently cripple the search for truth. Thus judgment, not perception, must determine the rational order of things. But perhaps the sensual world cannot be reduced to rational thought, but will always leave a perceptual or visual aspect unaccounted for, one which will reappear in fantasies and illusions.[14] Therefore this is not a problem involving the projection of a posthumanist body, nor of whether this body has a utopian or dystopian nature. Instead the issue rests on problems of perceptual disfigurement, and on whether we accept or reject the illusion that there is a self in the center from which to make these anthropomorphic projections.

In his discussion of utopias and "heterotopias" (places where incongruous things appear), Michel Foucault noted that there is a mirror standing between the utopian arrangements that have no real space but that reflect society in either its perfected (utopian) or dejected (dystopian) state, and the heterotopias that represent "other" spaces, spaces set up to counter arrangements or to offer compensatory places from those that exist in reality. Foucault uses the body's reflection in this mirror to help define this mixed-up, in-between space. This mirror is then a utopia, a placeless place where "I see myself there where I am not, in an unreal, virtual space, that opens up behind the surface;...a sort of shadow that gives my own visibility to myself there where I am absent..."[15] But the mirror is also a real place, a heterotopia: "It makes this place that I occupy at the moment when I look at myself in the glass at once absolutely real, connected with all the space that surrounds it, and absolutely unreal, since in order to be perceived it has to pass through this virtual point which is over there."[16] Thus at the center of any analysis of space and the body lies an illusion as to the constitution of the self, an illusion that endows the body with a false unity. In the mirror we find projected the rational self, privileged over the subjective emotional self. Here lies the basis for the Cartesian mind/body split which ascribes all things opposed to self-control, measurement, abstraction, or empirical verification to the feminized, sensual, inferior, or distrustful body. At the same time, however, Foucault's mirror image paradoxically seems to imply that the self is both disembodied and embodied, both absent and present, both an unreal utopian and a real heterotopian projection.

Michel Foucault reminds us not only that the self as a unity or whole may be an illusion, but also that the body's very skin has been written upon while the body itself has been constantly dismembered and disordered.

> The body is the inscribed surface of events (traced by language and dissolved by ideas), the locus of a dissociated Self (adopting the illusion of a substantial unity), and a volume in perpetual disintegration. Genealogy, as an analysis of descent, is thus situated within the articulation of the body and history. Its task is to expose a body totally imprinted by history and the process of history's destruction of the body[17]

> We believe, in any event, that the body obeys the exclusive laws of physiology and that it escapes the influence of history, but this too is false. The body is molded by a great many distinct regimes; it is broken down by the rhythms of work, rest, and holidays; it is poisoned by food or values, through eating habits or moral laws; it constructs resistances....Nothing in man—not even his body—is sufficiently stable to serve as a basis for self recognition or for understanding other men.[18]

In the bodily disenchantment that haunts our postmodern era, if the self is unstable, dephysicalized, and thus beginning to disappear, making projections from it ambiguous and unclear, then the image of the city as a normally functioning or healthy body also begins to be undermined. Thus the corporeal analogies of body/architecture and body/city under posthumanist, poststructualist thought are marked by zones of silence, estrangement, and emptiness.

The Illusions of Sight

One of the difficulties in both the modern and the postmodern problematic of the body lies in the emphasis on vision over all the other senses, because this preference greatly affects the so-called perception of disembodiment as well as the general disenchantment of art. Ever since Descartes called the intellect an "eye of the mind" and made vision, modeled on the camera obscura, the noblest of the senses, the Western world has assumed that the eye's perceptions are regular and reliable. We trust empirical evidence, even though Descartes actually established that there exists a triple displacement, setting up the mind's eye behind the physical eye that was itself looking out the window of a camera obscura. Because of this displacement—or so Leder posits in *The Absent Body*—visual experiences offer the body the strongest experience of disembodiment, as sight withdraws from its rootedness inside a body.

> Unlike the probing finger, the eye leaves its object of exploration unchanged… [and thus developed] in such features of vision the birth of the notion of *theoria*, a detached rather than praxical relation to the world. The body as the place of action and forceful interchange with the world for the moment fades away. This is intensified by the spatial distances sight opens, allowing the subject to dwell experientially far off. In touching, one's own body remains a proximate copresence with the touched, always immediately implicated.

But visual awareness, as when I gaze upward to the stars, can focus trillions of miles away.[19]

It must be argued, however, that when a body is in its most disenchanted and abstract state, there are always reminders of its localization in space and time that implicitly affect its vision. There is an experiential ambiguity to visual perception that both escapes from and is entangled within a body, as the modernists were well aware.[20]

Most rationalists believe that vision can corrupt the mind, leading it into the dark recesses of the archaic and phantasmagorical; therefore a constant war against its illusory effects must be vigorously waged. Barbara Stafford reports in *Body Criticism* that vision became identified with falsification and bodily-induced hallucination, while in contrast touch was linked to fleshless reason.[21] So, it has been argued, it is only when the sense of touch is transferred to the eye that one is able to identify things and to locate them in three-dimensional space. "Purely optical vision by an eye devoid of the synesthetic sense of touch would be a vision without pattern recognition in which only points, or at best two-dimensional extension, would be perceived."[22] Thus touch compensates for visual weaknesses by filling out the surface treatment or texture and the massing of structures. In any event, tactile sensations remind us that the senses are interactive, transferring body sensitivities into perception.

For example, the medical gaze as it developed in the late eighteenth century involved far more than sight: each sense organ was given a particular instrumental function, and the eye was certainly not considered the most important. As Foucault recounted,

The sight/touch/hearing trinity defines a perceptual configuration
in which the inaccessible illness is tracked down by markers, gauged
in depth, drawn to the surface, and projected virtually on the dispersed organs of the corpse....Through touch we can locate visceral
tumors, scirrhous masses, swellings of the ovary, and dilations of the

heart; while with the ear we can perceive "the crepitation of fragments of bone, the rumbling of aneurysm, the more or less clear
sounds of the thorax and the abdomen when sounded." The medical
gaze is now endowed with a plurisensorial structure. A gaze that
touches, hears, and, moreover, not by essence or necessity, sees.[23]

Nevertheless, the confirmations of the ear and the hand remained
under the domination of the eye—which was only temporarily limited to scanning the surface of the body, as eventually the ear and
the hand would become redundant when death and autopsy
revealed the heretofore hidden truth.[24]

Parallel to the rise of empirical techniques for medical diagnosis and pathological anatomy in the last decade of the nineteenth
century was the invention of medical instruments for the graphic
depiction of the body and its processes. For example, pulse rates
were rendered visible by the sphygmoscope, heartbeats were traced
by the cardiograph, and X-rays penetrated the flesh to produce
images of the skeleton system. All of these instruments led to the
common belief that the boundaries of the body were being invaded, exposing the private interior to the more public medical gaze.[25]
Late-twentieth-century electronic imaging technology, such as magnetic resonance imaging (MRI) and computerized tomography
(CT), has further decomposed the corporeal body into bits of data
and abstract images far removed from the classical hands-on probing and touching that were once hallmarks of a medical exam.
Disembodiment is exacerbated further when a woman's body is
treated as a passive reproductive machine and the "fetal person-
hood" as an autonomous patient with its own rights,[26] or when the
body is decomposed into a list of images and test results such as
blood smears, urine sediments, electrographic recordings, endo-
scopic views, sonograms, arteriograms, and venograms.[27]

While this sense of disembodiment haunts our postmodern,
poststructuralist, and posthumanist era, nevertheless, as George
Lakoff describes in *Woman, Fire, and Dangerous Things*, meaning-
ful cognitive structures arise from bodily experiences and from

imaginative processes such as metaphor and metonymy and mental imagery.[28] Lakoff argues that we understand our bodies as containers: they ingest, excrete, breathe in and out, and they contain emotions, such that we can be "filled with anger" or "brimming with tears." Furthermore, we conceptualize many activities in terms of this schema: the visual field, for example, is a container in which "things come in and out of sight." Moreover, the container schema involves a distinction between inside and outside, so that, for instance, we "wake out of sleep" or "we peer in." Rather than making anthropomorphic projections from an alien body in pain or a dematerialized, morcellated body, and rather than positing the rational and objective Cartesian mind as the source of knowledge, Lakoff proposes a material, tactile body that helps us establish our cognitive structures. In postmodern times, no matter how we try to efface the body as the center of our cognitive world, there always remains "the belief that the proper units of knowledge are primarily *concrete*, embodied, incorporated, lived."[29]

THE TACTILE EYE

So there is an inherent dilemma with respect to perception and embodiment: are the body and its senses in fact the source of cognition and knowledge? If, as Lakoff suggests, we cannot avoid projecting the body onto space, then perhaps we should investigate the synesthetic recordings of our body and our senses—especially a "tactile eye" or an "optical touch"—as it relates to the history of architecture and urbanism. After all, architecture is expected to serve the senses, while the city is an environment in which a frenzied attack on all the senses constantly takes place.[30] Yet we must remember that Aristotle believed the desire to touch was shameful, and that since then the sense of touch has usually been viewed with contempt and referred to as the lowliest of the senses. It is subject to the limits of the body and is treated as animalistic and erotic, evading the control of reason. Nevertheless, in the late eighteenth century Johann Gottfried Herder tried valiantly but unsuccessfully to establish haptic perception as the basis of all the other senses, believing that to understand a thing it was necessary for the hands to touch it before the mind could conceptualize or visualize it.[31] To the contrary, at the end of the nineteenth century Aloïs Riegl outlined what he considered to be a linear historical evolution in the arts from a haptic to an optic mode of spatial perception. "The history of art is, for Riegl," Meyer Schapiro explains, "an endless necessary movement from representation based on vision of the object and its parts as proximate, tangible, discrete, and self-sufficient, to the more distant continuum with merging parts, with an increasing role of the spatial voids, and with a more evident reference to the knowing subject as a constituting factor in perception."[32]

Certainly the Futurists advocated a new form of art based on tactile sensations alone. In a 1921 manifesto on "tactilism" Filippo Marinetti asserted that "a visual sense is born in the fingertips. X-ray vision develops, and some people can already see inside their bodies. Others dimly explore the inside of their neighbors' bodies. They all realize that sight, smell, hearing, touch, and taste are modifications of a single keen sense: touch, divided in different ways and localized in different points....With Tactilism we propose to penetrate deeper and outside normal scientific method into the true essence of matter."[33] Here the bodily senses are to be liberated, so that a rebellious energy flows through the body, a more tactile, erotic sensuality that allows the inferior sense of touch to be the primary mediator of matter. As it facilitates an energetic exchange between the body and mind, tactility leads to a sharpening or "funneling" of the senses, and eventually to the re-sensualization of the body.[34]

Walter Benjamin also hinted at an eye that touches when he wrote in *Moscow Diary*, "As I was looking at an extraordinarily beautiful Cézanne, it suddenly occurred to me that it is even linguistically fallacious to speak of 'empathy.' It seemed to me that to the extent that one grasps [that is, gets hold of, touches] a painting, one does not in any way enter into its space; rather, this space thrusts itself forward, especially in various very specific spots."[35] The work of art particularly seems to pierce the observer in fragmentary moments of illumination. But Benjamin also discussed this in terms of everyday artifacts, noting, for example, the visual tactility of modern advertisements: "Now things press too closely on human society.... Today the most real, the mercantile gaze into the heart of things is the art of advertisement. It abolishes the space where contemplation moved and all but hits us between the eyes with things as a car, growing to gigantic proportions, careens at us out of a film screen."[36]

Benjamin perceived that excessive stimuli found along the city streets of everyday life "hurtled things at" the spectator, bombarding the senses, and thus he believed these projectiles were recorded by the mind only as shock experiences. The concept of shock has a military origin: in war, the sudden consolidation of mechanical, electronic, and acoustical power into one single blow can cause the complete disorientation of the senses. When the body is under bombardment, shock overrides its ability to absorb all the stimuli. But it is primarily the visual spectacle—what the battlefield looks like during as well as after an onslaught—that causes this sensual derangement. Every soldier's frantic look from the besieged trenches into the theater of operations during World War I was accompanied by the risk of facial disfigurement. Of course the body tried to shield itself from such shocking stimuli and perversely fascinating views by developing a protective blank stare.[37] Nevertheless, the shocking sight was recorded, albeit in a peripheral manner, unwittingly avoiding the ego's censorship and depositing its hidden traces in the unconscious.

In his analysis of the optical unconscious, Benjamin borrowed the Russian cinematographer Dziga Vertov's portrayal of the hidden, invisible aspects of reality, of peripheral vision, brought into awareness through the prosthetic device of the camera.[38] Benjamin argued, "It is another nature that speaks to the camera than to the eye: other in the sense that a space informed by human consciousness gives way to a space informed by the unconscious....

Photography, with its devices of slow motion and enlargement, reveals the secret. It is through photography that we first discovered the existence of this optical unconscious, just as we discover the instinctual unconscious through psychoanalysis."[39] Thus the camera offered a new way of exploring reality, making visual images into a form of tactile knowledge in which contact, nearness, energetic forces, moving projectiles, and touching emotions became essential elements. It was the Surrealists who taught Benjamin to understand the revolutionary energies contained in unfashionable objects and outmoded architecture, bringing "the immense forces of 'atmosphere' concealed in these things to the point of explosion" so that the body was moved to action.[40] And architecture, normally viewed in a state of distraction, was primarily tactile, with its atmospherically charged spaces that reached out to touch or move the spectator and then radiated throughout the body and all the senses.[41]

We might begin to understand this tactile appropriation by examining Herbert Bayer's haunting photomontage of 1931–1932 entitled *Lonely Metropolitan*. Here sight and touch are juxtaposed in an emblematic image of an eye embedded like a stigma within an open palm. The hand becomes a background for the eye, which has left its socket in the head and moved to the center of the palm.[42] That these hands hold a view reveals the double function of seeing and interpreting. Once again, it is the eye that guides the hand, but it is touch that informs the eye; this makes reference to the new tactility of the dynamic city of the early twentieth century, to the metropolis that physically and emotionally reached out to hit the spectator between the eyes. By fetishizing the eyes and allowing them to become autonomous, however, the image is also a counterreaction to the tyranny of total vision over the other senses, and thus a celebration of the rise of the haptic experiences of the metropolis. This is a portrait of the big city: eyes that return the look, eyes that are not closed to reality, eyes that compel the spectator to unravel the mystery of the assembled image that disrupts the normal appearance of things. It calls out for a new vision, juxtaposing the sharp focus of rationality with the shadows of archaic powers that lurk in the background. And the transfer of the eye from head to hand is also representative of the lonely, uprooted traveller who has left home and emigrated to the big city. The upturned hands in the image suggest the stigmata imposed by the metropolis: the helplessness of the individual lost in the crowd, or the penetrating gaze of so many strangers, or the fear of unexpected violence from unknown persons. And hence the emblematic reference to the eye as an amulet to ward off evil. But rather than being a site that controls the future of humanity, that alienates and destroys the individual, the metropolis has in this case become the place where a person can manage his destiny. Space in the image and the metropolis are organized visually, as the eyes direct the hands.

But Bayer's image juxtaposes these hands with the walls of city buildings in the background, upon which their shadow is projected. The montage effect that merges the hands and the building within the same space sets up a second interaction between the eye and the hand: that of an optical unconscious in which we see and understand different aspects of familiar objects hidden in the shadows of obscurity. Benjamin wrote that the city revealed itself to those who traversed it absent-mindedly, doing so through the array of images that bombarded the spectator while in a semi-awakened state: a scenographic traveling shot seen from a moving vehicle, or a peripheral oblique view quickly glimpsed through the window of a moving train, or the sight of electric lights flashing and gigantic billboards adorning city walls.[43] These images invaded, probed, or penetrated the viewer, and by their very tactility they affected visual perception and critical awareness. As Benjamin noted,

> Architecture has never been idle. Buildings are appropriated in a
> twofold manner: by use and by perception—or rather, by touch and
> sight.... Tactile appropriation is accomplished not so much by atten-
> tion as by habit. As regards architecture, habit determines to a large
> extent even optical reception. The latter, too, occurs much less
> through rapt attention than by noticing the object in incidental

fashion....For the tasks which face the human apparatus of perception...cannot be solved by optical means, that is, by contemplation, alone. They are mastered gradually by habit, under the guidance of tactile appropriation.[44]

The Optical Unconscious

Evidently Franz Kafka discovered a movie theater in Prague that was named Cinema of the Blind, prompting him to write, "Every cinema should be called that. Their flickering images blind people to reality...[for photography] concentrates one's eyes on the superficial."[45] However, this result is quite at odds with the tactility provided by montage effects in film. Annette Michelson has explained that when montage theory first evolved (1924–1930), it was driven by an underlying general hypothesis: "that western man [was] now disposed of a new and powerful cognitive instrument which gave him access to a clearer and fuller understanding of existence in the world."[46] This new vision was exemplified by Vertov's film *Man with a Movie Camera*, for Vertov believed he was creating a "film-thing" with sufficient kinetic energy to affect the viewer's consciousness.[47] His "film-eye" (or "Kino-Eye") method used the camera's eye to reorganize the visible world, and to reveal aspects inaccessible to the naked human eye. In his street scenes of moving vehicles, for example, he took advantage of cinematic techniques and the ability of the camera to create fantastical visions by following a normal street scene with a scene in which vehicles move perpendicularly to each other.[48] The film is structured around the repetitive motifs of the circle, the vertical line, and the horizontal line: the circle represents the camera's lens or the human eye, and the lines refer to industrial construction, movement patterns, and communications. Circles in the form of film cans, projector reels, wheels, headlights, gears, valve controls, bicycles, eyeballs, and so forth are seen in close-up. These are contrasted with vertical patterns, which appear in architectural constructions, scaffolding, posters, newspapers, smokestacks, and telephone poles, and with the horizontal patterns of landscapes, bridges, railroad tracks, and vehicular movements.[49]

The "street and the eye" sequence in Vertov's *Man with a Movie Camera* first juxtaposes shots of human eyes and traffic scenes, and then shows a scene of traffic "severing" the human eye along with various accident scenes. It is meant to contrapose images "from the point of view of the human eye armed with the camera's eye" with images "from the point of view of the unaided human eye." Knowing that visual data is apparently filtered into the conscious mind through a small pinhole in the center of the retina, and that information registering in peripheral vision is subsequently routed to the unconscious, Vertov generated a variety of repetitive patterns in order to create a sense of kinetic power and subliminal psychological force. For example, he was able to arouse fear in audience members before they actually saw the accident scene.[50] Through his method of cutting between two shots, Vertov created optical "explosions." This "juxtaposition of different visual compositions and their insertions of unexpected light flashes (optical pulsations)" was intended to shock the spectators, and to engage them in perceiving the world in novel and unconventional ways.[51] Praising the camera's ability to aid the naked eye, Vertov ended his film by literalizing the film-eye metaphor and by noting the interrelationships between human perception and technology: the exit shot superimposes a human iris over the mechanical lens of the camera, thus asking the viewer to perceive more than the naked eye can detect, "to think not only about what appears right before us but also about what is hidden beneath the surface of reality."[52]

Along with the film-eye, Vertov also experimented with the radio-eye, or what he called "visually conveyed sound": a method of hearing based on elemental sound materials that were placed in sequence to form rhythmic pulsations of ascents, peaks, and declines. Thus seeing and hearing together organized a new mode of perception, one based on sounds and images drawn from everyday life. Vertov's work was an obvious influence on Walter

Benjamin as well as on Walter Ruttmann. The latter's montage documentary *Berlin—Symphony of a Great City* (1927) reveals his debt to Vertov. A year later, Ruttmann recorded a radiophonic montage for Berlin Radio entitled "Weekend," in which, from the moment the train leaves the city to the final good-byes of the lovers, sound fragments and silent intervals are woven together until they form an acoustical mosaic.[53] Interestingly, in 1924 Hans Flesch, the founding director of Berlin Radio, and his director Hans Bodenstedt had experimented with "sound portraits" of cityscapes—quick successions of one-minute street sounds, one-minute protest marches, one-minute stock market noises, and one-minute factory machines.[54]

If industrialization and urbanization created a crisis of perception by speeding up time and fragmenting space, which resulted in the individual's withdrawal as his senses were bombarded with too many images, then technical reproductions—the cinema, the radio, the photograph, and the phonograph—offered a palliative. They slowed down time and constructed synthetic realities through montage, reassembling these fragmented images and sounds under new guidelines. Thus Walter Benjamin spoke of the resurgence of mimicry within modernism, which allowed for the discovery of patterns that were once invisible or beyond recognition but now had become developed through a new consciousness, or a new physiognomic awareness of visual and acoustical information.[55] The ability both to perceive and to produce similarities or correspondences relied on a mimetic faculty, or so Benjamin argued.[56] But, as he wrote in "Doctrine of the Similar," "The similarities which one perceives consciously, for instance in faces, are, when compared to the countless similarities perceived unconsciously or not at all, like the enormous underwater mass of an iceberg in comparison to the small tip which one sees projecting above the waves."[57] Thus the development of modern mimetic machines enhanced the spectator's/listener's ability to play with and even to restore the lost powers of sensation. The optical unconscious offered new ways of perceiving and exploring "the physiognomic aspects of visual worlds" and thus of transforming culture and society in new and wondrous ways.[58] Benjamin pointed out, "Every day the urge grows stronger to get hold of an object at close range by way of its likeness, its reproduction."[59]

THE SKIN OF THE BODY

In an extended metaphor, Roland Barthes noted, "Language is a skin I rub against the other. It is as if I had words instead of fingers, or fingers at the tips of my words."[60] Thus physiognomy, Stafford claims, could be seen as a graphology of character, as it attempts to fathom the nature of an individual that lay behind the skin, to read legible signs that only the trained eye could decipher, and to probe beneath the external boundary of the body.[61] The skin is a metaphor that allows for both surface and depth, while simultaneously representing an absolute limit. Reading a text is a physiognomic activity, as it involves the peeling away of layer after layer of the palimpsest to reveal what lies below. It represents the decomposition of the body of the text, or the deconstructivist probing of an image with the eyes, exploring the gaps and fissures in and beneath the surface.[62] Optical proximity or tactile vision implies a dismembering or disordering of the structural whole, a focus on parts and fragments, and an imaginary reassemblage. Distance is smashed and order violated as touching proceeds part by part. While vision scans over the surface skin, taking in a panoramic whole, touching is personal; it particularizes and fragments as it precedes sequentially.

We might say the same of the popular "physiologies" of Parisian life in the mid-nineteenth century, which left neither a figure nor a place unsketched. As Walter Benjamin reported, these harmless scribblings describing Paris in detail veiled the surface of the city, yet were so removed from actual experience that larger motives lay hidden beneath. Benign and entertaining, these depictions helped adapt the initiate to the strange new conditions of big cities. Jorg Simmel knew it was through the bodily senses that urban individuals perceived each other, forming emotional likes and dislikes as well as feelings such as alienation and loneliness.

> Someone who sees without hearing is much more uneasy than some-
> one who hears without seeing. In this there is something characteris-
> tic of the sociology of the big city. Interpersonal relationships in big
> cities are distinguished by a marked preponderance of the activity of
> the eye over the activity of the ear. The main reason for this is the
> public means of transportation. Before the development of buses,
> railroads, and trams in the nineteenth century, people had never
> been in a position of having to look at one another for long minutes
> or even hours without speaking to one another.[63]

This unpleasant experience was exacerbated by the belief that every individual hid something secret within himself that made him fearsome to others. "The physiologies were designed to brush such disquieting notions aside as insignificant. They constituted, so to speak, the blinkers of the 'narrow-minded city animal' which Marx wrote about."[64] They assured people that even without the slightest empirical knowledge, they too could ascertain what profession, character, background, and lifestyle belonged to any anonymous passer-by.[65]

The movie camera, on the other hand, opened up new physiognomic aspects of visual worlds, giving them a magical aura: the smallest details were blown up into huge images that filled the screen, and slow motion revealed new visual patterns, while oblique views, tracking shots, and sequences of images caused new associative linkages in the spectator's mind. A "lust of the eyes" for phantasmagorical views as well as for unsightly scenes was the basic attraction of the new medium. It has been argued that the popular reception of film rested on the viewer's curiosity in visually examining the body's landscape—the nose, the eyes, the lips, the arms, the muscles, the hair—in the greatest of detail. Consequently, a parallel can be established between the cinematic eye and the anatomist's eye. Giuliana Bruno claims, for example, that the spectacle of the anatomy lesson was a predecessor of the cinema, for they both investigate and fragment the body.[66] But the parallels between film and the body can be extended further, for the very language of film construction bears similarities to anatomical analysis and epidermic operations, as it involves dismemberment or cutting and dissecting or decoupage of the celluloid skin of film.[67] To continue the analogy between the body and early cinema, the early twentieth-century film theorist Bela Balazs claimed that a director must be highly trained in physiognomy, especially for the use of close-ups.[68] "The camera close-ups aim at the uncontrolled small areas of the face; thus it is able to photograph the subconscious."[69] Film gave visual shape to physiognomic qualities in human beings, and to animate and inanimate nature.[70] Balazs wrote:

> We see how a film can make the machine acquire a face and how, in motion, these features assume a horrifying expression. Sometimes we see how an ostensibly neutral industrial "area" turns into a "landscape" full of ominous moods, a deadly animated landscape.[71]

> It is the task of a director to discover the eyes of a landscape. Such images, caught in the twinkling of an eye, have the expressive look of human eyes. Close-ups of such moments yield a subjective image of the world and succeed, despite the mechanical nature of the photographic apparatus, in showing the world as colored by a temperament, as illuminated by an emotion: poetry projected, objectified.[72]

Barbara Stafford draws a wonderful analogy between the physiognomic method of anatomical drawings and the figural and emotional etchings of Rome made by Giovanni Battista Piranesi in the late eighteenth century.[73] Piranesi's work was that of an anatomist uncovering information from a previous era, and he asked the beholder to wander slowly through the remnants of the city's morcellated past. He allowed the decaying bodies of his ruins to remain suffering surfaces, aging with dirt. Stafford believes that "he applied surgical procedures taken…from medical illustrations, to turn the still-living fabric inside out."[74] "Flayed bodies became analogues for temples peeled of their marble. Once the rind was removed, they exhibited the fissures and channels of underlying rubblework."[75] Following the way anatomical drawings depicted the body, Piranesi peered through holes into architectural ruins formerly covered with flesh and skin; he presented ruined remains in various stages, piling them up one on top of the other until they recomposed into one assemblage, and when confronted with interruptions and gaps, he sutured hypothetical views together which at best were only conjectures. Stafford explains, "Piranesi thus helped his contemporaries to recontextualize the ruins of the past into the living organism of modern urban Rome."[76]

But more than this, Piranesi saw architecture as an interplay of interior and exterior, and as an art of a very specific body, one that was fatigued and decaying, mutilated and disappearing. No detail appears to have escaped his view: ancient subterranean water pipes, tools, and decorative inscriptions were given as much attention as monumental structures such as the Castel Sant'Angelo or St. Peter's Square. In this sense, Piranesi's work was a forerunner of the Freudian model of remembering, for both linked the city of Rome to the acts of forgetting and repression. "In his manic reconstructions of Etruscan-Roman Antiquity, which had been suppressed by Classicism, Piranesi seems to have been following the basic psychoanalytic rule: everything is significant, particularly the incidental, the fragmentary, the ignoble and ugly as well as the base."[77] Sigmund Freud discussed the pathological hold the past had on the present if one did not resolve or come to terms with it but instead forced it underground and into hiding. Rome became his architectural metaphor for repressed memory, and psychoanalysis the technique for excavating this buried city and retrieving its lost past.

When images of the flayed man—used by Piranesi and exposed by Freud—first appeared in sixteenth-century mannerism, they did so at the very moment when the systematic, scientific exploration of the body became an artistic genre, when pleasure was obtained by laying bare one's interior mechanism, probing artistically into the depths of one's inner feelings and being.[78] Flaying as an artistic gesture derives from ancient Greek myth: Marsyas challenged Apollo to a musical contest and lost, so Apollo ordered him to be flayed alive for his "artistic hubris." Thus today we envision the creative process as a painful self-flaying.[79] For example, Michelangelo painted himself in the Sistine Chapel's Last Judgment fresco as an empty skin held up by St. Bartholomew. Such a visual probe of the body, exposing its inner self to view in such an extreme manner, represents a moment of transition, a moment when the artist sees himself as alienated from existing conditions, subject to their violation. "Indeed, Michelangelo produced his flayed bodies at a time of crisis: when Italy, shattered by the sack of Rome, was becoming more and more manneristic in its aesthetic ideals, and when the extreme opticity of the Renaissance was no longer regarded as compulsory by many artists."[80]

BONE STRUCTURES

Perhaps the most penetrating, tactile vision existing today occurs through the use of medical scanning and probing devices, from X-ray machines to magnetic resonance imaging and ultrasound. The Futurists seem to have been the first to address this technology's potential for a new art of transparency. László Moholy-Nagy borrowed a quotation from a 1912 Futurist statement that read:

> Who can still believe in the opacity of bodies, since our sharpened and multiplied sensitiveness has already penetrated the obscure manifestations of the medium? Why should we forget in our creations the doubled power of our sight, capable of giving results analogous to those of the X-rays?[81]

And Moholy-Nagy himself continued:

The X-ray pictures about which the Futurists spoke are among the most outstanding space-time examples on the static plane. They give a transparent view of an opaque solid, the outside and inside of the structure. The passion for transparencies is one of the most spectacular features of our time. We might say, with pardonable enthusiasm, that structure becomes transparency and transparency manifests structure.[82]

When director Sergei Eisenstein spoke about film as a mimetic art, he described two kinds of mimesis: one he called the magic type of imitation, which copies forms like a mirror, and for which he showed great disdain, while the other imitated the principle behind the obvious surface of an object. "The age of form," he proclaimed to a group of independent filmmakers at La Sarraz in 1929, "is drawing to a close. We are penetrating matter. We are penetrating [through analysis] behind appearance into the principle of appearance. In doing so we are mastering it."[83] Before manipulating montage effects, the artist proceeded through a decomposition—an X-ray "autopsy" of sorts—of the visible, of the "flesh." This X-ray vision penetrated beyond the exterior structure of an object to the skeletal form concealed within, and it involved a passage through flesh-like appearances that concealed the linear schema or line drawing. "The initial stage of the creation of meaning depends on the intuitively magic physiognomic disclosure of the line which lies concealed within the body of the object (or text)—of the 'bone-structure.'" Eisenstein used the image "of the skull squeezing through the surface of the face" as a metaphor for expressive movement or as a model to be imitated visually.[84]

This new penetrative method of seeing that revealed the underlying bone structure subsequently became the generative device for dissolving the old mode of vision and producing a new one. Thus the dream of transparency went hand in hand with new visual arrangements and with the idea of historical discontinuity. Paul Scheerbart wrote in *Glass Architecture* (1914) that to avoid the closed character of rooms, architecture must introduce glass in every possible wall, and it must also make liberal use of water, mirrors, and other reflecting materials, in order to illuminate a revolutionary new world. If man lives within a closed box, Scheerbart reasoned, his culture will likewise retain a closed character. To create a new culture, the architect must therefore create a new environment.[85] The recent inventions of the iron skeleton and the reinforced concrete skeleton framework made a new architecture of glass feasible. "Glass architecture," Scheerbart wrote, "will have a tough fight on its hands, but force of habit must be overcome.... Everything new has to wage an arduous campaign against entrenched tradition."[86] Glass architecture could transform the face of the earth, as it could be used to create towers of light in cities and under the sea, garden paths and majolica tiles, self-opening and self-closing doors, cars and motorboats in many colors, delicate ornamentation, and columns of colored light for use in the streets, just to name a few of Scheerbart's examples. "Glass architecture will only come if the city as we know it goes....This dissolution must take place."[87]

Walter Benjamin was clearly aware of Scheerbart's utopian visions, noting that the social conditions for such revolutionary technology are always late in arriving.[88] Benjamin believed that Scheerbart had championed the new glass architecture because transparency made secrecy and privacy impossible. Eventually this new glass architecture would cause human nature itself to be transformed.[89] Thus the early glass and steel arcades, which were precursors of modern architecture, were used by Benjamin to refer to his method of exposing truth: long corridors roofed with glass that cut through the thicket of the city became his metaphor for "historical illumination." Although considered regressive and outmoded by the 1920s, the arcade remained an image of transparency, offering a straight, clear path towards an emancipatory future. Everything that stood against innovation and promise was to be dissolved in the clear light that they afforded, but they also revealed regressions occurring underneath the dazzling appearance of progress. Scheerbart's glass architecture referred to a utopian potential: his was an aesthetic gesture that contained a suppressed social and political structure.[90] The transparency and commanding presence of glass architecture were juxtaposed against the opacity and impenetrability of subjective art and proclaimed the necessity of clearing a way through the latter's obfuscations.

Le Corbusier was also struggling to advance his revolutionary new architecture within a society that had failed to develop a directive line, a society that was without a rational order or plan. In his view, the dead skeletal structure of architecture was devoid of flesh and skin and needed be exhumed and turned into the very structure of life. Presenting the skeletal structure of a building that was purified of all material, devoid of organs, made its anatomy and its geometric order visible.[91] But, as Robert Romanyshyn has argued in *Technology as Symptom and Dream*, the corpse is the body in its most abandoned state, the body seen from the furthest distance. "Filtered through the grid, the body enters into the geometric space of linear perspective in pieces," where it can be more precisely analyzed, mapped, scaled, and then resurrected as a machine.[92] Le Corbusier broke down his skeletal structure into what he saw as the five points of architecture: pilotis, roof gardens, free plans, horizontal windows, and free facades. He reassembled these elements, all intimately tied to the body, into a machine for living by raising the floor slabs above the ground on feet, and cladding the building in the luminous skin of the facade. On the roof garden, the body found places to exercise and to absorb the sun; within the interior and along its ramps, movement was liberated; and outside the window, the framed spectacle of nature stood on review. In turn, he made his Radiant City a body filled with organs: a brain as the directive force of the nervous system, blood to circulate through the great transportation routes of its veins, lungs for breathing spaces, and a heart as its cultural center giving the entity life. The body was thus reworked—serialized, standardized, industrialized— by the machine.

As Benjamin warned, we also need to take into account the dark or
dystopian side of both progress and politics, and thus we turn to
examine the Man of Glass as a generic model of a human being.
For years unsubstantiated references appeared in the museum world
to the existence of a "Man of Glass" or an "X-Ray Man," which
supposedly had been a very popular display at various international
expositions in the 1930s. It was finally discovered that such a man
had indeed been made. The popular response had been so enthusiastic that many copies were created. The Man of Glass was a model
of a man standing erect, elevated on a podium. This was not the
image of a cadaver under dissection, a bloody, smelly, and putrefy-
ing body in a stage of decomposition; this was a purified model of
a man based on classical proportions. Constructed out of a material
that had the appearance of glass, it was thus entirely "whole" yet its
interior was completely visible. Spectators lined up for hours to
view this apparition—perhaps because they wanted to improve
their knowledge of anatomy, but more likely because they were fas-
cinated by this new technology capable of replicating the body, by
the illuminated organs, and by the new material that simulated a
shiny covering of glass. And this Man of Glass's arms, outstretched
as if in prayer, gave him a pose that since antiquity has symbolized
dialog with the divine spirits that transmit the power of life.[93]

It seems that this astonishing Man of Glass had first been presented to the German public in 1930 at the Dresden International
Exposition of Hygiene. Then in 1935 this "transparent citizen," as it
was sometimes called, was shown to the Berlin public during a pro-
paganda spectacle entitled "The Wonder of Life." At this event the
Man of Glass was the center of a sound and light show which slowly illuminated each of the carefully painted internal organs, beginning with the heart, until a complete explication of the human
anatomy had been made. The climax of the show, however, was the
appearance of a raised banner declaring, "Man is astonished before
the sea that knows no repose, rivers, the spectacle of a starry sky,

and he forgets that of all the wonders, it is he that is the greatest."[94] Man was no less than a technical and artistic masterpiece.

After considerable research, in 1990 Martin Roth discovered that three Men of Glass still existed in the United States. Two were offered to the German Historical Museum in Berlin and were painstakingly restored. Then, in collaboration with the Dresden museum, Roth mounted a very successful exhibit called "The Investigation of the Body."[95] Spectators entered the first room of the exhibit through a simulated vaginal opening and moved from there into the interior of a body. Here was displayed the Foucauldian body formed by the medical gaze, the body revealed by anatomy, and its vulgarization during the Enlightenment, as well as *memento mori* and instruments of dissection. But the exhibition also drew on Foucault's exploration of the side of humanism that intended to make the body into an optimally obedient and useful machine by developing a disciplinary policy, to change it into a docile form through coercion. As Foucault wrote,

> Discipline increases the forces of the body (in economic terms of utility) and diminishes these same forces (in political terms of obedience). In short, it dissociates power from the body; on the one hand, it turns it into an "aptitude," a "capacity," which it seeks to increase; on the other hand, it reverses the course of the energy, the power that might result from it, and turns it into a relation of strict subjection. If economic exploitation separates the force and the product of labor, let us say that disciplinary coercion establishes in the body the constricting link between an increased aptitude and an increased domination.[96]

Power over life, as Foucault detailed, developed around two different poles:

> One of these poles—the first to be formed, it seems—centered on the body as machine: its disciplining, the optimization of its capabilities, the extortion of its forces, the parallel increase of its usefulness

and its docility, its integration into systems of efficient and economic controls, all this was ensured by the procedures of power that characterized the disciplines: an anatomo-politics of the human body. The second, formed somewhat later, focused on the species body, the body imbued with the mechanics of life and serving as the basis of the biological processes: propagation, births and mortality, the level of health, life expectancy and longevity, with all the conditions that can cause these to vary. Their supervision was effected through an entire series of interventions and regulatory controls: a bio-politics of the population.[97]

Thus the organizers of the 1990 exhibition felt that the Man of Glass had a dual purpose: it was simultaneously a display of popular science—Foucault's anatomo-politics—and a normative model of a human being based on classical standards and proportions—bio-politics.

Consequently, the 1990 exhibition showed how the human being had been destroyed, mutilated, and dismembered during World War I, because the organizers felt that it was in this spirit that the Man of Glass had been conceived and presented as the ideal citizen of the Third Reich. Again we can refer to Walter Benjamin, who noted that the decline of direct experience in daily life stemmed in part from World War I, as men returned from war literally unable to recount what they had been through, numbed by the horrors of human destruction brought about through entirely new means of mechanical warfare. But the rise of dry and factual information was also to be blamed for the loss of directly felt experience. Extraordinary, implausible yet miraculous, and intensely personal accounts were replaced with verifiable data that was "understandable in itself" or "shot through with explanation." This replacement caused an aspect of humanity to disappear, as it placed too much reliance on anonymous authorities, such as the press, while it devalued the traditional influences that helped shape the way men reasoned reflectively and acted conscientiously in the world. Because of this history, modern man—silent and submissive—was ready to be organized in service to the fascist state.[98]

In the second and final room of the 1990 exhibition was presented information on the procedures that helped create a "normal healthy body" in the 1920s and 1930s. Shown here were the practices of the Third Reich that produced the "Body of the People": sports, dance, eugenics, and brutal racist and social policies. This display outlined the concepts and the mentality that had produced this "Citizen of Glass," and how this object came to represent a pure, transparent form, a mute body devoid of an inner self or a mind of its own, completely manipulable and controllable. The conclusion of the 1990 exhibition was an examination of the "New Man" as represented in the arts of the 1920s, particularly as articulated by the Bauhaus and in the work of Oskar Schlemmer and Herbert Bayer. Bayer's entry for "The Wonder of Life" exposition had been a human figure made of glass modeled after Polyclitus's *Doryphorus* sculpture (the apotheosis of youth, energy, and manliness), displayed before a large egg (the symbol of life). Alexander Dorner explained Bayer's image in the following manner: "All our traditional notions about classical antiquity, which make of it a haven of health, beauty, and virtue, become forces promoting our interest in medicine and turning research into an instrument for creating beauty. Two disparate things are again merged in interaction; they change and increase each other's essences and values, and energize life."[99] The sciences of life and artistic expression freshly reconciled lent themselves to the aestheticization of politics—in both its fascist and its avant-garde form.

THEATER AND THE BODY

For further definitions of the "New Man" of the 1920s we turn, as did the 1990 exhibition, to Oskar Schlemmer, who taught a "Course on Man" at the Bauhaus. Writing in 1928, Schlemmer noted, "My subject shall be a lofty one: man and everything connected with him: the nude, figural drawing, art history, hygiene, etc."[100] It was essential for the new life of the twentieth century that man be understood as a cosmic being. "His conditions of existence, his relationships with the natural and artificial environment, his mechanism and organism, his material, spiritual, and intellectual image; in short, man as a bodily and spiritual being is a necessary and important subject of instruction."[101] To achieve this, Schlemmer's course syllabus began with the history of man's development, a theory of race and sexual behavior, discussions of hygiene, and studies of the nervous system before branching into programs on figure drawing, as well as on man in the space of the stage or in his environment, which Schlemmer called "the scene."[102]

"Life has become so mechanized," Oskar Schlemmer wrote in his diary of 1922, "thanks to machines and a technology which our senses can not possibly ignore, that we are intensely aware of man as a machine and the body as a mechanism."[103] Therefore he argued that the theater should not ignore the impact of technology on the human body, but instead must present the latter as harmonious with yet superior to the machine, since man, despite all of his apparent breakages, fragmentations, and cripplings, is indestructible.[104] The human body would become the mediator of new configurations and spatial patterns, created out of a new organization of shapes, colors, and movements.[105] Schlemmer based his search for an eternal image of man, a quintessence of indestructibility, on abstract geometric forms:

> A square for the rib cage, a circle for the belly, a cylinder for the neck, and cylinders for arms and thighs; spheres for the joints of the elbows, knees, and shoulders; a sphere for head and eyes; the nose a triangle; a line to connect heart and brain, the ornament that takes shape between body and the outside world and symbolizes their relationship to one another.[106]

When these geometric forms were transferred to the body of an actor and transformed by costume, Schlemmer called the result "ambulant architecture."[107]

In Schlemmer's book *Man and the Art Figure* (1924), theater was assigned an intermediary position between religious cults and popular diversions such as clowns, acrobats, and jugglers.[108] But it was really the "effects of the body"—their precise, efficient, calculated gestures—that Schlemmer admired with regard to the theater. The purity of these movements was astonishing: they were unrelated to the spoken word and did not mimic anything in real life, instead establishing a drama of absolute artifice. The human body and the mathematics of cubic space followed the same laws: both were determined mechanically and rationally. Thus Schlemmer's "Dance of the Batons" or "Dance of the Circles" (1926–1927) focused the spectator's attention on the visible effects of body movements, particularly through the use of costumes and masks that transformed the actors into geometric shapes such as white bars or brilliant circles. "The Dance of Forms "(1926) and "Equilibristik" (1927) both had as a theme the confrontation between man and object. The body was visualized in its struggle to gain a state of equilibrium, and its motion recalled the art of juggling or the manipulation of objects such as bars, spheres, or giant letters of the alphabet. In these scenes, the lifting of an arm, a hand, or a finger was a triumphal act. The slightest movement became a unique event that was its own justification. Yet each actor worked outside of the traditional realm of spectacle; he never mimicked the actual performance of a juggler or an acrobat. What became important was the formal plan, the analysis of the movements, or the pattern these forms carved out of the space through which they moved. This art of pure artifice was not a spectacle purely meant to entertain, for it held a didactic role as well: it was intended to produce a new knowledge of the body. And it gave rise to a new aesthetics of purity and exactitude, one based on mathematical relationships.[109]

Schlemmer's "Triadic Ballet," for example, was a dance composed of three immutable elements: pure forms, colors, and movements. These elements were then based on the plane geometry of the dancing surface, divided into shapes, and the solid geometry of moving bodies, dressed in costumes that actually hindered natural movements. "In this way," he wrote, "dance, by origin Dionysian and full of emotion, becomes Apollonian and austere in its final form, a symbol of a reconciliation of polarities."[110] A performance conceived entirely as a mechanized drama would soon lose the spectator's interest if man himself were not the essential element of drama, but "he will remain so as long as there is a stage. He is the antithesis of the rationally constructed world of form, color and light; he is the vessel of the unknown, the immediate, the transcendental."[111] Thus it was the right—the imperative—of all Bauhaus artists to preserve this mystery, this enigma, of man.

In Schlemmer's view, the instinctual and sensual side of human nature were to be mistrusted and bypassed, and "every organic form…stiffened into geometry."[112] Abstraction facilitated the intellect's complete control over the body's emotional expressions and appearances, yet it allowed Schlemmer to turn the mechanical metaphor back on itself as he confronted the soullessness of the machine with the struggle of the human form to overcome nature and its elemental forces.[113] In 1926 he wrote:

> If contemporary artists love machines and technology, if they want
> to convey precision instead of vagueness and blur, this is an instinc-
> tual attempt to save themselves from chaos and find forms for our
> time. These artists are prepared to recast the disadvantages and
> angers of the machine age into the advantages of an exact meta-
> physics, to express the impulses of the present day and modern
> humanity and to lend them unique and unprecedented form.[114]

In an attempt to give metaphysics a body, which he termed "transcendental anatomy," Schlemmer developed an ideal form for the body that was a super-individual and timeless shape, a form that also could be projected onto architecture. In his sculpture *Architectural Sculpture R* (1919), for example, he presented a three-dimensional figure, both solid and surface, emerging from the plane of the background. The work linked the human figure with the elements of a hypothetical building facade onto which it might be attached, yet the architectural elements were referred back to the scale-determining human body.[115] All his metaphysical figurations of man were based on archaic Greek sculpture, which Schlemmer felt offered "nude and clothed figures, complementing one another, opposed to one another, overlapping, half right, left, and diagonal."[116] In these Greek precedents Schlemmer found that all the expressiveness of the human body had been distilled into the simplest movements, gestures, and poses. When translated into his puppet-like theatrical forms, they provided a compromise between his formalist, abstract utopia and his representation of a body in motion, between the human being and the mechanical demons created by man yet whose technological imperatives he needed to resist.[117]

DOLLS AND AUTOMATONS

Puppets, mannequins, and dolls represent the paradox of being both anthropomorphic projections and stuffed, lifeless things.[118] When in motion, they are illusions of living beings that can copy the movements of a human body; they define the meaning of the word "automaton." The nineteenth century's fascination with such models bears evidence of its anxiety over the unstoppable development of industrial production, and the accompanying interminable flow of commodities. Karl Marx explained that the first automaton used for practical purposes was the watch; after its introduction, all the theories of production of uniform movements were based on its measurements. This precision instrument gave rise to the gearworks of automated dolls that offered the spectacle of the same movements repeated over and over.[119] In the mid-eighteenth century, Jacques de Vaucanson amazed the French Academy with his magical dolls that could play musical instruments, write letters, and even dance. And another automaton maker, Pierre Jacquet-Droz, achieved considerable fame when he designed a young girl playing the harpsichord; it was described by contemporaries as "a vestal virgin with a heart of steel."[120]

Inevitably there arose the obvious fear that man himself might copy these automatons and begin to function with the precision of a well-constructed watch, or that by wearing prosthetic devices and relying too heavily on mechanical aids he might become a mere robot. Warnings were sounded in both amusing and alarming terms. In an 1859 *Scientific American* essay entitled "The Artificial Man," the author tells of a visit to a medical library, where he found a volume entitled *Biggs on Artificial Limbs* that described a London factory for prosthetic devices. He then visited the factory, where he saw a worker pass by with an artificial leg slung over his shoulder, and a severed hand lying was on a nearby table. As he walked thought the streets of London, he began to hallucinate—he saw artificial teeth, wigs, and eyes everywhere, which prompted him to ask,

> What member is there in this artful age that we can depend on as
> genuine? What secret bodily defect that we particularly desire to
> keep to ourselves that wicked *Times* does not show up in its advertis-
> ing sheet and tell us how to tinker?…If the individual can thus
> craftily be built up [as an artificial man], imagine, good reader, the
> nightly dissolution. Picture your valet taking off both your legs…
> carefully lacing away your arm, disengaging your wig, easing you of
> your glass eye, washing and putting by your masticators, and finally,
> helping the bare vital principle into bed, there to lie up in ordinary,
> like a dismantled hulk, for the rest of the night! [121]

But besides conjuring up fears of imitation as well as of the dehumanizing effects of the cycle of production and consumption, toys and automated dolls also held another role. In the nineteenth century, toys for adults were used in every department store as displays for commodities. Placed in these phantasmagorical milieus, they worked an intoxicating spell, irresistibly enticing the shopper. The fetishization of displayed merchandise disguised the complex ends and means of production: as items on display, these goods were divorced from any reference to the laborer who actually had produced them.[122] This phenomenon could be generalized to include the entire shop window or department store interior. Moreover, mechanical dolls tended to confuse the animate with the inanimate, and therefore they became perfect stand-ins for the commodity. And of course puppets, mannequins, and dolls represented the mass-production of identity, whether woman as commodity (that is, as prostitute or doll) or man as automaton. Fashion, Benjamin accounted, always had an ability to attach "sex appeal to the inorganic."[123] The woman who aligns herself with the fashionable through artifice and who represses her own natural decay mimics the mannequin: "Just as the much-admired mannequin has detachable parts, so fashion encourages the fetishistic fragmentation of the living body."[124] "For fashion was never anything but the parody of the gaily decked-out corpse....For this reason she changes so rapidly, teasing death, already becoming something else again, something new, as death looks about for her in order to strike her down."[125]

To rework the male body as automaton and to liberate it from both aestheticizing and effeminizing effects was Futurist Filippo Marinetti's goal. In this we see his desire to escape the limitations and transcend the boundaries imposed by a disenchantment with both the material and the maternal world. He wrote:

> With the machine, I intend to signify rhythm and futurity; the machine gives lessons in order, discipline, force, precision, and continuity....With the machine I mean to leave behind all that is languorous, shadowy, nebulous, indecisive, imprecise, unsuccessful, sad, and melancholy in order to return to order, precision, will, strict necessity, the essential, the synthesis.[126]

Thus Marinetti used the machine first as a model for the functional organization of the social and political body and of the aesthetic order, and second for instrumental control over the transgressive energies of the material body. And he believed this mechanized body to be a productive force, functioning at full capacity, fully plugged in, with every sense aroused:

> Your machine of fused iron and steel, this motor built to exact speci-fications, will give you back not only what you put into it, but dou-ble or triple, much more and much better than the calculations of its builder—its father!—made provision for.[127]

By neutralizing oppositional forces, Marinetti was able to define a perfected, and productive, superhuman male machine, modeled after and disciplined by the instrumental laws of science and technology. This male automaton was even created outside the body of a woman:

> Well then: I confess that before so intoxicating a spectacle we strong Futurists have felt ourselves suddenly detached from women, who have suddenly become too earthy, or to express it better, have become a symbol of the earth that we ought to abandon. We have even dreamed of one day being able to create a mechanical son, the fruit of pure will, a synthesis of all the laws that science is on the brink of discovering.[128]

This automaton questions not only what it means to be human—fallible, mortal, and irrational yet simultaneously controllable, fecund, efficient, and organizable—but also where the ambiguous and antagonistic boundary between the body and the machine lies.

WHAT DOES IT MEAN TO BE HUMAN?
ROBOTS AND REPLICANTS

In order to answer the inevitable questions that machines and robots pose, let us turn to two movies that express the modernist and the postmodernist city. The first, Fritz Lang's *Metropolis* (1927), has been called the "first great achievement of the SF [science-fiction] cinema,"[129] and was a precursor to the second, Ridley Scott's *Blade Runner* (1982). Each film organizes the space of the city in anthropomorphic terms of high and low. In *Metropolis*, the master of Metropolis (the brain) and the divine machines that power the city live high above the dehumanized laborers' underground town (the hands and feet). In *Blade Runner*, the corporate boss Tyrell lives well above the dark and ominous cityscape of post-nuclear-holocaust Los Angeles, while the city itself is crowded with "inferior" people abandoned long ago by most of the superior beings, who moved to "Off-Planet" colonies.[130]

Both films are also based on the use of the robot or double. In *Metropolis*, the human Maria, the lead female character, is connected with the Virgin Mother by name and action: she is the protector of children, a teacher inspiring her fellow workers to resist violence until the mediator comes to unite their city. Maria's mechanical double is the other, darker side of woman, directly linked with the fear of sexuality, who tries to lead the workers to riot and to destroy the city they built. The two Marias establish the underlying theme of the movie: will machines control and eventually destroy humanity, or will they liberate it? Lang also questions the Cartesian duality of human nature, the mind/body split, that by the year 2000 has turned Metropolis into a divided city in which the power of the brain and the power of the hands can be both geographically and pictorially contrasted. Eventually humanity triumphs over machines and over the divided city, as "there can be no understanding between the hands and the brain unless the heart acts as mediator."[131] In *Blade Runner*, the Tyrell Corporation makes "replicants," also called "skin jobs," that are perfect copies of humans, with the exception that their lifetime is limited to only four years. Banished to outer space, where they fulfill tasks too dangerous for human beings or they become personal servants to Off-World emigrants, they have been forbidden to return to earth. They are inevitably feared, both as doubles that might replace or eradicate the uniqueness of man and as mistreated slaves who might escape control, rebel, and spread destruction.[132] In the story, four replicants want to have normal human life spans and want to develop the emotions of normal human beings. This desire has fueled an intense anger over both their biogenetic (or programmed) enslavement and their non-human condition. When they do revolt and return to earth, they must be eliminated. Rick Deckard, the protagonist, has been ordered to hunt down and "retire" these rebellious replicants.

THE CONDITION OF POSTMODERNITY

While *Metropolis* involves the projection of the body onto the city, *Blade Runner* emphasizes the problems with this projection, as it is about the dissolution of the mind/body duality in which the mind is conceptual, rational, and masculine while the body is spatial, emotional, and feminine. *Blade Runner* is not about modern production but about postmodern reproduction, both genetic and mechanized —a virtual body both abstract and real, as Foucault described, that is constructed or inscribed by a series of events (the body as computer software), plus a body that is also plastically rearranged and de-natured at will with organ transplants, cosmetic surgery, and artificial implants (the body as computer hardware). The film plays with visceral emotions such as sorrow, fear, loathing, and desire, but assigns unexpected, irrational feelings to nonhuman bodies in order to question the nature of humanity and to consider what it means for the human self to become a computerized machine.

In addition, the treatment of space and time in *Blade Runner* is a metaphor of our postmodern condition, as the film presents a concentration of space, in which distances coalesce into a single point, coupled with a division in time, in which simultaneity and seriality define a temporal order of replication or repetition. Scott wanted to shock his audiences by exploiting the tactility of the setting, which was an extrapolation of the condition of contemporary American cities. "If the future," he commented, "is one you can see and touch, it makes you a little uneasier because you feel it's just round the corner."[133] *Blade Runner* takes place in Los Angeles in 2019, and its urban space is composed through a series of eye-level images and orchestrated camera movements that skim over the surface of the city, cutting back and forth and travelling in all directions at varying tempos. David Harvey proclaims in *The Condition of Postmodernity* that this rapid travel across the city as well as through outer space is patterned on the implosion of space and time that international global communications engender. It represents a postmodern time-space compression that allows for separate existences to occur on different time-scales, for historical memories to be simulated on the basis of photographs, and for futures to be determined on principles of uncertainty and undecidability.[134] Adding to the spectacle of random images in the film, the towering skyscrapers of Los Angeles are covered with advertisements, and in the narrow canyon air space we see people transporters, surveillance machines, searchlights, and a mixture of building-size billboards and neon signs advertising Coca-Cola, Pan Am, and Budweiser moving at oblique angles. Meanwhile, advertising blimps repeat the delights of "Off-World" places, and loudspeakers announce, "A new life awaits you in Off-World colonies."

As for *Blade Runner*'s dystopian urban vision, the set designer Syd Mead, when asked about the architectonic views, replied that he imagined a future when buildings in giant cities such as Chicago or New York could no longer be torn down and replaced but had to be retrofitted by applying new wiring, air conditioning, and elevators onto their faces. Thus three-thousand- to five-thousand-foot-high megastructures might be built over the lower ten- to twenty-story buildings, to produce a cityscape that contrasted spectacular towers in the stratosphere with shabby, eroding infrastructure on the ground.[135] In contrast to the architectural pastiche in most of the city, two seven-hundred-foot-high twin ziggurats house the headquarters of the Tyrell Corporation. Not only do they look like enormous microchips, replicating the interior electronic circuitry of a giant computer, but they are also reminiscent of Mayan temples and other vast monuments that symbolize control over life and death, order and sacrifice. The Tyrell Corporation's specialty is genetic engineering—the ultimate power to create human-like mannequins and to control them like slaves. Thus the movie also highlights the postmodern dependency on both biotechnology and computers.[136]

DISCIPLINARY CONTROL

Blade Runner can also be seen as a science-fiction interpretation of Foucault's societies of disciplinary control. When surveillance becomes pervasive, allowing for absolute control by a corporation, and simulation of life becomes the ultimate power, the issue is necessarily the kind of influence the body retains over these surveillance and simulation machines. That is, can inanimate machines have a will of their own? Can they control the human body? How do humans interact with these nonhuman, programmed images and environments? And is the simulacrum immune to intervention and recoding when it begins to act autonomously? In addition, control over the boundary between man and machine is slippery when the body itself can be perfectly reproduced, when its parts can be replaced and its memory constructed and reconstructed by historical photographs. Thus what protects the separation between man and machine, and who has the right to hold the power over life and death for others when these others are less than human?

In *Blade Runner*, control is so powerfully and uniformly deployed that the disciplinary order and rational management of urban form have been long abandoned. Police cruise over the city in their airborne surveillance vehicles, dispersing any attempted congregations of isolated inhabitants. Traditional urban space has been supplanted by a city of simulation, an agglomeration of media surfaces and retrofitted structures. Consequently, the postmodern cityscape of Los Angeles is portrayed as a generic dystopia where violent eruptions and gas flames symbolize repressed energy forced underground and restrained beneath its surface. Los Angeles in

2019 reflects a post-industrial, post-nuclear-holocaust, decomposed, disintegrated, and decayed city where technological systems have gone awry.[137] Seen through a dark filter of smog or persistently dripping acid rain, its small-scale street markets and low-ceilinged malls give the appearance of a labyrinthian underground enclosure choked with refuse. All of the vendors in these crowded street markets, as well as the individually subcontracted manufacturers of eyes or various other body parts, are third-world Asian immigrants whose language is "city-speak," a meltdown of English, Japanese, Spanish, and other vocabularies. The murky streets are clogged with a mass of isolated individuals who no longer have the effective means or even the desire to communicate with each other.

OPTICAL CORRECTNESS

As is typical in postmodernism, no sense of place nor unity of urban space is ever developed in *Blade Runner*.[138] When spectators travel through the space in the film they are assaulted by a flood of imagery, as if they were standing on an escalator or seated behind the windshield of a moving vehicle. The movie replicates and exaggerates a common postmodern experience in which images travelling at top speed flash briefly in front of our eyes and constantly interrupt our view. Generalizing beyond the film but reflecting on questions it raises, we might discuss Paul Virilio's concern that the postmodern eye has produced a disturbed and dependent perception that affects every spectator. This fact

may rightly prompt us to consider the ethics of common perception as a serious matter. Do we want to lose our role as *eye-witnesses* of perceptible reality and be replaced by technology with its multifarious substitutes, its "artificial limbs" (video, television surveillance, etc.)? Do we want to lose the ability to see for ourselves? Will we become visually handicapped, succumbing to a kind of blindness which is paradoxically caused by overexposure to the visual image, as well as by the development of unseeing "vision machines" powered by the "indirect light" of electro-optics, as opposed to the "direct light" of the sun and electricity?[139]

We need, Virilio says, "a committee for the ethics of perception" or "optical correctness."[140]

Blade Runner does raise questions about postmodern vision, since in the film the eye has become so dependent on electronic devices that it cannot determine the difference between man and machine. Disembodied eyes are emphasized in the film: we see close-ups of eyes on video monitors, eyes that are gouged out, a bottle full of genetically-engineered eyes, a manufacturer of eyes whose costume parodies that of a giant eye with connective nerves, and the glaring eyes of an artificial owl. Distortions of perspective seen by the normal eye are underscored by the human reliance on computerized scanning devices. One technological invention used in the film is the Esper machine: it enhances normal vision by using photographic images to create a three-dimensional space which is then explored by the user. It becomes an analogy for the visual manipulation that machines such as the camera and the movie camera provide.[141] Yet another machine used in the film is the Voight-Kampff Empathy Test, which distinguishes between replicants and humans by enlarging and subsequently examining the respondent's eye on a video monitor. Since the eye and its emotive responses may not be the best test for the identification of humanity, the film often positions the spectators so that they are required to look at images of eyes enlarged to huge proportions and thus are forced to question the validity of using the eye as a signifier of human life.[142] The film also casts doubt on the ability of the human eye to discern our human-ness in an age of electronic technology when our perception is saturated and we have become passive, dependent, unemotive, and often dehumanized. This dependency on the computer to test what constitutes humanity sets up an ambivalent dilemma: can impersonal machines evaluate emotional life? If life can be reproduced in a laboratory, then doesn't the assessment of what is human necessarily change, as do other binary oppositions such as male/female, animate/inanimate, natural/artificial, self/other, and I/it?[143] These devices ask us as spectators to question our own controlling perspective, to question what we see and what we do not see. They expose our dependency on programmed outcomes that electronic optical devices command, requiring us to open our own eyes to the impact of science and technology not only on social and biological bodies but on perception and experience as well.

However, as Michel Foucault criticized, the fetishization of one body part—the eye—is a cover-up for an internal experience that cannot be whole.

> The eye, in a philosophy of reflection, derives from its capacity to observe the power of becoming always more interior to itself. Lying behind each eye that sees, there exists a more tenuous one, an eye so discreet and yet so agile that its all-powerful glance can be said to eat away at the flesh of its white globe; behind this particular eye, there exists another and then still others, each progressively more subtle until we arrive at an eye whose entire substance is nothing but the transparency of its vision. This inner movement is finally resolved in a nonmaterial center where the intangible forms of truth are created and combined, in this heart of things which is the sovereign subject.[144]

As does Foucault, *Blade Runner* questions the illusions of a sovereign self by raising the issue of what it means to be human, and, in the case of the film, what it means to be a human within a world of simulated replicants by examining the very nature of that humanness. This blurring of the boundary between man and machine also raises the issue of whether artificial life forms can achieve humane-ness—can think and act morally—if humans are known to act inhumanely and unethically. In other words, science and technology fluctuate around ambivalent poles: they have been put to the most beneficial as well as the most destructive uses.

THE VALORIZATION OF THE BODY
THE ISSUE OF DISEMBODIMENT

Blade Runner raises the interrelated issues of the disappearing city and the dematerialized body. In today's world, the real space of the city is displaced by computerized cyberspace and by the decentered global network of information flows; de-industrialization is promoted as manufacturing production relocates to offshore locations; there has been an elimination of the social welfare programs that used to provide a safety net for urban existence; and most of the moderately well-to-do population have long since moved to the edge of the city. All of these factors add up to the dominant contemporary perception that the city is physically disintegrating and beginning to blur as a physical entity and as a point of focus. The human body seems to be disappearing as well, becoming disposable as human memory is downloaded into computer programs, while a sense of disembodiment grows as actual body organs are replaced by electronic prosthetic devices and bodily sensorium augmented by biological and computer technologies that remain external to the body. One advocate of cyberspace has put it this way: "Nothing could be more disembodied or insensate than…cyberspace. It's like having had your everything amputated."[145]

Blade Runner tries to insert the spectator into the virtual space of the film in a manner that simulates the experience of travelling in cyberspace where perception is controlled by a computer program or, in the case of the film, by the director's or the camera's view. However, in the Cartesian world of computers there is no longer any reference to the body, for the internal matrix of the computer's memory is an extended grid of zeros and ones without dimension. "Operating independently of the body, and of the senses, computers have simply reduced visualization to an aspect of mathematics."[146] Thus the body remains on one side of the screen and the representation on the other, which privileges linear perspective and objective realism, and assumes a detached point of view. In virtual space, moreover, the so-called "self" is uncoupled from the body, projected into computerized space, and reconstructed in digital form. Information that used to be called input/output to the machine is now constructed from and processed by this projected "self." It is coded according to the bodily senses: it can be visual, auditory, haptic, "propriocentric (current body configuration)," or "vestibular (orientation, movement, acceleration)," and it sometimes even involves the senses of smell and taste. Unquestionably, however, visual information predominates, and haptic information is reduced to the touch of a button, glove, or joystick. The point is that both the body and the "self" are represented within virtual space in a disembodied manner: the body by an arrow cursor, a data glove, or a mechanical arm; the "self" by a computer software program or a set of rules, commands, and functions.[147]

As has been discussed, when it is in pain or is having negative feelings the body can be experienced as "other," from which there is a desire to escape or retreat. But these fantasies of escape ignore the fact that the real body is fragile and mortal. The sense of disembodiment involved in Virtual Reality tends towards a sense of abstraction, a translation of vision through the camera or computer, and an ultimate reduction of experience (or experiential information) to synthetic digitization. Not only is virtual space based on Cartesian space, but it also reasserts and continues to develop the Cartesian mind/body split and all of its related problems. The exploration of artificial worlds through computer memories or with prosthetic body parts forces us out of our bodies and out of the material physical world. As Sally Pryor writes,

> VR [Virtual Reality] can be seen to represent a retreat from direct experience of the senses, the body, each other, and our (polluted) environment. Is this really a solution to the problem of modern life—to turn a blind eye to what is happening and to what we are doing to this world by re-mapping ourselves into digitally-mediated, synthetic fantasy worlds?[148]

We have seen how the body throughout history has been projected onto the image of the city, and how the city has been described as the simulacrum of the body. As body awareness withers, space becomes immaterial; as we retreat into the privacy of our media-altered realms, direct experience of the city disappears. We can no longer read the city as a totality: it is heterogeneous, fragmented, dismembered, decentered. And this marred and disfigured city, this "other" from which we retreat and which we feel limits our self-expression, may be a major cause of our late-twentieth-century fascination with the computer as a "clean machine." As we emerge from the synthetic world of machine codes and Boolean algebra, it is the machine that appears to be clean, and man guilty, abject, and unclean.[149] We can compare this retreat to the warnings of both Walter Benjamin and Michel Foucault.

THE DECLINE OF EXPERIENCE AND THE DEPOLITICIZATION OF AESTHETICS

Obsessed with the latest electro-optical devices and their reproductions and appropriations, we experience an extreme sense of disembodiment that inhibits the projection of body metaphors onto architectural or urban form. We have arrived at the ultimate stage of disenchantment with the city, in which phantasmagorical illusions that urban form might hold have been dissipated and dematerialized into thin air. The city no longer evokes our involvement; it has become numbed, speechless, without a story to tell. We are unable to develop architectural forms that are engaged politically with the urban environment. Perhaps this is simply the extension of the modern rationale that engenders a widespread disenchantment with the world and relegates art to the private sphere. But we have failed to develop a critical understanding of the internal logic of these new electro-optical devices, even though they have become our everyday tools. Nor have we examined them as technical apparatuses that activate procedures of perception and expression, thus having both liberating and reifying potential.

This disembodiment can also lead to the feeling that multi-sensory, multi-media sensibilities engendered by electronic technologies control our all-but-redundant bodies. As physical experiences decline, our bodies begin to act like puppets with strings that are pulled by somebody else. How else can we explain the French performance artist Orlan, whose medium is her own body? She has endured at least seven different plastic surgery operations as she attempts to make her own face resemble a computerized composite likeness based on the images of five mythic women. One of Orlan's latest operations was recorded on video, and was simultaneously broadcast in gallery spaces around the world. Using telephones, fax machines, and picture-phones, viewers could interact with the artist, asking her questions about her work as she underwent her operation.[150] While this is an extreme and outlandish case of the co-mingling of image and body, it raises troubling questions. Why in these postmodern times have we failed so completely to arrive at a "politicization of aesthetics" first outlined by Benjamin? Why have we refused to develop a new political awareness suitable to an age of electro-optical reproduction—an engaged, embodied position that would utilize our new technology in a liberating and critical manner?

One response to this retreat from a politicized aesthetic, as discussed by Dean MacCannell, is to blame postmodernism (which includes poststructuralism, posthumanism, postindustrialism, and so forth), which he sees as a late expression of Euro-fascism. He believes, "There are too many points of correspondence to ignore: the death drive, the attack on the notion of truth as so much metaphysical baggage, the sense of living in an infinite instant at the end of history, nostalgia for the folk-primitive peasant, schizophrenia at the level of culture, and general ennui periodically interrupted by euphoric release from all constraint."[151] MacCannell argues that both fascism and postmodernism lose contact with "real reality" as they valorize surface expressions, raising the ordinary and banal to aesthetic heights. Everyday reality is hidden behind a "fetishism of the ordinary" or an "overstated version of the Real" or a "Technicolor version of what is."[152] Thus the popularity of theme parks and Disneyland, and the outpouring of fakes that appear to exceed the realism of their originals. Both fascism and postmodernity, MacCannell continues, cover up the fact that violence has become routine, as they move towards a conservative politics of the individual. Postmodernity admits race, gender, ethnicity, and class to the podium of Western white males at the same time as it spuriously claims that difference no longer makes a difference. Everyone is supposedly brought together under one huge multicultural banner that transcends all divisions, but the result is a kind of "United Colors of Benetton" philosophy, an illusion of a happy ending that disavows the uneven development of cities and neighborhoods around the world by suppressing the acceptance of real differences that painfully still exist.[153] When Guy Debord defined the "society of the spectacle" he said that "everything that was directly lived has moved away into representation," and warned that the spectacle was "not a collection of images, but a social relationship among people mediated by images."[154] Nevertheless, postmodernism has not listened to his warning as it revels in reproductions and reified images.

> [Like] documentary photography and the photojournalism of glossy magazines such as *Life* and *National Geographic*, books and museums serve to reassure us of our own social position and provide an outlet for our fears. They are putting a face on the fear and transforming threat into fantasy, into imagery, into a photograph, an object which we can look at and deal with by leaving it behind, because it is "them" not "us" who suffer.[155]

Another response to postmodernity's aesthetic depoliticization can be found in Andrew Hewitt's *Fascist Modernism*. The issue is how to develop a politics of representation without compromising the reality of the representation and without treating it as a degenerate form.[156] This concern, Hewitt continues, can be traced back to Walter Benjamin's analysis of aestheticization in "The Work of Art in the Age of Mechanical Reproduction." In this essay, Benjamin examined how the very techniques of reproduction that were supposedly opposed to fascism were actually used to empower it. In a footnote to this essay, Benjamin wrote:

> Mass reproduction is aided especially by the reproduction of masses. In big parades and monster rallies, in sports events, and in war, all of which nowadays are captured by camera and sound recording, the masses are brought face to face with themselves. This process, whose significance need not be stressed, is intimately connected with the development of techniques of reproduction and photography. Mass movements are usually discerned more clearly by a camera than by the naked eye....This means that mass movements, including war, constitute a form of human behavior which particularly favors mechanical equipment.[157]

> Fascism sees its salvation in giving the masses not their right, but instead a chance to express themselves....The logical result of Fascism is the introduction of aesthetics into politics.[158]

Thus fascism sates the public's legitimate desire for self-expression by staging theatricalized spectacles as a substitute for their political demands. But, as Hewitt recounts, Walter Benjamin discussed two opposing aspects of this aestheticization. He saw it both as the reduction of reality to representation and as the loss of power of the spectator, who is crushed into silence by the overwhelming nature of the spectacle. By conflating reality with representation, Hewitt argues, fascism ushered in the concepts from which stem all of our contemporary concerns with simulation and theatricality. But Benjamin saw that the very processes that integrated the spectator into the spectacle also brought a loss of critical distance, which actually legitimated the political performance but disempowered the public.[159] As Benjamin put it, "Fascist art is executed not only *for* the masses, but *by* the masses," so that they actually bring about their own disempowerment through the spectacle.[160] Through the absence of any critical space, of any position from which to oppose being reduced to a passive onlooker, fascism eliminated the public sphere where reason could once be exercised.

Consequently, any confrontation with fascism must be a confrontation with theatricality, particularly when expressed in aesthetic terms; it is both "the possibility of a critique of the visible as an organizing epistemological category"[161] and "the processual nature of the spectacle."[162] Hewitt argues, "Fascism's 'truth,' the 'truth of politics,' is…that politics, despite its self-effacing modesty, is not simply a ragbag of contingencies, a domain of the hopelessly empirical, but an aesthetic—a discourse for the staging of history."[163] Benjamin's argument that fascism is one reaction to the loss of history and the decline of experience is extended by Hewitt, who searches for the reasons why contemporary theory since World War II has been so concerned with aesthetic intrusions into the political realm.

> It is not enough to trace the obsession of postwar theory back to the experience of the war or of fascism. Quite to the contrary, the confrontation with fascism seems, in its most interesting forms, to consist in the attempts to come to terms with a loss of experience—the loss, that is, not only of the war and the extermination as an experience, but the loss of the very possibility of experience itself.[164]

And so we return once again to the issue of contemporary reality mediated by technological devices, which transform it into an abstract and rationalized experience, a distanced and cold existence, radically affecting all fields of perception.

THE RETURN TO THE BODY

Finally, we have to question the ethics that are contained within postmodernism's return to the body. A close look at Michel

Foucault's *The History of Sexuality* draws a compelling picture of the reasons why the body became a central focus for the bourgeoisie in the nineteenth century, and these reasons form the basis of our present obsessions. Foucault argues that the primary concern over—and invention of—sexuality was not to repress the sexual expressions of the exploited classes, but rather to preserve and invigorate the body and to protect the longevity and descent of the ruling classes. This is what Foucault called

> the self-affirmation of one class rather than the enslavement of another: a defense, a protection, a strengthening, and an exaltation that were eventually extended to others....With this investment of its own sex...the bourgeoisie underscored the high political prices of its body, sensations, and pleasures, its well-being and survival.[165]

The bourgeoisie's affirmation of its own body was a "primordial form" of class consciousness. It took a long time to acknowledge that the classes the bourgeoisie were exploiting also had a body and were sexual beings. If we look at the living conditions of the poor in the first half of the nineteenth century, we can see that it was of no importance whether these people lived or died, since in any event, it was argued, they reproduced themselves naturally.

> Conflicts were necessary (in particular, conflicts over urban space: cohabitation, proximity, contamination, epidemics, such as the cholera epidemic of 1832, or again, prostitution and venereal disease) in order for the proletariat to be granted a body and a sexuality; economic emergencies had to arise (the development of heavy industry with the need for a stable population flow and competent labor force, the obligation to regulate the population and apply demographic controls); lastly, there had to be established a whole technology of control which made it possible to keep that body and sexuality, finally conceded to them, under surveillance (schooling, the politics of housing, public hygiene, institutions of relief and insurance, the general medicalization of the population, in

short an entire administration and technical machinery made it possible to safely import the deployment of sexuality into the exploited
class; the latter no longer risked playing an assertive class role opposite the bourgeoisie; it would remain the instrument of the bourgeoisie's hegemony).[166]

[Thus] the bourgeoisie endowed itself, in an arrogant political
affirmation, with a garrulous sexuality which the proletariat long
refused to accept, since it was foisted on them for the purpose
of subjugation.[167]

In short, an entire administration and technical machinery made it
possible to safely import the deployment of sexuality into the
exploited class. The proletariat no longer risked playing an assertive
role opposite the bourgeoisie; it remained the instrument of the
bourgeoisie's hegemony.

Like the computer, the clean machine, the contemporary val-
orization of the body produces important effects of gender, race,
and class; these effects marginalize and exclude, they make invisible
and disavow. We must heed Foucault's message that knowledge
is power: it imposes itself and it is imposed. And through these
impositions it leaves metaphorical voids and blacked-out spaces.
How else can we explain our academic ignorance of minority experience or our fears of others that are based entirely on generaliza-
tions or on inherited hierarchies that categorize different kinds of
people? Or why James Q. Wilson and Richard Hernstein in their
book *Crime and Human Nature* develop such spurious and pseudo-
scientific concepts as "Anatomical Correlates of Crime," suggesting
that physical shape and appearance might contribute to criminal
behavior?[168] As American society shifts away from the panopticon
surveillance of bodies (that is, based on spatial organization) and
becomes more reliant on the diffused observation techniques provided by video monitoring, this sort of shorthand identification
becomes handy for controlling the population: "The more modest
task of the monitor [is] to provide partial coverage of dangerous

spaces, not to pretend to make surveillance perfect, but only to ensure that in protected zones defensive actions might be taken in response to invasions."[169] And how else can we explain that the fastest growing communities in America are "common-interest developments," which privatize public spaces, erect gates of entry and exit, and monitor every action, vigilantly scanning for elements perceived as deviant, dangerous, or criminal?

This paper was originally written for the Committee on Theory and Culture 1993–1994 seminar series entitled "Body/Space/Machine" held at New York University, 25 March 1994.

1   Maud Ellmann has raised similar issues with respect to anorexia and hunger strikes in her book *The Hunger Artists: Starving, Writing, and Imprisonment* (Cambridge: Harvard University Press, 1993).

2   Terry Eagleton, *The Ideology of the Aesthetic* (Cambridge: Basil Blackwell, 1990), 13.

3   William Spanos, *The End of Education: Toward Posthumanism* (Minneapolis: The University of Minnesota, 1993).

4   Barbara Stafford, *Body Criticism* (Cambridge: MIT Press, 1991), 15.

5   Geoffrey Scott, *The Architecture of Humanism* (New York: W. W. Norton & Company, Inc., 1969), 159. The italics are Scott's.

6   Anthony Vidler, "The Building in Pain: The Body and Architecture in Post-Modern Culture," *AA Files* 19 (Spring 1990): 3–10.

7   Elaine Scarry, *The Body in Pain* (New York: Oxford University Press, 1985), 281–286; the quotation is on page 285. The italics are Scarry's.

8   Quoted in Vidler, "The Building in Pain," 8.

9   Susan Buck-Morss, "Aesthetics and Anaesthetics: Walter Benjamin's Artwork Essay Reconsidered," *October* 62 (Fall 1992): 38.

10   Drew Leder, *The Absent Body* (Chicago: University of Chicago Press, 1990), 84.

11   Ibid., 86–87.

12   Ibid., 70.

13   Quoted in Leder, *The Absent Body*, 129.

14   Allen S. Weiss, "Cartesian Simulacra," *Persistence of Vision* 5 (1987): 55–61.

15   Michel Foucault, "Of Other Spaces," *Diacritics* 16, no. 1 (Spring 1986): 24.

16   Ibid.

17   Michel Foucault, "Nietzsche, Genealogy, History," in *Language, Counter-Memory, Practice*, trans. Donald F. Bouchard and Sherry Simon (Ithaca: Cornell University Press, 1977), 148.

18   Ibid., 153–154.

19   Leder, *The Absent Body*, 118.

20   Ibid.

21   Stafford, *Body Criticism*, 11–12.

22   Claude Gandelman, *Reading Pictures Viewing Texts* (Bloomington: Indiana University Press, 1991), 6.

23   Michel Foucault, *The Birth of the Clinic*, trans. A. M. Sheridan Smith (New York: Pantheon Books, 1973), 164.

24   Ibid., 165.

25   Lisa Cartwright, *Screening the Body: Tracing Medicine's Visual Culture* (Minneapolis: University of Minnesota Press, 1995), 10–12, 107–109, 121.

26   Carol A. Stabile, "Shooting the Mother: Fetal Photography and the Politics of Disappearance," *Camera Obscura* 28 (January 1992): 180.

27   Paula A. Treichter and Lisa Cartwright, "Introduction," *Camera Obscura* 28 (Winter 1992): 7.

28   George Lakoff, *Women, Fire, and Dangerous Things* (Chicago: University of Chicago Press, 1987), 271–281.

29   Francisco J. Varela, "The Reenchantment of the Concrete," *Zone* 6 (1992): 320.

30   This section on the tactile eye and the optical touch follows the work of Claude Gandelman in *Reading Pictures Viewing Texts* (see note 23 above). On the eye as the organ of tactility, see Michael Taussig, *Mimesis and Alterity: A Particular History of the Senses* (New York: Routledge, 1993).

31   Gert Mattenklott, "The Touching Eye," *Daidalos* 41 (September 1991): 106–113.

32   Meyer Schapiro, "Style," in *Aesthetics Today*, ed. Morris Philipson and Paul J. Gudel (New York: New American Library, 1961), 157.

33   F. T. Marinetti, *Let's Murder the Moonshine: Selected Writings* (Los Angeles: Sun and Moon Classics, 1972), 120.

34   Andrew Hewitt, *Fascist Modernism* (Stanford: Stanford University Press, 1993), 152.

35   Walter Benjamin, "Moscow Diary," trans. Richard Sieburth, *October* 35 (1985): 42.

36   Walter Benjamin, *One Way Street*, trans. Edmund Jephcott and Kingsley Shorter (London: New Left Books, 1979), 89.

37   Gregory Whitehead, "The Forensic Theatre: Memory Plays for the Post-Mortem Condition," *Journal of the Performing Arts* 35/36 (1990): 99–109.

38   Dziga Vertov proclaimed in the 1920s, "Kino Eye is the possibility of seeing life processes in any temporal order or at any speed inaccessible to the human eye." Quoted in Annette Michelson, "The Wings of Hypothesis," in *Montage and Modern Life 1919–1942*, ed. Matthew Teitelbaum (Cambridge: MIT Press, 1992), 79. Also quoted in Vlada Petric, *Constructivism in Film* (New York: Cambridge University Press, 1987), 4.

39   Walter Benjamin, "A Small History of Photography," in *One Way Street*, trans. Edmund Jephcott and Kingsley Shorter (London: New Left Books, 1979), 243.

40   Walter Benjamin, "Surrealism," in *Reflections*, trans. Edmund Jephcott (Ithaca: Cornell University Press, 1978), 182.

41   Gernot Bohme, "On Synaesthesiae," *Daidalos* (September 1991): 26–36; Taussig, *Mimesis and Alterity*, 20–32.

42   Gandelman, *Reading Pictures Viewing Texts*, 4.

43   Walter Benjamin, "The Work of Art in the Age of Mechanical Reproduction," in *Illuminations*, trans. Harry Zohn (New York: Schocken Books, 1969), 238–240.

44   Ibid., 240.

45   Weiss, "Cartesian Simulacra," 56.

46   Michelson, "The Wings of Hypothesis," 62.

47   Petric, *Constructivism in Film*, 130.

48   Ibid., 132.

49   Ibid., 134–135.

50   Ibid., 146–148.

51   Ibid., 29.

52   Ibid., 200.

53   Douglas Kahn and Gregory Whitehead, eds., *Wireless Imagination* (Cambridge: MIT Press, 1992), 340–341.

54   Ibid., 339–340.

55   Susan Buck-Morss, *Dialectics of Seeing: Walter Benjamin and the Arcades Project* (Cambridge: MIT Press, 1989), 268.

56 John McCole, *Walter Benjamin and The Antinomies of Tradition* (Ithaca: Cornell University Press, 1993), 269–272.

57 Walter Benjamin, "Doctrine of the Similar," *New German Critique* 17 (1979): 65.

58 Taussig, *Mimesis and Alterity*, 23–24; the quotation is on page 24.

59 Benjamin, "The Work of Art in the Age of Mechanical Reproduction," 223.

60 Quoted in Gunnar Olson, *Lines of Power/Limits of Language* (Minneapolis: University of Minnesota Press, 1991), 143.

61 Stafford, *Body Criticism*, 84, 96.

62 Gandelman, *Reading Pictures Viewing Texts*, 140.

63 Jorg Simmel, quoted in Walter Benjamin, *Charles Baudelaire: A Lyric Poet in the Era of High Capitalism* (London: New Left Books, 1969), 38.

64 Benjamin, *Charles Baudelaire*, 38.

65 Ibid., 39.

66 Giuliana Bruno, "Spectatorial Embodiments: Anatomies of the Visible and the Female Bodyscape," *Camera Obscura* 28 (1992): 239–261.

67 Gandelman, *Reading Pictures Viewing Texts*, 67.

68 Gertrud Koch, "Bela Balazs: The Physiognomy of Things," *New German Critique* 40 (1987): 171.

69 Quoted in Koch, "Bela Balazs," 173.

70 Koch, "Bela Balazs," 167–177.

71 Quoted in Koch, "Bela Balazs," 168.

72 Ibid., 170. The film director Sergei Eisenstein disagreed with Balzas. For him, the figural value of an individualized shot could not be the decisive factor; instead it was the relationship, superimposition, sequence, or collision between shots that was important. Context and juxtapositions determined figurative expressions, not the other way around. "The shot merely interprets the object in a setting to use it in juxtaposition to other sequences....The shot is merely an extension of selection....The conditions of cinema create an 'image' from the juxtaposition of these 'cuts.'" Quoted in Richard Taylor, ed., *Eisenstein Writings 1922–1934* (Bloomington: Indiana University Press, 1988), 80.

73 Stafford, *Body Criticism*, 58–70.

74   Ibid., 59.

75   Ibid., 61.

76   Ibid., 70.

77   Ulricke Brunotte, "The Construction of the Underworld on the Architecture of Memory in Cults and Psychoanalysis," *Daidalos* 48 (June 1993): 81.

78   Gandelman, *Reading Pictures Viewing Texts*, 113.

79   Ibid., 114–115.

80   Ibid., 129.

81   Quoted in Kriztina Passuth, *Moholy-Nagy* (London: Thames and Hudson, 1985), 350.

82   Ibid.

83   Quoted in Mikhail Yampolsky, "The Essential Bone Structure: Mimesis in Eisenstein," in *Eisenstein Rediscovered*, ed. Ian Christie and Richard Taylor (London: Routledge, 1993), 177.

84   Yampolsky, "The Essential Bone Structure," 187–188.

85   Paul Scheerbart, *Glass Architecture*, ed. Dennis Sharp (1914; reprint, New York: Praeger Publishers, 1972), 41.

86   Ibid., 43.

87   Ibid., 71.

88   Benjamin, *Reflections*, 147, 149.

89   McCole, *Walter Benjamin and the Antinomies of Tradition*, 186.

90   Pierre Missac, *Passage de Walter Benjamin* (Paris: Editions du Seuil, 1987), 157 184.

91   Marc Perelman, *Urbs ex machina Le Corbusier* (Paris: Les Editions de la passion, 1986), 30–32.

92   Robert D. Romanyshyn, *Technology as Symptom and Dream* (New York: Routledge, 1989), 116.

93   Rosmarie Beier, "Regarder l'interior du corps," *Terrain* 18 (March 1992): 95–102.

94   Quoted in Martin Roth, "L'homme de verre," *Terrain* 18 (March 1992): 105.

95   Roth, "L'homme de verre," 103–115.

96 Michel Foucault, *Discipline and Punish*, trans. Alan Sheridan (New York: Pantheon Books, 1977), 138.

97 Michel Foucault, *The History of Sexuality*, trans. Robert Hurley (New York: Pantheon Books, 1978), 1: 139.

98 Walter Benjamin, "The Storyteller," in *Illuminations*, trans. Harry Zohn (New York: Schocken Books, 1969), 89.

99 Alexander Dorner, *The Way Beyond "Art": The Work of Herbert Bayer* (New York: Wittenborn, Schultz, 1947), 172.

100 Quoted in Heimo Kuchling, ed., *Oskar Schlemmer: Man*, trans. Janet Seligman (Cambridge: MIT Press, 1971), 228.

101 Ibid., 25.

102 Ibid., 30.

103 Quoted in Tut Schlemmer, ed., *The Letters and Diaries of Oskar Schlemmer* (Evanston: Northwestern University Press, 1972), 126. To explore a completely new way of looking at things was also the aim of El Lissitzky's electro-mechanical show "Victory over the Sun," which was planned in the early 1920s but never realized. The theme of this futurist opera was modern man enhanced by technology; man was able to tear down the sun, the emblem of old world energy, and replace it with his own source of energy. Lissitzky stated, "No one seems to pay any attention to the magnificent spectacle of our cities, simply because 'everyone' has become part and parcel of the spectacle himself. Each particular energy is harnessed to its own individual purpose. The whole is amorphous. All energies must be organized to achieve unity." Thus in the middle of a city square, Lissitzky intended to build a large scaffolding that would support a director who could control electromechanical forces and devices to make skeleton-like figurines or various objects move, turn, stretch, slide, roll, and hover. "At the flick of a switch," Lissitzky noted, "the sound system is turned on and the whole place may suddenly reverberate with the din of a railroad station, or the roar of Niagara Falls, or the pounding of a steel-rolling mill." El Lissitzky, *Russia: An Architecture for World Revolution*, trans. E. Dluhosch (Cambridge: MIT Press, 1970), 136.

104 Mathias Eberle, "Oskar Schlemmer: Adam Transformed into Prometheus by Geometry," *World War I and the Weimar Artist* (New Haven: Yale University Press, 1985), 106–127.

105 Oskar Schlemmer, "Theater," in *The Theater of the Bauhaus*, ed. Walter Gropius, trans. Alan S. Wensigner (Middletown: Wesleyan University Press, 1961), 81–101.

106 Quoted in Eberle, "Oscar Schlemmer," 109.

107 Quoted in Gropius, ed., *The Theater of the Bauhaus*, 26.

108 Gropius, ed, *The Theater of the Bauhaus*, 18–19.

109 Ibid., 21–32.

110 Quoted in Eberle, "Oskar Schlemmer," 111.

111 Herbert Bayer, Walter Gropius, and Ise Gropius, *Bauhaus 1919–1928* (Boston: Charles T. Branford Company, 1959), 164.

112 Quoted in Eberle, "Oskar Schlemmer," 118.

113 Eberle, "Oskar Schlemmer," 109.

114 Quoted in Eberle, "Oskar Schlemmer," 109.

115 Eberle, "Oskar Schlemmer," 113.

116 Quoted in Eberle, "Oskar Schlemmer," 119.

117 Eberle, "Oskar Schlemmer," 120, 122; Plassard, *L'acteur en effigie* (Lausanne: Editions L'Age d'Homme, 1992), 208.

118 Rainer Näele, *Theater, Theory, Speculation: Walter Benjamin and the Scenes of Modernity* (Baltimore: The Johns Hopkins Press, 1991), 75, 162.

119 Walter Benjamin, *Paris capitale du XIXe siècle* (Paris: les Editions du Cerf, 1993), 706.

120 Julie Wosk, *Breaking Frame: Technology and the Visual Arts in the Nineteenth Century* (New Brunswick: Rutgers University Press, 1992), 82.

121 "The Artificial Man," *Scientific American* 1 (8 October 1859): 285; quoted in Wosk, *Breaking Frame*, 88.

122 Jeffrey Mehlman, *Walter Benjamin for Children* (Chicago: The University of Chicago Press, 1993), 67–69.

123 Quoted in Buck-Morss, *The Dialectics of Seeing*, 101.

124 Ibid.

125 Ibid.

126 Quoted in Hewitt, *Fascist Modernism*, 146.

127 Ibid., 147, 152.

128 Ibid., 150.

129 David Desser, "Race, Space and Class: The Politics of the SF Film from *Metropolis* to *Blade Runner*," in *Retrofitting Blade Runner*, ed. Judith B. Kerman (Bowling Green, Ohio: Bowling Green State University, 1991), 112.

130 Ibid., 111–112.

131 Fritz Lang, *Metropolis* (London and Boston: Faber and Faber, 1973), 130.

132 Josepha Francavilla, "The Android as Doppelgänger," in *Retrofitting Blade Runner*, ed. Judith B. Kerman (Bowling Green, Ohio: Bowling Green State University, 1991), 4–15.

133 Quoted in Judith B. Kerman, "Technology and Politics in the *Blade Runner* Dystopia," in *Retrofitting Blade Runner*, ed. Judith B. Kerman (Bowling Green, Ohio: Bowling Green State University, 1991), 18.

134 David Harvey, *The Condition of Postmodernity* (Cambridge: Basil Blackwell, 1989), 308–314.

135 John J. Pierce, "Creative Synergy and the Art of World Creation," in *Retrofitting Blade Runner*, ed. Judith B. Kerman (Bowling Green, Ohio: Bowling Green State University, 1991), 201–211.

136 Steve Carper, "Subverting the Disaffected City: Cityscape in *Blade Runner*," in *Retrofitting Blade Runner*, ed. Judith B. Kerman (Bowling Green, Ohio: Bowling Green State University, 1991), 188.

137 Giuliana Bruno, "Ramble City: Postmodernism and *Blade Runner*," *October* 41 (1987): 61–74.

138 Carper, "Subverting the Disaffected City," 185–195.

139 Paul Virilio, "Speed and Vision: The Incomparable Eye," *Daidalos* 47 (1993): 97.

140 Ibid., 98.

141 Jack Boozer, Jr., "Crashing the Gates of Insight: *Blade Runner*," in *Retrofitting Blade Runner*, ed. Judith B. Kerman (Bowling Green, Ohio: Bowling Green State University, 1991), 216.

142 Ibid., 212–227.

143 Ibid., 216–217.

144 Michel Foucault, *Language, Counter-Memory, Practice*, trans. Donald F. Bouchard and Sherry Simon (Ithaca: Cornell University Press, 1977), 45.

145 Vivian Sobchack, "New Age Mutant Ninja Hackers: Reading *Mondo 2000*," *The South Atlantic Quarterly* 92, no. 4 (1993): 577.

146   Andrew Menard, "Art and the Logic of Computers," *Art Criticism* 8, no. 2 (1993): 62.

147   Ibid., 169–171.

148   Ibid., 177.

149   Sean Cubitt, *Timeshift: On Video Culture* (New York: Routledge, 1991), 178.

150   Roberta Smith, "Surgical Sculpture: The Body as Costume," *New York Times*, 17 December 1993.

151   Dean MacCannell, "The Desire to Be Postmodern," *Empty Meeting Grounds* (New York: Routledge, 1992), 187.

152   Ibid., 188.

153   Ibid., 183–229.

154   Guy Debord, *Society of the Spectacle* (Detroit: Black and Red, 1983), unpaginated.

155   Susan E. Edwards, "Photography and the Representation of the Other," *Third Text* 16/17 (1991): 164.

156   Hewitt, *Fascist Modernism*, 161–209.

157   Walter Benjamin, "On Some Motifs in Baudelaire," in *Illuminations*, trans. Harry Zohn (New York: Schocken Books, 1969), 249; quoted in Hewitt, *Fascist Modernism*, 167.

158   Benjamin, "On Some Motifs in Baudelaire," 243; quoted in Hewitt, *Fascist Modernism*, 167–168.

159   Hewitt, *Fascist Modernism*, 171–175.

160   Quoted in Hewitt, *Fascist Modernism*, 175.

161   Hewitt, *Fascist Modernism*, 183.

162   Ibid., 186.

163   Ibid., 192.

164   Ibid., 193.

165   Foucault, *The History of Sexuality*, 1: 123.

166   Ibid., 126–127.

167   Ibid., 127.

168 James Q. Wilson and Richard Hernstein, *Crime and Human Nature* (New York: Simon and Schuster, 1985).

169 Thomas L. Dunn, "The New Enclosures," in *Reading Rodney King Reading Urban Uprising*, ed. Robert Gooding-Williams (New York: Routledge, 1993), 186.

IMAGING THE CITY IN THE AGE
OF ELECTRONIC COMMUNICATION

M EMORY SYSTEMS AND IMAGING THE CITY

Developing an image of the city in an age of visual saturation appears to be a problem, precisely because awareness of the physical space of the city is disappearing or dematerializing—the result, we are told, of new digital information and communication technologies. Paul Virilio says that every city is over-exposed and its physical sense of space decomposed as our eyes are constantly bombarded with ephemeral and interchangeable images, visions that move along the constant space of flows called the informational city.[1] It is then no accident that William Gibson's account of cyberspace in *Neuromancer* is conflated with an account of a city that no longer has any imageable form or definable boundary. He says this metroscape called "BAMA" (Boston–Atlanta Metropolitan Area) reaches from Boston to Atlanta along the eastern seaboard.

> Program a map to display frequency of data exchange, every thousand megabytes a single pixel on a very large screen. Manhattan and Atlanta burn solid white. Then they start to pulse, the rate of traffic threatening to overload your simulation. Your map is about to go nova. Cool it down. Up your scale. Each pixel a million megabytes. At a hundred million megabytes per second, you begin to make out certain blocks in midtown Manhattan, outlines of hundred-year-old industrial parks ringing the old core of Atlanta.[2]

Gibson introduces us to the American space of "the sprawl" by mapping the cyberspace of the computer onto the physical space of a regional city.

And what else, we might ask, is the American city of today but a gigantic, boundless metroscape like "BAMA"? Its appearance seems to simulate a complex switchboard of plug-in zones and edge cities connected through an elaborate network of highways, telephones, computer banks, fiber-optic cable lines, and television and radio outlets. There is an intentional conflation of the physical and the electronic city in Gibson's science-fiction accounts, which is an acknowledgment that a gap exists between the city that we can visualize and the invisible city that is constituted in and through its fields of information circulation. Furthermore, the radically decentered non-place of the metroscape defies existence as an imageable form because of its very dispersal, as do the matrices of cyberspace.[3]

And what of the knowledge and power that Michel Foucault once described as being embodied in disciplinary places of enclosure such as prisons, hospitals, factories, and even the city as a whole? These spaces or systems, which combined discourses and architectures, programs and mechanisms, also seem to be dislocated from space, deeply hidden within the electronic matrices of a global computer network that connects all points in space and directs our lives from some ethereal "other" location.[4] The processes of city planning once imposed a rational form on the modern metropolis to make it efficiently managed and machine-like. But how do we begin to organize this new metroscape that defies any imageable form, at a time when the role of the planner has been displaced as a coherent site of command and control over the space of the city and when new positions within postmodernity have yet to be defined?[5]

Images, imagination, and memory of cities are intimately linked, and thus I want to turn to descriptions of two different types of artificial memory, so that they may give us some insights into our contemporary crisis of representing invisible cities. The "classical art of memory," as described by Frances Yates,[6] depended on the mental construction of an imaginary but complex architectural setting that contained a series of places, or *loci*. In these places, vivid images or icons symbolically representing what was to be recollected were mentally stored. In order to remember the parts of a speech, for example, the orator imaginatively followed a path through the sequence of rooms, or *topi*, where the symbols had been placed, encountering the images one by one and recalling the ideas or arguments that the images represented.[7]

Yates also describes another, lesser-known art of memory. Developed by Ramon Lull, it differs considerably from the classical method in that there are no striking images, and there is nothing to excite recall though resemblance or similitude. Instead, the concepts were designated by letters; it was, in other words, an abstract art of memory. Movement and change were introduced into this static system not by mentally reenacting a promenade through a fixed and memorized spatial container of icons, but instead by using a set of revolving concentric circles marked with letters standing for concepts, which enabled a recombinatory play of these concepts. In this mathematical art of memory, the meaning thus changed with respect to the level of the circle on which a given letter was located—that is, the context that was being used. It required memorizing the principles and procedures of Lull's art and then investigating the combinations through a series of questions and answers.[8]

These two arts of memory can help us explore the question of the imageability of cities in the age of electronic communication. For the classical art of memory was embedded within modernists' visualizations of the space of the city, while the combinatorial art of memory appears to be more closely related to the postmodern view of a city that is increasingly disappearing or invisible. Kevin Lynch's *The Image of the City*[9] can provide a brief explanation of how the classical art of memory has informed the visual aspect of the city. Lynch was interested in the capacity of the image of a city to generate the kind of order that made a city a legible, memorable, and coherent place—in other words, he sought to describe the spatial container that would hold the icons of memory. This systematic structure, or cognitive map, would be used to guide subsequent design interventions, for Lynch's work was developed during the decades of urban renewal and renovation, when programs focused on improving the image of American cities. He argued,

> Orientation in space (and time) is the framework of cognition. We
> have powerful abilities for recognizing places and for integrating

them into mental images, but the sensory form of those places can make that effort at understanding more or less difficult.[10]

Lynch's analysis of the city rested on five different elements: paths, edges, landmarks, nodes, and districts. He noted that problems could arise in this system, which would disorient the viewer by blocking the road to recall. For example, edges could be too weak to delineate a place, or too wide, leaving a district exposed to view; a landmark could be too great or too alien to the character of a district; paths might lead towards but not to a node; or parts within a district might be loosely connected, roughly related, or without a structure of any kind. It then became the planner's task to restore order to the spatial container of memory icons by eliminating these visual inconsistencies in a city's imageable form.

As for the combinatorial art of memory, let us first explore Italo Calvino's *Invisible Cities* before quickly reviewing Michael Sorkin's book entitled *Local Code: The Constitution of a City at 42° N Latitude*. In a 1967 talk entitled "Cybernetics and Ghosts," Calvino described the tendency at that time to consider the world, in all its various aspects, as "discrete" and not continuous in form.[11] He used the word discrete in mathematical terms, meaning composed of separate, divisible parts. Instead of a series of linear images that formed a sequence or a system of places, thought now appeared as a series of discontinuous states and combinatorial relays. Calvino claimed that early computer scientists such as Claude Shannon, Norbert Wiener, John von Neumann, and Alan Turing had radically changed the theoretical image of our mental processes.[12] Computers could now instantaneously create a combinatorial complexity unattainable by human minds. They had, he noted, finally displaced the classical art of memory, and had realized the combinatorial art first imagined by Ramon Lull.[13]

We can turn to Calvino's *Invisible Cities* to see this art in action: here a series of city descriptions fail to geographically connect the discrete elements located within each city.[14] Though each element is endowed with startling visual presence, when assembled they remain merely a listing of icons. There is no mental map to tie these piecemeal images together so that they describe or structure the elusive journey from city to city; instead, there is only a combinatory system of rules and relationships at play. Indeed, only a great atlas containing the maps or forms of all possible cities allows for an imaginary projection of what otherwise remain invisible places.[15] Marco Polo, the protagonist, tells Kublai Kahn,

> Traveling you realize that differences are lost: each city takes to resembling all cities, places exchange their form, order, distances, a shapeless dust cloud invades the continents. Your atlas preserves the differences intact: that assortment of qualities which are like the letters in a name.[16]

Thus the combinatory order of the atlas enables Marco Polo to

> put together, piece by piece, the perfect city, made of fragments mixed with the rest, of instants separated by intervals, of signals one sends out, not knowing who receives them. If I tell you that the city toward which my journey tends is discontinuous in space and time, now scattered, now more condensed, you must not believe the search for it can stop.[17]

Recombined and reordered, these visual configurations take on their own imaginary force, helping to overcome the failure of vision in a culture so saturated with visual forms that images often fail to register at all. *Invisible Cities* represents a network much like the matrix of a hypertext, in which the reader can select multiple routes and draw a variety of conclusions.[18]

Since all representational forms can now be subjected to the algorithmic manipulations of abstract computer logic, it is not surprising to find that a contemporary account of city order, Michael Sorkin's *Local Code,* is based on the listing of a discrete set of places that have no relation to each other save the common set of rules or regulations that generate elements within them. A comparison of "adjacency restrictions" is the basic mode of operation in this game of set theory. Each set is a vector of information that encounters other vectors constituting the city matrix; as in set theory, these vectors are transformers with an ability to grow and change direction. While borrowing much from the paths, edges, nodes, and districts first outlined by Lynch, Sorkin compounds the contemporary problem of imageability by developing his own vocabulary for urban planning: districts have been changed into "Nabes" and residential areas become physical places of inhabitation or "Habs," paths are now "Nets," air and light considerations are labeled "Heliotropisms," the garden city model is referenced as "Territory and Ring," the civic center is now a "Mosaic" oriented to the cardinal points of the compass, and so forth.

This cool mathematical approach to the problems of the contemporary city is the result of Sorkin's singular failure to provide the reader with the wealth of symbolic and visionary incitement that words and signs can provide. In an afterword, Sorkin admits this failure, and says that it was only after much consideration that he decided to exclude visual imagery such as drawings and diagrams. Underscoring his ambivalence over the power of images, both verbal and visual, he notes,

> The medium [of text] has its limitations: verbal, it lacks a dimension of precision that more literally architectural media might provide....The code recognizes that a vision already concretized preempts the greater possibilities of an incitement open to many interpretations. Like all building codes, this one is an essay in the limits of specification...[but at the same time the code] seeks a city designed not simply through the deductions of a dominating generality [the kind that always inhabit a master plan] but also via induction from numberless individual points of departure [by comparing adjacent elements in a series]....Codes are Rosetta Stones, keys or prescriptions for acts of translation. Poised between fantasy and construction, codes—if they are both broad enough and precise enough —can be the channels of urban invention.[19]

But are codes or are images the generators of imagination and memory? Is it the structural formation of the city—the listing of relations that govern a set of vectors and the elements within each vector, similar to the static system of rooms and icons that define the classical art of memory—or is it the mental objects and visual images embedded in structural form that generate magnificent and evocative patterns of thought? Again I want to return to Calvino, for he is a master at structural combinations and ordered abstractions as well as an expert conjurer of the evocative power of words. At one point in his accounting of invisible cities, Calvino describes poor Kublai Kahn focusing so narrowly on a chessboard of black and white squares that the game's meaning has eluded him—it has become simply an abstract square of planed wood. Then Calvino has Marco Polo point out that this wonderful board was "inlaid with two woods: ebony and maple," and from there the Kahn's imagination takes flight, moving from the images of ebony forests and rafts laden with logs, to river docks and welcoming women, and so on.[20] In this manner, Calvino taught a lesson: either readers can reduce events to abstract patterns that facilitate the procedures of logical operations and the demonstration of theorems, or they can make words reveal the very tangible aspects of the objects to which they refer, thus engendering imaginary visions while allowing that something unfathomable will always remain.[21]

Following the lessons of Calvino, we have to ask: in the presence of invisible images of the city and of the kind of combinatorial play that Sorkin's manual entails, is the widespread failure to understand the evocative power of images of all types a result of the dulling of visual sensibilities too accustomed to looking at cities through the distancing device of a television screen, or too saturated with the flood of prefabricated scenes presented on any ramble through the metropolis? In his very last lectures, Calvino wondered,

What will be the future of the individual imagination in what is usually called the "civilization of the image"? Will the power of evoking images of things that are not there continue to develop in a human race increasingly inundated by a flood of prefabricated images?…We are bombarded today by such a quantity of images that we can no longer distinguish direct experience from what we have seen for a few seconds on television. The memory is littered with bits and pieces of images, like a rubbish dump, and it is more and more unlikely that any one from among so many will succeed in standing out.[22]

THE HYPER-VISUAL AMERICAN CITY

So let us turn to the problems of hyper-visuality in the space of the contemporary city. What might be the image of the city in a culture—such as America—that constitutes itself as an image, a culture in which the public spaces have been usurped by a series of simulations or variations on a theme park, and in which every aspect of metropolitan life seems thoroughly impregnated by the logic of the private market? As discussed in a previous essay, science-fiction accounts seem to offer a way to explore the dislocating power and decentered space of the urban realm, as they consider it to be a designed construction, a made thing, a play of shapes and places. They also overtly acknowledge the fact that both cyberspace and city space are artifices, intentionally constructed "zones" under the sign of computer algorithms that must function in precisely the manner their programs or design codes allow. But cyber-"zones" and urban "zones" also allow a number of possible worlds to coexist; they insert alien places into familiar ones or harmoniously juxtapose two non-contiguous and incongruous spaces as if no separation existed between them. Images of the city matrix become that of the computer's, and vice versa; any sign, word, or place is susceptible to being converted into something else, for in these artifices there is no center, there are no spatial coordinates to tie down the shifting "zones" and meanings of urban reality.[23] How do we begin to describe the emerging invisible realms and the fragmented "zones" of the metroscape? We can draw examples from contemporary New York and Atlanta. Perhaps we may start by inspecting clever artifices designed to advertise cities.

THE ART OF SELLING CITIES

In the 1930s, Walter Benjamin wrote:

> Today the most real, the mercantile gaze into the heart of things is the advertisement. It abolishes the space where contemplation moved and all but hits us between the eyes with things as a car, growing to gigantic proportions, careens at us out of a film screen. And just as the film does not present furniture and facades in completed forms for critical inspection, their insistent, jerky nearness alone being sensational, the genuine advertisement hurtles things at us with the tempo of a good film....What in the end, makes advertisements so superior to criticism? Not what the moving red neon sign says...but the fiery pool reflecting it in the asphalt.[24]

Since the rise of commercial capital in the nineteenth century, city streets have been littered with advertisements that assault us, calling out for our attention and arresting our thoughts. And consumption has always been stimulated by sumptuous visual displays. What Benjamin pointed out, however, is that the contemplative, passive, and distanced mode of viewing—and criticizing—cities as works of art could no longer be harnessed to awaken visual awareness. Printing had been dragged out into the street, where it literally assaulted the eye. Writing had been blown up to gigantic proportions, so that its very nearness prohibited avoidance. These forms of writing, this instantaneous language—in publicity brochures, in slogans, in advertisements, in posters—were direct and resourceful communications provoking the public to act. A language of the image spoke directly to its spectators, it anticipated and guided their reactions, it struck an optical unconscious. Before visual sensibilities became dulled and distracted by a repetitive succession of city sights and an overstimulation of urban sensations, these simple spectacles held the potential, so Benjamin thought, to have a revolutionary effect.

Although New York City's streets have been blocked from such forceful experiences, for more commercialized purposes they have been refigured, recently and cleverly, with illusory scenes that reflect an ideal city image back at the spectator. Knowing that the public space of the city is animated and mediated by the economy, advertisers have become facile manipulators of this public sphere. Donna Karan, a New York fashion designer who has used urban images to great effect in her advertisements, claims that "I kept saying DKNY is about the streets and Peter [Arnell, the director of her advertising agency] said, 'If it's about the streets why aren't we out there on the streets?' And that's how the billboards, bus shelters, and [paintings on sides of buildings] came about."[25]

City officials have learned that as their budgets shrink during economic recession, they have to find creative ways to raise money. One recent development is the city store, a shop that sells items such as old voting machines, stop signs, and steel bars from an old city jail, thus offering an idealized and commodified urban image to the consumer. Replicas of street signs such as Wall Street and 42nd Street are big sellers in New York.[26] Recently the creative director of a New York advertising agency, Drenttel Doyle, designed the Transit Museum Gift Shop in Grand Central Terminal, which sells all sorts of subway-related paraphernalia such as earrings and cufflinks made of old tokens, or a "Rush Hours" watch on which the numbers are the familiar symbols of the 1, 2, 3, 4, 5, 6, 7, and 9 subway lines.[27]

Based on Andy Warhol's remark that "business art is the step that comes after Art. Being good in business is the most fascinating kind of art,"[28] it seems obvious that the rampant commodification of the art world in galleries, museums, and auction houses during the 1970s and 1980s would extend itself to the art of selling cities, as has happened in Atlanta. "The image that best sums up Atlanta," the novelist Anne Rivers Siddons believes, "is the cash register....

So far, the soul of the city has been money and business."[29] With this reputation at stake, Atlanta did not rely on product advertisers or the usual city memorabilia to put its name and image on the map, but hired its own director of marketing and communications, Joel Babbit, to polish its image and "put the city up for sale and [eventually] for ridicule."[30]

Babbit's position with the government was short-lived: he resigned in July of 1993 after a year or two of employment. But before he left, this image doctor made Visa the "official credit card of Atlanta" so that for three million dollars, payable over five years, Visa's marketing program is allowed to be a part of city promotions, as well as being able to bill itself as the official city credit card.[31] Babbit spoke proudly of this sale, proclaiming that "what we're doing here in Atlanta will become standard operating procedure for cities in the next ten years."[32] He also wanted to sell the names of parks and streets to corporate buyers: Broad Street might have become Coca-Cola Boulevard, and Atlanta itself could have been renamed Coca-Colaville (after all, Atlanta has been the home of Coca-Cola since its invention in 1886). He dreamed that city side-walks might be implanted with high-tech advertising machines and that corporate logos would be mounted on city garbage trucks. For a price, an automobile maker might have received the exclusive right to have its automobiles be the city's official taxis.

Babbit claimed, "We're sitting, as most cities are, with thou-sands of non-income-producing assets that can easily be converted to income-producing assets....We don't get a penny from calling Piedmont Park, the largest in Atlanta, Piedmont Park."[33] The stratosphere itself might have been filled with Atlanta advertise-ments if Babbit had not resigned: he wanted the city to sponsor "an outer space billboard: a mile-wide balloon that would orbit the earth bearing clearly visible corporate logos. It would look about as big as a full moon....The city, as broker of the ad space, would get a fifteen percent cut." Babbit called the space billboard "one of the biggest ideas ever to cross my desk....The concept of having a billboard...seen by sixty percent of all the people on earth is incredible. And the idea that such an opportunity would come and align itself with the city of Atlanta is equally incredible."[34] Babbit also called a special "image summit" to arrive at a new slogan for Atlanta. The best he was able to develop was "Atlanta: Home of the American Dream" and "Atlanta: What the World Is Coming To," while his critics' responses were "Atlanta: What's Pride Got to Do with It?" and "Atlanta: The Price Is Right."[35] However, other cities have quickly followed Babbit's lead.

So the legends of advertising go: "From infancy to adulthood, advertising is the air Americans breathe, the information we absorb, almost without knowing it. It floods our minds with pictures of perfection and goals of happiness easy to attain."[36] Why not advertise perfected cities? It seems that people around the world are connected through brand names as much as through anything else. A recent marketing sample of young people from eleven different countries found that forty percent could recognize the United Nations logo while eighty-two percent knew the Coca-Cola logo.[37] Since the public sphere, consisting of squares, streets, the press, and public opinion, has been eviscerated by the market tactics of advertising and underwriting, the image of the city has also been sundered into self-contained, artificially constructed "zones" that repetitively circulate identical messages, drawing the public together as global consumers of products, places, and images.

When it comes to the art of selling cities, however, we have to ask, whose dreams are being packaged and sold back to us, and for what purpose? However paradoxical advertising messages may appear, their function is to distort, not to mask. They are an intentional staging of the signifier. But in a culture saturated by images, the signifier no longer points to solid ground outside of its structure of signification. The sign is all there is, in this play of appearances in which the image has become transcendent.[38] In the gap between image and object—or signifier and signified—there can be a skewed representation and a great deal of instability of meaning. Perhaps the outpouring of advertisements using nostalgic forms or providing the appearance of unity for a city that has long since been divided reflects the difficulty of giving any representational image to urban reality in the late twentieth century.[39]

In the end, this flood of images of the city fails to offer the spectator a stable sense of physical reality, because public space appears impermanent and nondescript within the persistent flow of information. Thus perception of the physical city begins to shift. We divert our eyes to protect ourselves from the tyranny of constant visualization. Our sense of sight is dulled by this hyper-imageability that makes everything appear familiar and already known. And the reliance on stereotypical images erases the complexity and the nuances of the physical form of the lived city. Escape into the visual excess that images can provide also distorts or disguises traumatic material that the public may wish to deny.[40]

To give a few examples, during the last two decades, American cities have begun to disinvest massively in many of their older and poorer neighborhoods, deindustrialization has erased many working-class jobs and devastated their communities and homes, city doorways have become the places where the homeless and drug abusers lurk, crime and physical assault have seemed to threaten the pedestrian at every corner—and the list can go on. In these times, the spectacle of phantasmagorical city images, whether they appear in old-fashioned billboard advertising or in newly-designed architectural "zones," become pleasurable diversions that mask what is disturbing and destabilize what we deny. Images that imaginatively take us from absence to presence, from deficiency to excess, and that do not move us beyond the pre-packaged intent enable us to disengage what exists from what we imagine to exist, thus disavowing that the American city is increasingly divided, both economically and racially. And this gap between reality and representation also works to make the experience of the actual city disappear behind a screen that juxtaposes discontinuous images, eradicates connecting spaces, and manipulates our sense of history and time.[41]

The Retreat into Privatized "Zones"

We can argue that revolutions in communications, such as the computer, the highway, and the jet airplane, have made almost every metropolitan area and every highway interchange an equivalent location point within the global network. And there have been shifts within the workforce which support this argument: for example, in 1975 twenty-five to thirty percent of the jobs in New York were in manufacturing. But by the beginning of the 1990s, manufacturing jobs had declined to less than fifteen percent.[42] However, fear and physical repugnance are also the basis for the latest depopulation of the city and the current exodus to the suburbs: in 1975 New York did not suffer from AIDS, crack, or homelessness. As a newspaper article written in 1991 commented, New York has been transformed into a spread-out, automobile-reliant, peripheral community, not unlike Los Angeles or Atlanta. The generation that grew up in suburbia appears to hold no nostalgia for the old New York; these people prefer the suburbs, where they are surrounded by like-minded people and provided with the type of security they have known since childhood.[43] It has been said that "the broad retreat to the suburbs over the last twenty or thirty years correlates to the fear of the future and the wish to make time stand still. The politics of the Nixon, Reagan, and Bush Administrations made manifest a San Diego realtor's dream of heaven and defined the great, good American place as an exclusive country club."[44]

There is a new civic culture taking root in these suburbs and at the edges of cities: walled-in, private enclaves called common-interest housing developments (CIDs). Evan McKenzie reports in "Trouble in Privatopia" that over the last thirty years, large-scale community builders have erected more than 150,000 of these developments, and some thirty million Americans—one-eighth of the American population—live in CIDs today.[45] McKenzie notes,

> The rapid spread of CID housing is the largest and most dramatic privatization of local government functions in American history.

> CID residents pay monthly assessments to a homeowners association
> that provides exclusive services. Within their gates and walls, CID
> dwellers are protected by their own private security guards. They
> drive on streets that are privately lit, cleaned, and maintained. Their
> swimming pools, gyms, parks, and golf courses are private. Many
> CIDs also have exclusive access to shopping centers and even their
> own schools.[46]

Now, of course, what these predominately white, middle-class
citizens of Privatopia give up is their freedom and privacy, as
they become the subjects of surveillance by video monitors and
private eyes. What they are offered in return is an alternative quasi-
governmental regime exclusively for the well-to-do, which is tanta-
mount to a secession from urban America. Their retreat into privatized "zones" enhances the view of the city as a site of deprivation
and dysfunction.

There are many suburban communities that want to secede
from the city. One of these, discussed in the *New York Times*, is
one of the most conservative, prosperous, and fastest-growing counties in America: Cobb County, Georgia, which includes the town
of Marietta. Located just north of Atlanta, the county's main
stretch of interstate highway is named for a former neo-Nazi John
Birch Society president, and one of its towns passed an ordinance a
few years back that required all residents to keep a gun and ammu-
nition at home. Recently this same county passed a notorious reso-
lution condemning homosexuality, and decided to terminate all
government funding for the arts rather then determine what is
offensive versus what is in keeping with its "community values."[47]
The explicit distinctions between the good life the county offers
and the negative influences emanating from the city of Atlanta are
exacerbated, precisely because of Cobb County's economic success.
The county has grown explosively over the last decade, increasing
its population by fifty percent and doubling its number of jobs.
Too much growth in such a short time has brought in its wake the
fear that jobs and economic security might just as quickly be

reversed.[48] As the *Times* noted, Cobb County is "the fastest growing part of America, and what goes on there says as much about the
nation as it does about the South." But it says less about the South
than about suburban America, as its politics resemble those of other
suburban counties in the southwest regions of the country.[49] Cobb
County is separated by the Chattahoochee River from Atlanta,
which is now seventy percent black, and it treats that division as if
it were a moat. Refusing to join the MARTA rapid-transit system
that would link the area to Atlanta, one county official said, "We
would stock the Chattahoochee with piranha" to keep out the transit system.[50]

Whatever the form, the move to the periphery of an American
city is a gesture that stands dramatically against the concept of the
metropolis and the meaning of public space. The wasteful and
increasingly untenable dreams of single family homes, suburban
isolation, and shopping malls, all of which depend on the automobile and highway systems, have dispersed these privatized "zones"
throughout the landscape. This "new American urbanism," as it has
been called, has nothing to do with the city; in fact, it is to be
blamed for the city's disappearance.

THE MALLING OF AMERICAN CITIES

Since the early 1970s, the private market has penetrated deeply,
without the slightest struggle, into every aspect of American lives.
In fact, advertising in the public realm and marketing images
now appear to be the only mechanisms that offer isolated individuals in the decentered non-place of the American city access to
meaning and well-being, albeit through the form of consumption.
As the awareness and use of public space disappears, these types of
places have been reconstituted in privatized "zones" such as the
shopping mall. When the old central business districts of American cities declined after World War II, the retail establishments,
banks, offices, and business services fled towards the periphery,

transforming the shape of cities throughout the country. Joel Garreau has termed these new agglomerations "edge cities." They are developments that begin with a suburban shopping mall and a few offices located at the intersection point of two major highways and then quickly begin to spread out, becoming low-density edge cities within a few years—a phenomenon commonly referred to as "sprawl." By the 1990s, however, the existence of every Main Street and every commercial strip dating back to the 1950s has been threatened, and most often its economic viability destroyed, by the appearance of a shopping mall nearby.

The American middle class had already moved to the suburbs in the 1950s and 1960s, for the most part, but now most metropolitan residents not only sleep and eat but also relax and work outside the center of the city. Garreau claims that America contains more than two hundred edge cities, and that two-thirds of American office space is already located there.[51] For the most part, architects have ignored this phenomenon, and rather myopically have kept their focus on the center of the city, hoping for its imminent revitalization. But a few, such as Stephen Kieran and James Timberlake in their article entitled "Paradise Regained," have begun to outline the spatial transformations and morphological types that these edge cities represent. Rather than the familiar relationship of building-to-building or building-to-roadway that American Main Streets have traditionally been, and which dematerialized into the 1960s Las Vegas-type strip, these new commercial and residential centers have no relationship to the abstract circuitry of the spreading highway system. Instead, they insulate their clusters of buildings behind large green lawns and juxtapose their contained garden areas against the highway network. Isolated and self-contained, these high-speed centers become icons of cyberspace, or, as the authors describe, an "electronic or hydraulic circuitry with each line representing an individual automotive passage, each overlay an interchange, and each node in the diagram corresponding to a destination."[52]

Kieran and Timberlake argue that the morphological arrangement of streets in these centers is no longer a traditional gridiron pattern with its multiple series of choices and its stop-start rhythmic motion. Instead, it is an hourglass shape, in which drivers' choices narrow down to the one desired interchange as their automobiles approach their destination points on limited access highways. The basic unit of blocks and lots, which is the standard American building parcel in the center of the city, has been transformed in these new suburban centers into the "land bay." This is defined as a "ready-for-development parcel" that comes complete not only with looping access roads but also with all of its utility infrastructure and planning permits.[53] These centers may be anchored by one major tenant (to continue the nautical metaphor), or they may become "deliberate collections of individual land bays docked against one another; [but as a whole] they are developed as privatized gardens in which one works, markets, and resides and that define a collective realm of sorts, interconnected by green-veiled roadways."[54]

Kieran and Timberlake use as an example of these privatized garden areas Perimeter Center Mall, a mall that began its development in the 1960s when a regional highway was intersected by the new perimeter beltway north of Atlanta. Here they find a combination of urban utopias that borrows from Ebenezer Howard's Garden City, Frank Lloyd Wright's Broadacre City, and Le Corbusier's Radiant City. In this place, architecture has been located in or perhaps replaced by the garden.[55] The design of separate building complexes draws from a pattern book of garden typologies: for example, Ravinia, a mixed-use office and hotel complex in Perimeter Center, is a hybrid of two landscape types: "ravine" and "arcadia." This ravine, with its stream and waterfalls, is located in a wooded arcadian landscape, and this garden veil through which the spectator must peer—not its nondescript architectural structures—dominates the visual appearance of Ravinia.[56] In these new American places, architecture has been reduced to a prosaic background prop, and the command over space that it once might have achieved has disappeared behind the nostalgic dream of a garden paradise.

Closer to New York, or at least on its periphery, we could use as another example of the garden land bay Princeton Forrestal Center, launched in 1973 by Princeton University along the Route One corridor linking Trenton to New York City. Taking 1,600 acres of land on either side of the road, its plan allocated 308 acres for anticipated university expansion, 628 acres for a research and office park, 190 acres for a residential village, retail center, and hotel, and 482 acres of protected green space. By 1988, Princeton Forrestal Center's labor force exceeded five thousand, as it had attracted such corporate tenants as American Re-Insurance, Dow Jones, IBM, Merrill Lynch, The National Science Foundation's John von Neumann Supercomputer Center, Prudential Insurance, GE-RCA, Siemens, Xerox, and the Robert Wood Johnson Foundation.[57] Forrestal Center, called a "symbolic-analytic zone," is also a cybernetic "zone," "staffed by highly skilled employees stationed at networked computer terminals, [who] receive, analyze, and transmit data essential to the daily transactions of far-flung, large-scale corporate and research operations."[58] Yet Forrestal Village has not fared well: though its design was carefully constructed to emulate the imagery associated with the open-air streetscape of a New England shopping and business street, and though it provides room for 125 retail specialty shops, a hotel, and several restaurants, vacancies abound, there are no residential areas within walking distance, and it is only accessible by means of a $20.4-million vehicular overpass and cloverleaf that Princeton University constructed in 1989. It is a ship marooned in its garden landscape.

In what can be construed as an offensive against suburban mallification and against the general disappearance or abandonment of the American city, the old central business districts are bringing suburban amenities back to the center. This sort of inversion is taking place in centered cities such as New York, as well as in centerless cities such as Atlanta. Fear of the real city, however, has resulted in an outpouring of simulated metropolitan enclaves, which are cut out and juxtaposed against the city itself. In the safety of the privately policed and monitored new center city, the nostalgic images of the old city have been artfully rearranged and reprocessed into new theatrical spectacles.

In the late 1970s and 1980s, the Rouse Company was a pioneer developer that brought the suburban mall back to the center of the city by recycling old historic structures and areas into the well-known "urban festival marketplaces" such as Boston's Quincy Market, Baltimore's Harborplace, and New York City's Fulton Market in South Street Seaport. But the days of new malls and festival marketplaces are past, and now the area of growth seems to be in managing or remerchandising already existing places. In 1969, Atlanta decided to redevelop the Underground—a very steep center-city six-block area lying underneath the old 1929 viaducts—in an attempt to re-establish a downtown lost when the area was turned into a hotel and convention center, as well as to provide a nighttime entertainment "zone" for conventioneers and tourists. But crime, the fear of downtown, and the constant construction and reconstruction of nearby land spelled out economic disaster for the recycling of this railway-era theme park. The Rouse Company, subsequently given the contract to manage this area, has taken this losing marketplace and turned it around, making the Underground into a shopping center that sports a grand new staircase connecting Peachtree Street with a performance plaza on the lower level.

The Rouse Company was also one of the original developers of South Street Seaport in lower Manhattan. The *New York Times* said of the reinvention of this area: "The old buildings, miraculously preserved, and the eclectic armada, lovingly preserved, retain the flavor of the days a century and a half ago when the environs of Fulton Street and the East River were at the hub of world commerce.... [However,] along Fulton itself, the Seaport has become a gaudy Disneyland strip for shoppers and, weekend evenings, white-collar roisterers who detract from a recollection of earlier incarnations."[59] This festival marketplace remains relatively unsuccessful as it enters its second decade. Its annual sales may exceed one hundred million dollars, but nevertheless, the Rouse Company is busy remerchandising the place.[60] Since its opening in 1983, more than one hundred shops have gone out of business, making the turnover rate higher than ten percent every year. Most of the merchants in the Fulton Festival Market have been forced to sign temporary leases so that they can be removed as soon as more lucrative retailers are found. Originally, the Rouse Company predicted that the Seaport would be doing four or five times the business it actually does, and that it would welcome one hundred thousand tourists each year rather than the twenty to thirty thousand it currently draws. The entire story of South Street Seaport's redevelopment and historic preservation is the result of a long battle over contested terrain, land uses, and conflicting images of the city; in the end, the mall-like marketplace was approved only as a way to support the South Street Seaport Museum and Historic District. Rouse was supposed to give the museum five million dollars a year from collected revenues generated by the $3.50-per-square-foot rent that it charged its retailers, plus a share of their profits. To date, the museum has received one million dollars a year. After paying off its own debts and rents, the museum is left with little more than three hundred thousand to four hundred thousand dollars to carry out its programs and to maintain all of the historic structures under its care within the Historic District.

In order to raise more revenue, the Rouse Company has tried to turn the area into a primary shopping district by replacing small-scale operations with national chain stores. Of course, this violates the intent of the original agreement that Rouse struck in the 1970s with the city and the Seaport Museum—an agreement that states, "There are supposed to be a 'reasonable number' of stores devoted to the promotion of maritime and sea-related activates and products." One of the only remaining such shops, Captain Hook's, which offers a variety of maritime kitsch, received an eviction notice from the Rouse Company in 1993. Many found that to be a betrayal of all the Seaport was supposed to be.[61] There had been six tenants predating the arrival of Rouse's Fulton Marketplace, but three of these were already gone. The proprietor of Captain Hook's told the *New York Times*, "There's a man-eating shark in our midst and the citizenry must be warned. A shopping mall monster is try-ing to devour our city's history."[62] In retort, Rouse's Marketplace marketer argued, "Our intent is to preserve the integrity and feeling of nineteenth-century New York. But our audience is very much part of the twentieth century." If that means bringing a virtuality shop or a miniature golf course into the Fulton Marketplace, they argue, then so much the better, even if it inevitably trivializes the maritime milieu.[63]

South Street Seaport is not the only shopping mall that has experienced difficulties in the 1990s. After all, some American malls are nearing their fiftieth birthdays, and at that age they need to be reinvented. The earliest shopping centers, built on the edges of sub-urbia in the 1950s and 1960s, were long, shedlike structures with cement canopies to keep off the rain. Soon thereafter, when out-door weather was taken into consideration, the closed mall was born: a massive, boxlike structure marooned in a sea of cars. It has been argued that in the 1980s shopping became an "intensified American experience," and malls suddenly needed glamour and curbside appeal to survive in the war against their competitors. "It was the era of epic outdoor logos, splashless fountains, marble floors, and postmodern pitched roofs. Vast expanses of skylights—Vaults 'n' Stuff—came to define what a mall should be."[64]

Atlanta has become preeminent in terms of developing new malls and enhancing existing ones—in fact, the only remaining public area in Atlanta is the shopping mall plaza. Because there has been a steady growth in population and income north of Interstate Highway 285 outside of Atlanta, a battle of malls has been waged at this site. One major standoff pits the two-year, $40-million expan-sion and redesign of Phipps Plaza against the $40-million overhaul of Lenox Square. These two malls are located across the street from each other on Peachtree Street, Atlanta's most famous thoroughfare. In order for the prestigious Phipps Plaza, already the home of Saks Fifth Avenue and Lord & Taylor, to siphon off its competitor's shoppers, it added a Parisian, Inc. department store, a twelve-screen movie theater, a food court, and over four thousand new parking spaces. To meet this competition, the twenty-year-old Lenox Mall is remodeling its food court, raising its roof, creating a series of indoor plazas, and adding skylights, vaulted ceilings, and arches. A second Atlanta mall war finds the newly-constructed North Point Mall off Highway 400 fighting against the existing Rouse Company's Perimeter Mall, located fourteen miles away inside Atlanta city limits.[65]

THE OLYMPIC GAMES

Atlanta will be hosting the Olympic Games in 1996, and it knows that Barcelona will be a hard act to follow. What, after all, does Atlanta have to offer? Founded in 1842, burned to the ground during the Civil War by General Sherman in 1866, it has few historic memories to offer the Olympic spectator. Its monuments are such outstanding buildings as "the Dump," which is the name for the boarded up hovel where Margaret Mitchell wrote the celebrated *Gone with the Wind* (and which in fact burned down in 1995), and the Varsity Drive-In Restaurant, where the world's greasiest hamburgers are cooked. What Atlanta does have is the Rouse-managed Underground as well as the Coca-Cola Museum; as one hopeful entrepreneur plans, it may also have a Gone with the Wind theme park ready to open its plantation-like arms in time for the Games.[66] As Atlanta's marketer Mr. Babbit seemed to have known, "In a city where overachieving is a central part of the local mythology, it's an article of faith here that the 1996 Olympics will be a future-oriented, high-tech pageant of New South prosperity and interracial harmony, able to compete with any host city that came before it."[67]

The Olympic Games should also offer Atlanta a lasting legacy, and planning for them should be an empowerment process for its inner-city black neighborhoods. For while Atlanta has experienced a boom in its northern white suburbs over the last decade or two, the old financial heart of downtown known as Five Points has lost

dozens of banks, corporate clients, and department stores.[68] Having
won the coveted Games based on a mythically constructed image of
itself as an amicable, multiracial civil rights capital in a world
increasingly torn by conflicts of race and nationalistic uprisings,
Atlanta has a lot to address if it is to remove the racial and economic boundaries that actually exist. A wish list of more than five hundred million dollars in hoped-for projects for downtown Atlanta,
where most of the games will take place, reveals the fragmentation
of the city, for this list includes hundreds of units of affordable
housing, new parks in black South Atlanta, new stores in abandoned downtown areas, renovations of public housing projects,
extensions to the MARTA rapid-transit systems, and expanded cultural facilities, as well as the requisite list of stadiums and sports
facilities that the Olympics require.

Most of the $1.35-billion budget will not go toward the human
and urban revitalization that many expect from the games, but will
instead be spent on projects directly related to sports. The Georgia
Dome, a 70,500-seat stadium begun before Atlanta was chosen to
host the coveted Olympic Games, is where basketball and gymnastic events will be housed; it was the site of the 1994 Super Bowl and
will eventually become the home stadium of the Atlanta Falcons. A
new Olympic stadium, to be built with private money, will be
home to the Atlanta Braves. And the fifty-six-year-old Techwood
Homes, one of the nation's first public housing projects, will be
renovated as the place for the Olympic athletes to live. After the
Games it will be given to the adjacent Georgia Institute of Technology, rather than being returned to the public as mixed-income
affordable housing.[69]

With expectations running high, the drama of race and poverty
relations has already appeared. When the Olympic flag arrived in
Atlanta in September 1992, it was met by five thousand demonstra-
tors protesting what they believed were plans for "an exploitative
low-wage Olympiad," and a planning process that might have been
sold on the peace-keeping image of Martin Luther King Jr. but was
being controlled by rich white suburbanites. The reality is that

there are two Atlantas, one of those who have and the other of those who do not.[70] The projected image of the city glosses over these discrepancies, and thus the actual city disappears, enveloped in a haze of media pretensions.

REDEVELOPMENT "ZONES"

The spatial restructuring of American cities, which sets up the dystopian city center as the mirror image of the spreading, sprawl-like suburbs, or which tries to insert a random series of suburban amenities into the heart of the city, is partly the effect of shifts within the economy of late capitalism. But fear is the root cause, and fear can be contagious when fueled by a constant diet of negative media caricatures that represent the city as a nightmarish place of crime and horror. Social scientists have not helped either, for they constantly talk about the perpetual crisis that confronts the city, inevitably focusing on the city's worst problems and devastated neighborhoods, which they describe as "overrun by drug wars, controlled by gangs toting Uzi machine guns, and [filled with] dangerous deviants lurking in darkened corners."[71] And while Manhattan, New York City's center, may still retain a concentration of more than a quarter of all the jobs in the thirty-one-county metropolitan district, the *New York Times* still proclaims, "It is becoming increasingly necessary to 'reinvent New York' economically and in terms of an image that sells."[72]

We find the ninety-one-acre landfill in New York's Hudson River called Battery Park City to have been created in the 1970s and 1980s as a luxury upper-middle-class neighborhood. This area, another instance of the reinvention of the city, has been discussed in the *New York Times*: "One need not live there to appreciate the presence of an undeniable enhancement in the urban vision, one that is perhaps a trifle too clean-cut, too sanitized for the incorrigible New Yorker. But its majestic Winter Garden, its jolly marina, its incomparable esplanade all contribute to the realization of the city

as one of the great harbors of the world."[73] The sylvan 8.2-acre,
$18-million Hudson River Park that was added in the summer of
1992 to Battery Park City's constructed cityscape is considered a
preview for what might follow along the city's river edge between
14th Street and 72nd Street, if it survives its marketing test. It is
also an example of how new "zones" must represent what the city
once might have been, as well as duplicating all the necessary
amenities. The park bears witness that the city is shifting—without
much comment or complaint—from an old industrial landscape
where shipping and manufacturing were dominant activities to
a consumer cityscape where consumption and pleasure are the primary focus.

Before Hudson River Park was built, the adjoining neighborhoods of Tribeca and Battery Park City drew up a list of things they
wanted the Battery Park City Development Authority to provide.
They strongly protested the meager public spaces such as Vesey
Park and the Winter Garden that had been squeezed between
blocks of buildings in the lower parts of Battery Park City. Nor did
the "community" want more critically-acclaimed public art projects.
Instead they sought more popular waterfront pleasure spots and
places for active recreation, such as basketball courts, volleyball
lawns, and children's swings. In addition, they wanted, albeit in
miniaturized form, the kind of amenities that Central Park offered
its neighbors: green lawns, winding paths, fountains and lily ponds,
even a rest station; and they wanted these located in a swath of
open landscape.[74] As a result, Hudson River Park resembles a laun
dry list of park-like elements: serpentine promenades, recreational
and sports areas, pavilions, and ponds, with a series of art projects
dotting its terrain.[75] Thus at Hudson River North a suburban paradise has been recreated. As Herbert Muschamp recounts, "It's the
natural consequence of Battery Park City's mission to woo upper-
middle-class residents back from suburbia."[76] But public subsidies
for luxury housing and for privatized parks within the city have
stretched the meaning of "public" beyond comprehension. Here,
too, we can argue that the space of the city has disappeared behind

newly erected garden walls that secure its protected "zone." But, as Muschamp warns, "For decades, other cities have fought against the 'Manhattanization' of their skylines. For New Yorkers, the prospect may well be the suburbanization of the shoreline, if not the entire metropolis."[77]

Government development policies are essential in sustaining a city's market position. That is why some critics believe that New York is falling behind in the competition among cities—because it has failed to develop a forceful economic development policy over the last two decades. These critics blame New York for focusing on shoring up sagging businesses and repairing antiquated infrastructures such as bridges that are falling down and roadways that are filled with holes, rather than investing in projects that would attract growing industries and generate employment. Thus the city has allocated one-third less than other large American cities to economic development projects such as new airports, sports arenas, and a larger convention center. In addition, New York invested three-fourths of its development capital in the construction of office spaces in downtown Brooklyn's MetroTech, hoping that this lower-cost location would enable New York to hold on to the businesses that New Jersey was drawing away. Once again, its critics complained, New York had failed to underwrite its high-growth sectors such as finance, communications, and international trade.[78]

However, during the last twenty years in New York, real estate tax concessions have been the primary negotiating tool with real estate developers. Designed during the fiscal crisis of 1975–1976 when the city was nearly bankrupt, they have been used to spur on new construction, to generate the preservation of historic structures, to lure businesses to the outer boroughs, and to keep big corporations from leaving the city for less costly locations. As well as through tax incentives, real estate development during the boom years of the 1980s was helped along through zoning bonuses for office and hotel construction, which until 1987 especially targeted the western sections of midtown Manhattan.[79] Because many of these expenditures have no immediately visible effect on the city's public budget and because people believe that they stimulate future growth and do not cost the city a penny, the disproportion- ate benefits that real estate developers have reaped have generally gone unchallenged.[80]

Bernard Frieden and Lyn Sagalyn have described the new forms of urban redevelopment that many American cities under- took during the 1970s and 1980s: "By now most cities have the basic equipment to attract development: a new office district, good hotels and restaurants, a shopping mall, a convention center, a his- toric neighborhood or two. They have projects that keep downtown competition as a place for business, as well as ornaments that make it enjoyable for the public."[81] And the privatization of public space must be added to this redevelopment checklist. As Magali Sarfatti Larson has noted, during these same decades architects forged new development teams with "public-private ventures."

> The commercial need for "product differentiation" and the com- petition among cities to create a sense of their own uniqueness were thus perfectly attuned with the evolution of architectural discourse…hard-pressed city managers, hard-headed businessmen, and architects in retreat from modernism discovered that the pro- duction of ever-renewed and ever-diversified images and meanings is a constitutive dimension of postindustrial economic activity.… Commodities (among them buildings), valued more for what they mean in terms of status than for their actual use, are the lifeblood of late capitalist commerce.[82]

Architect-developer John Portman's Atlanta Hyatt Regency Hotel was the first atrium-style postmodern extravaganza to blaze a path for downtown revitalization when it first opened its doors more than twenty-five years ago. With its world-famous interior of elevator banks adorned with light bulbs, escalators and bubbling fountains surrounded by trees, and red-carpeted balconies adorning all twenty-three stories, the Hyatt Regency and other Portman atri- um hotels became exemplary of a postmodern aesthetic of luxury and entertainment. Not only were these hotels sanitized human terrariums fortified against the turmoil and crime believed to have captured the streets outside, but they also offered a dazzling array of internalized, festive forms that were both entertaining and confusing. Since they allowed the spectator to view the city only through the windows of a revolving cocktail lounge, a lobby, or a pedestrian bridge raised eight stories above the street, they inhibited the spectator from critically understanding and mapping the urban terrain. Muschamp believes that by drawing on rocket imagery, "Portman [soon became]…our leading scientist of inner space. Psychologically as well as physically introverted, his voids maintained a constant emotional pitch with their suave blend of pleasure and terror, cocktails and vertigo."[83] These dizzying voids were carried out in Portman's Bonaventure Hotel in Los Angeles, his Peachtree Center Plaza in Atlanta, his Detroit Renaissance Center, and his Marriott Marquis Hotel in New York City. But what was the program's mission if everything outside of the space capsule was alien to human life? Of his planned development of fifteen contiguous blocks in downtown Atlanta, Portman told one reporter, "I'm building a city that will become a modern Venice. The streets down there are canals for cars, while these bridges are clean, safe, climate-controlled. People can walk here at any hour.…I'm giving the city new spaces away from the turmoil of urban life. I like to think of this lobby as a new town square. Here's a sidewalk cafe. And look over there.…Name me a public place in a city today where you can see outdoors without someone bothering you."[84]

TIMES SQUARE

New York City's Times Square is a prime example of these redevelopment projects that make public space private and private space public. In addition, it has a place in the postmodern debate over the position to be offered popular culture in the architecture of the city. No American place stands out as a monument to raucous commercial enterprise more than Times Square. After two decades of discussions as to its future, this famous space has been placed in a state of suspension. Even though the city promised the developers of the four planned towers known as Times Square Center—designed several times by Philip Johnson and John Burgee—unbelievably large tax abatements that may extend as long as fifty years in return for their land costs,[85] in 1992 it was decided to postpone the controversial project until the twenty-first century, when the real estate market is expected to have regained its strength. In the meantime, the public and the architects have been given time to rethink the importance of Times Square as the crossroads where consumers and producers of popular culture inevitably meet.

In the interim, several New York design firms were asked to imagine how they would celebrate Times Square as an upgraded "international landmark to popular culture."[86] James Wines of Site Projects, an advocate of "green architecture," proposed turning Duffy Square, the area just to the north of 42nd Street, into a publicity-minded commercial art park. Focusing on the vernacular iconography of urban signage systems, the plan utilized a series of kiosks adorned with icons from America's environmentally aware commercial enterprises, such as the golden arches of McDonald's. In its kiosk, McDonald's could explain to visitors how it plans to save the ecologically-threatened planet through its nature-friendly packaging. Studio Asymptote, under the direction of Hani Rashid and Lise Anne Couture, proposed a health club in a deconstructed glass-walled high-rise—a round-the-clock physique folly to titillate the gaze of passersby. Along with aerobics and weightlifting activities there would be virtual-reality bungee jumping, experimental theaters in black box retreat, storefront cable television news bureaus, and a Hip-Hop Hall of Fame. Tibor Kalman, the creative director of *Interview* magazine, and who eventually became part of Robert Stern's plan team, imagined that Times Square could be turned into a twenty-four-hour News Cafe located in a two-story pavilion beneath a facade of posters displaying magazine covers.

Electronic news strips, also on the facade, would continuously flash out news headlines, stock market prices, poems, and short stories. Finally, a plan for a new subway station designed by Craig Hodgetts and Hsin Ming Fung displayed cars on revolving platforms, borrowing the look of automobile showrooms, and had giant stuffed animals and toys from F.A.O. Schwarz Toy Store hanging from the rafters. All these commercial icons and whirling stages would be housed in a barrel-vaulted, glass-canopied shed that celebrated the subway as pop art as much as it integrated the subterranean level with the commercial world on its surface.[87]

Of course it is still an open debate whether 42nd Street—or "the Deuce," as the block of 42nd Street braced by Times Square and Eighth Avenue is called—is seamy, honky-tonk, and full of sleazy characters, or whether it is grim and eerie, a reminder of its old glitter and bustle, as some accounts insist. Rebecca Robertson, the president of the 42nd Street Development Project, believes "that 42nd Street is a street that means New York to a lot of people, but for many years what 42nd Street has meant is six to seven crimes a day....It's meant child prostitution. It sometimes seems to me the people who sentimentalize it are up in their houses in northern Connecticut."[88] The development corporation claims that even many of the legitimate businesses were no better than stash houses for drug dealers or for manufacturers of false identification cards. The area is seen as a cancer holding back Times Square's recovery and as long as dozens of private owners control it, Robertson contends, there is no chance for revitalization.[89] As Herbert Muschamp put it,

> The goal of the $20-million plan is not so much to overhaul the street physically as to reconstruct people's perception of it....A lot of time, money, and public relations have gone into constructing the image of 42nd Street as a squalid corridor of horrors that can only be redeemed by ripping it apart. The image is not unconnected to reality. The decay, crime, drugs, pornography, and prostitution are real, and no one thinks that these are civic assets. Still, even in its

most blighted state the street continued to draw people who came to enjoy the bright lights, crowds, and budget movie tickets. And it has never been clear that real estate development is the ideal deterrent to squalor or crime.[90]

When the four jumbo towers known as Times Square Center were put on hold, the interim project of fixing up 42nd Street was moved to the fore. It appears, however, that the guiding light behind the 42nd Street revitalization plan is Robert Venturi's 1966 proclamation that "Main Street is almost alright."[91] New Yorkers will be given an opportunity to learn from 42nd Street as they once learned from Las Vegas, for the new plan—paradoxically based on a principle of no plan at all—is a set of design guidelines that extrapolates from the street's popular features, so that privileged spectators will be able to relish the illusion of commercial enterprise in a sanitized and protected "zone." Each of the thirty-four refurbished structures that line the street between Broadway and Eighth Avenue will be wrapped and layered with spectacular signs, some animated and some lighted, but all legible from a distance and displaying outstanding visual impact. A chart of coordinated colors has been developed, diversity in styles, scales, and materials encouraged, and a mélange of restaurant and retail types expected.[92]

> In short the plan is devised to reinforce the street's existing characteristics. The layered accretion of forms over the past century. The mix of styles and scales. The lack of visual coordination.... Above all, the street will be unified by the prominence given to signs: video screens, painted billboards, theater marquees, faded murals from the past, LED strips, holograms—an uninterrupted commercial interruption.[93]

This play with popular forms drawn from America's image-saturated commercial landscape helps to destabilize the position that architecture once held in the city. For architecture no longer determines a city's unique visual identity, but is reduced to nostalgia stereotypes generating what Gilles Deleuze termed "any-space-whatever."

> Any-space-whatever is not an abstract universal, in all times, in all places. It is a perfectly singular space [such as Times Square], which has merely lost…the principle of its metric relations or the connection of its own parts, so that the linkages can be made in an infinite number of ways [such as in Calvino's *Invisible Cities*]. It is a space of virtual conjunction, grasped as pure locus of the possible. What in fact manifests the instability, the heterogeneity, the absence of link of such a space, is a richness in potentials or singularities which are, as it were, prior conditions of all actualization, all determination.[94]

The plan for Times Square will incorporate it into a larger sense of assembled space, where all of its simultaneity and immediacy will evaporate. It will show what Times Square was and how it achieved that form, but not how those elements will affect its future. Its definitive image will be blurred by the confused visual allure of consumer culture and by the use of historicized themes, even while it will direct our visual perception into yet another well-articulated "zone" of the city.

BUSINESS DISTRICTS AND SAFETY "ZONES"

There are other ways to "zone" the city into privatized enclaves and protected areas. Another not-for-profit private corporation in charge of the cityscape in New York is the Grand Central Partnership, formed in 1985. This is one of several business improvement districts (BIDs) carving up the city into special private-interest containment "zones," not unlike the common-interest districts (CIDs) active in the suburbs, and these quasi-governmental authorities are never fully accountable to public review. There are more than twenty of these BIDs in New York City, thirteen in Manhattan alone. The largest is the Grand Central BID, which contains at least fifty-one million square feet of space—just about the same size as downtown Los Angeles—in an oddly shaped fifty-three-block district that runs from 38th to 48th Street and from Third to Fifth Avenue. Its master plan mixes improvement of public space with revenue-earning commercial development. Assessing higher property taxes on its member businesses in order to pay for its projects, this BID has already improved sidewalk and storefront maintenance, hired one hundred private security guards, and contracted for special garbage collectors. In addition, it has initiated a facelift around Grand Central Terminal, with the installation of new street signs, trash bins, pollution-resistant trees, and lampposts.

Another way to cordon off crime is to "zone" the city into high-crime areas or drug sites, and to propose special disciplinary control districts that merge the city's land use controls with its criminal codes, which no doubt oversteps individual liberties. One such area in New York City is the East Village just below Tompkins Square Park, where more than thirty-four sites were identified as locations of drug sales and consequently padlocked by Mayor David Dinkins's anti-crime enforcement officers. Padlocking is a quick and dirty remedy that requires only police testimony of repeated drug purchases at the site. Evidently the city's nuisance-abatement law allows a site to be padlocked for a year and imposes a fine on landlords that can amount to one thousand dollars for each day of violations. Of course, not everyone supports these disciplinary strategies, and the New York Civil Liberties Union has noted that such action violates due process by seizing property without a hearing and ignores the presumption of innocence before being proven guilty.[95] A number of cities have begun to test the legality of applying various ordinances on vagrancy, loitering, and disorderly conduct, and of imposing dress codes and curfews in order to eradicate the homeless, drug addicts, prostitutes, and homosexuals from their public spaces. But carving up the city into districts and "zones" may further marginalize the homeless and unwanted.

"Not in my back yard" or NIMBY neighborhood movements are also in the process of cordoning the city off into safety "zones."

Recently a vigilant neighborhood group located on the Upper West Side of Manhattan above 96th Street and just below Columbia University protested plans to turn two buildings on Broadway into housing for the homeless. This NIMBY group believes its area is already saturated with nuisance sites. Through a neighborhood survey, it found that eighty social-service sites such as single-room occupancy hotels, mental health housing and facilities, and drug programs and facilities were already located in the area. Most often, however, it is the poorest neighborhoods that have a disproportionate share of these services. The highest concentration of these sites can be found in East Harlem, Central Harlem, and the Lower East Side from Houston Street to Gramercy Park, while virtually no such sites can be found on the affluent Upper East Side between 86th and 96th Streets. The poorest neighborhood communities already have their problems with drug addiction and alcoholism, unemployment and absentee landlords, poor schools and crime—to cite a few of their grievances—and they argue that dumping more and more troubled and destitute people onto their streets is a sure way of pushing their entire district beyond the brink of stability.[96]

CONCLUSION

In terms of the imageability of our contemporary cities, there appears to be a double process of remembering and forgetting at work, an aggressive emphasis on conventional "zones" where images are cast from archives and databanks alongside a refusal to address forgotten, in-between spaces from which reason, capital, services, and visual focus have all been withdrawn. Images that imitate city scenes from the past, images that are orchestrated by unseen master codes never confronted by the average spectator, and images that separate private sites from the excesses and wastes of the city are concrete projections on the disintegrating plane of the metroscape. Yet there is simultaneously a retreat from this world into unmappable lands beyond memory and recall, into spaces that have disappeared by disruption into the black holes of an expanding terrain. These forgotten sites represent a different scale of space and time, a different order of reality and experience, beyond that imagined in a "zone." They are the amorphous interstitial spaces that accrete in every direction just beneath visual awareness. It is as if we perceive our contemporary metroscape on two different levels: one that we frame from pre-established codes and that we believe to be freed from the confines of reality, and one erased by projections that block our sight yet return in an uncanny manner to haunt perception.

Quite clearly, those responsible for the image of American cities have learned a lot from the concepts of the strip, Main Street, small-town America, and the garden city as part of a generalized rapprochement with popular culture. But focusing on the graphic sign and the advertising billboard until they become the image of a more "realistic" metroscape is now a commonplace. The planners who cite the past in order to popularize the urban landscape, who stabilize the image of the city using comfortable and conforming pictorial representations that address middle-class fears about the dangers of downtown, are not reinterpreting the metropolis; they are simply reapplying conventional forms to new situations. These sorts of city images which arise out of popular culture fail to address people's true fears, which instead have established the contemporary metro-map of enclosed "zones" and privatized enclaves.

On one hand, this type of listing of safety areas and monitored spaces, of commercialized areas and protected "zones," while it does offer a way to manage spatial data, is yet another device that disturbs our visual perception, for the array of nodes never congeals into a totality representing the metropolitan whole, but remains indeterminate and open to innumerable recombinations of self-contained, self-referential processes that define and redefine each "zone." Since they adapt to any-space-whatever, be it in the center of the city or on its periphery, there is no referential specificity to which these "zones" can be tied, there is no external referent that can be held responsible for what, after all, have clearly been constructed from design codes and simulation processes.

But on the other hand, in each of these "zones," perfected images of the city or suburbs have been projected onto pre-established frames or onto well-defined scenes. They direct and organize the spectator's visual perception. In *A Framework for Representing Knowledge* (1974) Marvin Minsky noted,

> Whenever one encounters a new situation (or makes a substantial change in one's viewpoint) he selects from memory a structure called a frame: a remembered framework to be adapted to fit reality by changing details as necessary. A frame is a data-structure for representing a stereotyped situation, like being in a certain kind of room, or going to a child's birthday party. Attached to each frame are several kinds of information. Some of this information is about how to use the frame. Some is about what one can expect to happen next. Some is about what to do if these expectations are not confirmed.[97]

Hence the "zones" of the city are like these visual frames, and they are organized by urban planners into memory networks that require a structural map to be accessed. In an attempt to impose a systematic order onto the city, to give a representational form to structure reality, we once again fall back on the spatial container and on the archives of images that are a part of the classical art of memory.[98]

Yet as I explored above, it is not the static container of memory —or the map—that informs our postmodern visual perception, as much as it is a combinatorial play of discrete bits and pieces that can be randomly selected, combined, replayed, and rerun. The apparatus that best displays this virtuosity is a matrix or a grid, a network with its cuts, disconnections, blank spaces, and intervals inserted between the serial entries of its rows and columns. This is the instrument to screen, cover over, and master the multiple; it is the hyperspace that simulates the whole from the characteristics of its parts; and it is, of course, the replica of a computer memory. Unlike the classical art of memory, a grid or computer matrix offers no singular focus, clear image, or plan—only multiple scannings, spatial interruptions, fractures, and lags. Hence disjunctive sequences of intensively realized "zones" may form the generating matrix of contemporary American city plans, from New York to Atlanta, but they represent the remembering and recollecting of urban parts when the whole has gone to pieces and no longer has an imageable form.

This paper was originally written for the Programme Interdisciplinaire de Recherche (PIR) sur la Ville Conference on the American City, sponsored by the Centre National de la Recherche Scientifique (CNRS), held in Paris, 23 October 1993.

1   Paul Virilio, "The Overexposed City," *Zone* 1/2 (1987): 14–39.

2   William Gibson, *Neuromancer* (New York: Ace Books, 1984), 43.

3   Scott Bukatman, *Terminal Identity: The Virtual Subject in Postmodern Science Fiction* (Duke University Press, 1993), 123.

4   Ibid., 149.

5   Ibid., 164.

6   Frances A. Yates, *The Art of Memory* (Chicago: University of Chicago Press, 1966), 3–4.

7   Ibid., 172–198.

8   The comparison of these two forms of the art of memory as they relate to the work of Italo Calvino is fully described in Ellen J. Esrock, "A Proposal for Integrating Readerly Visuality into Literary Studies: Reflections on Italo Calvino," *Word and Image* 9, no. 2 (April/June 1993): 114–121.

9   Kevin Lynch, *The Image of the City* (Cambridge: MIT Press, 1960).

10   Kevin Lynch, *Managing the Sense of a Region* (Cambridge: MIT Press, 1976), 23.

11   Italo Calvino, *La machine littérature* (Paris: Editions du Seuil, 1984), 11–29.

12   Ibid., 14.

13   Ibid., 15.

14   Italo Calvino, *Invisible Cities*, trans. William Weaver (New York: Harcourt Brace Jovanovitch, 1972).

15   Ibid., 164.

16   Ibid., 137.

17   Ibid., 164.

18   Italo Calvino, *Notes on Six Memos for the Next Millennium* (Cambridge: Harvard University, 1988), 71.

19   Michael Sorkin, *Local Code: The Constitution of a City at 42° N Latitude* (New York: Princeton Architectural Press, 1993), 127.

20   Calvino, *Invisible Cities*, 131–132.

21   Calvino, *Notes on Six Memos for the Next Millennium*, 75.

22   Ibid., 91–92.

23   Scott Bukatman, *Terminal Identity*, 168–170.

24   Walter Benjamin, "The Space for Rent," in *Reflections*, trans. Edmund Jephcott (New York: Schocken Books, 1978), 85–86.

25   "Fashion Marketing," *Advertising Age* (9 August 1993): s–10.

26   Seth Mydans, "From Signs to Pistols, Cash-Short Cities Sell Past," *New York Times*, 6 September 1993.

27   Liz Logan, "Yes, You Can Buy the Subway," *New York Times*, 19 September 1993.

28   Quoted in Mark C. Taylor, *Disfiguring: Art, Architecture, Religion* (Chicago: University of Chicago Press, 1992), 145.

29   Quoted in Peter Applebome, "Atlanta: The City without a Slogan," *New York Times*, 6 October 1993.

30   Joseph M. Winski, "Marketing Run Amok: The Adman who Sold Atlanta," *Advertising Age* (2 August 1993): 14.

31   Peter Applebome, "How Atlanta's Adman Pushes the City to Sell Itself," *New York Times*, 9 February 1993.

32   Quoted in Winski, "Marketing Run Amok," 14.

33   Quoted in Applebome, "How Atlanta's Adman Pushes the City to Sell Itself."

34   Quoted in Winski, "Marketing Run Amok," 14.

35   Winski, "Marketing Run Amok," 14.

36   Mark Pendergrast, *For God, Country and Coca-Cola* (New York: Charles Scribner's Sons, 1993), 406.

37   Ibid., 407.

38   Roland Barthes, referenced in Taylor, *Disfiguring*, 179.

39   For a similar account of city imageability, see Ackbar Abbas, "Building on Disappearance: Hong Kong Architecture the City," *Public Culture* 14 (1994): 441–459; and Paul Virilio, "Speed and Vision: The Incomparable Eye," *Daidalos* 47 (1993): 96–105.

40   Laura Mulvey, "Some Thoughts on Theories of Fetishism in the Context of Contemporary Culture," *October* 65 (1993): 3–20.

41   Abbas, "Building on Disappearance," 441–459.

42   Jack Newfield, "Optimism in the City Is Gone," *New York Observer* (15 April 1991): 1.

43   William Glaberson, "For Many in the New York Region, the City Is Ignored and Irrelevant," *New York Times*, 2 January 1991.

44   Lewis H. Lapham, "Fear of Freedom," *New York Times*, 6 June 1992.

45   Evan McKenzie, "Trouble in Privatopia: Residents Check Their Rights at the Gates," *The Progressive* (October 1993): 30–33.

46   Ibid., 30.

47   Peter Applebome, "County's Anti-Gay Move Surprises Only a Few," *New York Times*, 29 August 1993.

48   While Cobb County rejected a minuscule federally-sponsored arts program, its employment growth is largely based on Lockheed Aeronautical Systems plants, and thus the county receives more federal money than any other suburban county except Arlington County, outside of Washington, D.C., and Brevard County, the home of the Kennedy Space Center. There are fears that employment will decline if federal funds are lost. Applebome, "County's Anti-Gay Move Surprises Only a Few."

49   Peter Applebome, "A Suburban Eden Where the Right Rules," *New York Times*, 1 August 1994.

50   Ibid.

51   Joel Garreau, "Cities on the Edge," *Architecture* 80 (December 1991): 45–47, 114–115.

52   Stephen Kieran and James Timberlake, "Paradise Regained," *Architecture* 80 (December 1991): 48–51; the quotation is on pages 48–49.

53   Ibid., 50.

54   Ibid.

55   Stephen Kieran and James Timberlake, "A Tale of Two Cities," *Architectural Design Profile* 108 (1994): 30–35.

56   Kieran and Timberlake, "Paradise Regained," 51.

57   Michael H. Ebner, "Experiencing Megalopolis in Princeton," *Journal of Urban History* (February 1993): 11–53.

58   Ibid., 35.

59   Richard Shepard, "The Real New York? It's There, All Right, but It's Hiding," *New York Times*, 2 August 1991.

60   Claudia H. Deutsch, "Rouse's New Strategy: Mixed Use and 'Remerchandising,'" *New York Times*, 13 May 1990; and Douglas Martin, "South Street Seaport: Just Another Mall?" *New York Times*, 17 October 1993.

61   Michael McAuliff, "Abandoning Ships: Has a Shopping Mall Submarined History at South Street Seaport?" *Downtown Express* 7, no. 15 (19 July–2 August 1993): 12–13.

62   Douglas Martin, "South Street Seaport: Just Another Mall?"

63   Ibid.

64   Patricia Leigh Brown, "Turning Back the Clock to Reinvent the Mall," *New York Times*, 15 March 1992.

65   Shepard Barbash, "A Retail War Waged North of Atlanta," *New York Times*, 25 November 1992.

66   "But Will They Burn Atlanta? Theme Park Will Rise on Ashes of the Old South," *New York Times*, 15 December 1992.

67   Peter Applebome, "Striving to Outshine Barcelona's Aura," *New York Times*, 11 August 1992.

68   Peter Applebome, "Some Say Recent Unrest Broke More than Glass," *New York Times*, 12 May 1992.

69   Ronald Smothers, "Barcelona Games Start, and Atlanta Is Starring," *New York Times*, 27 July 1992.

70   Peter Applebome, "Turf Wars Are Beginning over Atlanta Olympics," *New York Times*, 19 September 1992.

71   Josh Barbanel, "Some Signs of Hope Glint from New York's Clouds," *New York Times*, 30 July 1991.

72   Glaberson, "For Many in the New York Region, the City Is Ignored and Irrelevant."

73   Shepard, "The Real New York?"

74   Herbert Muschamp, "Manhattan Samples Suburbia," *New York Times*, 28 August 1993.

75   Michael Kimmelman, "Sculpture, Sculpture Everywhere," *New York Times*, 31 July 1992.

76   Muschamp, "Manhattan Samples Suburbia."

77   Ibid.

78   Sarah Bartlett, "Leaders Call New York City a Tongue-Tied, Off-Target Suitor of Business," *New York Times*, 8 March 1992.

79   Thomas J. Lueck, "Time for a Change in Builder Incentives?" *New York Times*, 8 December 1991.

80   Michael Peter Smith, *City, State and Market* (New York: Basil Blackwell, 1988), 58–59.

81   Bernard J. Frieden and Lynne B. Sagalyn, *Downtown, Inc.: How America Rebuilds Cities* (Cambridge: MIT Press, 1989), 314–115; quoted in Magali Sarfatti Larson, *Behind the Postmodern Facade: Architectural Change in Late Twentieth-Century America* (Berkeley: University of California Press, 1993), 83.

82   Sarfatti Larson, *Behind the Postmodern Facade*, 85.

83   Herbert Muschamp, "The Thrill of Outer Space for Earthbound Lives," *New York Times*, 20 September 1992.

84   Steve Oney, "Portman's Complaint," *Esquire* 107, no. 6 (June 1987): 182–189; the quotation is on page 184.

85   Thomas J. Lueck, "Financing for Times Square Leads to Harsher Criticism," *New York Times*, 28 July 1994.

86   Herbert Muschamp, "Time to Reset the Clock in Times Square," *New York Times*, 1 November 1992.

87   Ibid.

88   James Bennet, "Taking the Deuce," *New York Times*, 9 August 1992.

89   David Dunlop, "Times Square Plan Is on Hold, but Meter Is Still Running," *New York Times*, 9 August 1992.

90   Herbert Muschamp, "42nd Street Plan: Be Bold or Begone!" *New York Times*, 19 September 1993.

91   Robert Venturi, *Complexity and Contradiction in Architecture* (New York: The Museum of Modern Art, 1966; reprint New York: The Museum of Modern Art, 1977), 104.

92   Robert A. M. Stern Architects and M & Co., "42nd Street Now! A Plan for the Interim Development of 42nd Street" (report prepared for the 42nd Street Development Project, Inc., the New York State Urban Development

Corporation, and the New York City Economic Development Corporation, New York, 1993), 2.

93   Muschamp, "42nd Street Plan."

94   Gilles Deleuze, *Cinema! The Movement Image*, trans. Hugh Romlinson and Barbara Habberjam (Minneapolis: University of Minnesota, 1986), 109.

95   Bruce Lambert, "More 'Padlocking' to Close Drug Sites," *New York Times*, 10 October 1993.

96   Susan Chira, "New York's Poorest Neighborhoods Bear the Brunt of Social Programs," *New York Times*, 16 July 1989.

97   Marvin Minsky, "A Framework for Representing Knowledge," in *The Psychology of Computer Vision*, ed. P. H. Winston (New York: McGraw Hill, 1975), 211–277; quoted in Bartels, "The Box of Digital Images: The World as Computer Theater," *Diognenes* 41, no. 3 (1993): 50.

98   Bartels, "The Box of Digital Images," 45–70.

Electronic Disruptions and Black Holes of the City: The Issues of Gender and Urbanism in the Age of Electronic Communication

Cross: You may *think* you know what you're dealing with, but, believe me, you *don't*.
Gittes: That's what the D.A. used to tell me in Chinatown.

—*Chinatown*, screenplay written by Robert Towne

CRIMES IN AND OF THE CITY

At least one feminist critic of urban form, Rosalyn Deutsche, has criticized a few white male theorists of the postmodern urban condition for adopting the personae of *film noir* detectives. Pitting the force of rational detection against the irrational power of money (real estate investors, elite residents, and their allies in municipal governments or special municipal authorities), these neo-*noir* detectives attempt to uncover the violent results that criminal acts of wealth have brought about in terms of the production of urban space.[1] "Men in space," another label Deutsche gives these theorists of the postmodern city's spatial form,[2] are far from innocent investigators of treacherous urban terrain and of dangerous encounters with those in power, for they perpetrate their own set of crimes against women and hide their own masculine traces behind veiled comments and disguised positions. Specifically, these men fail to address the role that women traditionally hold in *film noir*—that of the *femme fatale*—and thus they link the dangers of the city with the dangers of sexual liaison. By hiding the presence of women—making them either disappear or appear invisible—these critics desexualize the terrain of the postmodern city. Such criminal acts against women subsequently enable these same detectives to become the rational masculine subject who gives form and shape to or who controls what they consider to be indeterminate, characterless, and neutral feminine matter.[3]

In *noir* detective stories, the *femme fatale* is characterized as a destabilizing force that "resists confinement—in—or as—space":[4]

she crosses boundaries and thus threatens male subjectivity. The subsequent work of *film noir*, Deutsche relates—and of the writings of these "men in space"—is to suppress her image and restore the male to the center of the picture. I read the ambiguous phrase "resists confinement—in—or as—space " to mean that the *femme fatale* resists categorization: she cannot be pinned down to a place or made accountable to public norms, and escapes the space of disciplinary order and the meticulous gaze of the detective. In short, she embodies the irrational and spreads disorder and disruption. She must not be allowed to appear in the same space as the rational detective, lest he be seduced by her powers and deterred from solving the crime; thus she must be suppressed or made invisible in the space in which he appears.[5]

In other words, the feminine is doubly encrypted: it has affected the manner in which space is conceptualized and theorized, yet it is simultaneously denied an appearance in that space. This feminization is implicit in the way metaphors and concepts carry the imprinting of sexual terms—for example, space "naturally" receives the so-called feminine characteristics of passivity, inertness, staticness, even speechlessness—but this connection of space and gender is never made explicit and thus escapes analysis. As Sue Best writes in "Deconstructing Space,"

> This is all done, as it were, under cover [like a true detective]. These theorists continue to do what man has always done: hog the subject position and thereby masquerade as the human. It is as if contemporary male writers are played by the binary system and the violent sexual hierarchies it installs, but even after two decades of feminist scholarship the writers in question still proceed as if sexuality has nothing to do with textuality.[6]

There is, however, a long history to this sexualization of space, going back at least to the time of Plato, when the transference of feminine attributes to spatial concepts appears to have been clearly established. Plato wrote that space can always be called the same because it never alters its characteristics. For it continues to receive all things, and never itself takes a permanent impress from any of the things that enter it, it is a kind of neutral plastic material on which changing impressions are stamped by things that enter it, making it appear different at different times. And the things which pass in and out of it are copies of the eternal realities, whose form they take....We must make a *three-fold* distinction and think of that which becomes [birth], that in which it becomes [womb], and the model which it resembles [father]. We may indeed use the metaphor of birth and compare the receptacle to the mother, the model to the father, and what they produce between them to their offspring.[7]

The metaphor of the female womb as the spatial receptacle waiting for male impregnation, as well as that of the masculine abstract model as the disembodied form-giver, were clearly delineated by Plato. Sue Best briefly outlines the history of this metaphoric transference found in male discourse, focusing on the writings of contemporary "men in space." Edward Soja exemplifies the detour men take through the matter of woman while simultaneously disavowing the feminization of space even while seeking to impose themselves in that domain. In his *Postmodern Geographies*, Soja claims that space has been reduced to passive and inert matter by the theorization of historians who, on the other hand, have elevated time and motion to the status of the active and dynamic. His desire is to activate feminized space by injecting masculine vigor into it. Thus geography would be reconceptualized and revitalized by "the modern and/or postmodern, urban, public man." But Soja or any man can only revalorize space by rupturing women's position in it.[8] As Deutsche and Best proclaim, postmodern space has become the object of a reformulated cartography which exercises renewed jurisdiction over the urban terrain and which is allied with the urban violence perpetrated in and against the city and women.[9]

In particular, Deutsche discusses the writing of Mike Davis. The image of the urban analyzer or theorist as neo-*noir* detective can be seen in Davis's analogy between Roman Polanski's movie *Chinatown* and the state of contemporary Los Angeles, found in his essay "*Chinatown*, Part Two?"[10] Davis bases this comparison on the fact that the real estate crisis of the downtown section of the city, which came to a head in the 1980s, originated in the same decade in which the film *Chinatown* was set—the 1930s. In the fictional movie, Los Angeles is a city under siege by a drought and falling prey to villains who manipulate the Municipal Water Works and thus add considerably to their real estate holdings purely for the sake of greed and desire. They do so by illegally rerouting water away from a valley of orange groves and subsequently accumulating all the ruined land in the valley at rock-bottom prices. In the real world of today, the city is threatened by the automobile and the spreading highway system which since the 1920s have drawn the well-to-do citizens away from the center of the city and into the suburbs. Real estate values in the downtown area spiralled downwards as a result until, as Raymond Chandler (the author of celebrated *noir* detective stories) wrote, it became a "lost town, shabby town, crook town" where "women with faces of stale beer…[and] men with pulled-down hats" reside.[11] After several decades passed, depressed real estate holdings in the downtown area eventually became ripe for redevelopment, and the owners of these properties, with the help of municipal authorities, began to subsidize their investments by redirecting substantial tax revenues away from deindustrialized zones such as black South Central and toward low-interest loans for downtown redevelopment, as well as reallocating these monies to infrastructure development and coordinating a series of tax abatements as incentives for developers. This process also took place in many other so-called "soft spots" surrounding the core of central Los Angeles. Thus in the film as well as in reality the city is threatened, as either the flow of water or the tax revenues are being criminally tampered with, to the financial advantage of real estate operators.

Davis's "*Chinatown*, Part Two?" can be analyzed not as a simple example of how women are rendered invisible by postmodern theorists of space, but as a layered reading of one text through another, facilitating a metaphorical transference of the *femme fatale* onto figurations of place. I assume that Mike Davis was aware— probably unconsciously—of this allegorical reading of the post- modern city as the *femme fatale*; nevertheless, his choice of a neo- *noir* film entitled *Chinatown* allows for a more complex re-reading of "men in space." So, while not disagreeing with Deutsche, I want to extend her argument in order to determine how the condition of the postmodern city affects how we represent the feminization of space. This allegorical re-reading of *film noir*, and specifically of neo-*noir Chinatown*, enables the issues raised initially in the 1940s to resurface under new conditions of postmodernity. As we shall see, the rational male gaze of the *noir* detective not only connotes the power to render the feminine invisible in space but also signi- fies the impotency of the passive observer who witnesses criminal deeds but cannot act to alter the outcome, and thus in the end encourages the dissolution of both the public and private spheres.

Why did Davis use *Chinatown* as his central metaphor, and what does it mean that the postmodern city is allegorized as a *femme fatale*? We have to assume that if the modern city was invisi- ble, then the postmodern city is doubly invisible or doubly encrypt- ed, as I discussed above. Walter Benjamin claimed that the "crowd" was never visible in the prose poems of Charles Baudelaire because it was not described according to the standards of social realism, being both a source of anxiety and a source of pleasure, both a utopian and dystopian place; similarly, the irrational in *Chinatown* cannot be represented, nor its ambiguities and anomalies resolved. Thus Jake, the detective in the film, reveals the loss of his powers of detection and the failures of representation. Chinatown is never really represented as a place, and appears only at the very end of the film; it remains an invisible site where everything and anything can happen. Also, if the modern city can be characterized as a space of panoptic surveillance subjected to the gaze of the white male voyeur, then the postmodern city reflects a fragmented look that not only evades representation but also witnesses the impotent

powers and innumerable failures of neo-*noir* detectives. In this
sense, *Chinatown* represents the city of too much knowledge, of
enigmatic judgments, of distasteful information. Displaced from
the city of patriarchal dominance, we hear the fatal warnings of
film noir: the breakdown of paternal authority, the increasing number of crimes against the daughter, the disappearance of spaces of
enclosure, and the decline of the public sphere. Finally, we also
have to deal with the inheritance of the allegory of modernity,
which is the violence perpetrated in and against the space of the
city and the *femme fatale*. But here, too, there is a twist of difference, as contemporary violence reflects the postmodern city's
increasing immateriality and its temporal and spatial eclipse, a
result of the pervasive representations of the privatized, virtual gaze
of television and the computer. Let us look at the subversive aspects
of *film noir* and the inheritance of a technology of violence. But
first we need to explore both the history of the detective story and
the allegories of nineteenth-century cities, which is where the pathways of the feminine and the detective first cross.

THE BIRTH OF THE DETECTIVE STORY

The development of the detective story, psychoanalysis, and archaeology were three different products of the nineteenth century,
each displaying the same desire to dig into the past, to uncover
what had been concealed, or to reconstruct what was lost from
sight in order to reveal truth in the light of reason and to inculcate
a sense of order. For nearly the entire century, cities in the West
suffered the repetitive disruptions of revolution, industrial capitalism, and urbanization. Cities were places of constant turmoil and
unrest, of alienation and crime, of the irrational and the unknowable, and they needed to be subjected to disciplinary control. The
detective story, in particular, explored these uncanny and unfathomable aspects of large cities where traces were easily covered and
evidence quickly eradicated, where people could simply vanish into

a crowd. London was the city where the detective story achieved its narrative form—for example, in Charles Dickens's *Bleak House*—as nineteenth-century London was a city enveloped in fog, smoke, and dust, a city growing without a plan, neither knowable nor decipherable. Everything and everyone converged on this metropolis of darkness and light; it was a place where every individual seemed lost in a crowd of strangers and disoriented by the maze of tangled streets.

Ernst Bloch noted that the birth of the detective story also depended on shifts in nineteenth-century legal procedures. Criminal investigations began to place an emphasis on the detective, because trial by evidence now demanded that sufficient information be gathered not only for an initial arrest warrant but also for the trial.[12] Urban detective stories represented wish-fulfillment fantasies of knowlege and control; they were narrative descents into the labyrinthian netherworld of marginalia hidden beneath a surface covering expected to both protect bourgeois morality and simulate rational order. The detective attempted to decipher clues, rearrange evidence, and restore order through the power of knowledge.[13] But these narrations were constructed on a fictional paradox that linked the awareness and mastery of the clues with the production of anxieties and fears, because the knowable might turn out to be the irrational, and because readers were often humiliated when they failed to spot the clues during the pleasurable reading of the story. Thus detective stories intertwined abstract knowledge (the rational powers of detection) with carnal knowledge (the erotic or sensual fears produced in the reader).[14]

Moreover, detective stories arose in tandem with a range of disciplinary practices—which Michel Foucault called "parasciences"—that were spreading their web throughout Western society in the late nineteenth century. In medicine, for example, diagnostic practice, based on examining a patient's symptoms or complaints, was giving way to the knowledge of the specialist, grounded in objective observation and detection of specific signs. Thus in Sir Arthur Conan Doyle's Sherlock Holmes stories, Dr. Watson's diagnostic point of view, his repetitive failure to observe the clues or solve the mystery, holds a subordinate role to Sherlock Holmes's exact or microscopic view of detection. In *The Sign of Four*, Watson said to Holmes, "You really are an automaton—a calculating machine!... There is something positively inhuman in you at times." Whereupon Holmes replied, "It is of the first importance...not to allow your judgment to be biased by personal qualities. A client is to me a mere unit—a factor in a problem. The emotional qualities are antagonistic to clear reasoning."[15]

Evidently it was Joseph Bell, Conan Doyle's anatomy professor, who provided the model for Sherlock Holmes. Dr. Bell had written that "radical peculiarities, hereditary tricks of manner, accent, occupation or the want of it, education, environment of all kinds, by their little trivial impressions gradually mould or carve the individual and leave finger marks or chisel scores which the expert can recognize."[16] Thus a myriad of details or signs, not symptoms, are collected and read by the detective, who exalts in the pleasure that comes—as Foucault would later describe—"of exercising a power that questions, monitors, watches, spies, searches out, palpates, brings to light...the power that lets itself be invaded by the pleasure it is pursuing; and opposite it, power asserting itself in the pleasure of showing off, scandalizing, or resisting."[17] And, of course, the reader masochistically identifies with Doctor Watson's bumbling attempts and his humiliating subordination to the detective, whose specialized knowledge allows brilliant and flamboyant leaps of rational judgment.[18]

Another development of the nineteenth century (specifically, in the period 1830–1848) that influenced the rise of the detective story was the birth of statistics. Statistics is a disciplinary science that emerged in order to count individuals, to locate them in space, to classify them into types, to judge their deviances from a generalized norm, and so to control indeterminacy and chance.[19] The development of this science of numbers was due not only to the modern welfare state's growing concern over the well-being of its people, but also to its interest in securing a stable social order in a century of revolutions and change. There are other relationships between statistics and the detective story as well: statistics was initially called "moral science," because it primarily studied immoral behavior and deviances from the norm, such as the rates of crime, suicide, prostitution, labor protest, and divorce. Moreover, it investigated calculated risks and causes that could not be reproduced but that could be analyzed only by examining their effects: for example, the probability of contagion (in the cholera epidemic of 1832); the probability of workers' sicknesses, strikes, or protests (Frederic Le Play's 1855 study of European workers); the probability of deviance from a normal distribution of human, social, and biological traits (Adolphe Quetelet's social statistics of 1833); the chances of criminal recidivism (Alphonse Bertillon's 1879 studies); or the chances of improving hereditary traits to produce more suitable races and ethnic strains and thus to ensure the "survival of the fittest" (Frances Galton's 1907 studies of eugenics).[20]

Finally, we must link the development of the detective story with imperialism and with the so-called white man's burden of bringing rational order to the primitive world. The colonies were unknowable places, beyond the realm of everyday life and normal experience. Thus in the nineteenth-century detective story, the Orient became a code word for the unknown, the different, the mystery, which the detective needed either to resolve or to repress.[21] Further-more, as Jon Thompson has written in *Fiction, Crime and Empire*, "Crime fiction's intrinsic interest in society—in the law and in the violation of the law—inevitably involves an exploration of the experience of modernity, of what it means to be caught up in this maelstrom of perpetual disintegration and renewal, of struggle and contradiction, of ambiguity and anguish."[22] Thompson argues that much of this tension came from the investment America and England made in imperialism. Hence he sees the detective story as an antidote to this uncertainty and risk, as a reduction of life to the conventions of form and to rules of a game that were—at least in terms of the narrative—unchangeable and knowable.

I want to return to the focus on the feminine, which—as mentioned above—has often been a metaphor for modernity. This motif has been subjected to devaluation and disfigurement, but nevertheless it embodies all the flux, uncertainty, exoticism, sensuousness, wealth of meaning, and otherness that both the modern metropolis and the nineteenth-century Orient unleashed. Christine Buci-Glucksman has written that "the feminine constitutes one of the nineteenth century's 'original historic forms'....The feminine becomes the inevitable sign of a new historic regime of seeing and 'not-seeing,' of [the] representable and [the] unrepresentable."[23] As allegory, the feminine depends on "images, sight, scenes that link the visible and the invisible, life and dream. History presents itself to be seen with all its ambivalence fixed in *tableaux*."[24] The feminine symbolizes all the phantasmagoria and artifice of modernity—in terms of images, styles, spectacles, and fictions—as well as the destructive tendency of false promises and unfulfilled desires, and the melancholic loss of equilibrium and the emptying of experience. It captures the double nature of things, being both the source of anxieties and the promise of pleasures.

Writing of his youth in Berlin, Benjamin described the maze or labyrinth of the city as the place he first understood love. In the twisting streets of large cities, women were offered the visible role of the prostitute. In the streets, the prostitute came to be the possessor of new secrets, for the labyrinth was also the symbol of desire: secrets of men led astray, or of men who did not want to know where they were going; secrets of the hidden doorways and places of the city; secrets of the passage down into the underworld.[25] And the female body in the city became the sign of commodity or of the mass-production of sex, for the prostitute was an interchangeable item up for sale. The conflation of the prostitute with the commodity is grounded in the phantasmagorical spell each has spun over innocent spectators and the empathy each has generated through the promise of pleasure and complete satisfaction.

And thus the prostitute exemplified the unreality of any love object, as well as the impotency of the male to curb or alter the loss of the maternal body, of a real love object, and of aura. She could only be re-idealized and re-presented as a false simulation, as a fiction of style and artifice.[26] Thus the feminine characterizes or delineates modernity: as sexual desire was never satisfied by the prostitute, so the commodity never fulfilled its promises, and women were always deceptive in their use of style and makeup. These primal scenes of modernity spreading alienation and melancholy inevitably shattered the integrity of the self.[27]

The prostitute was more than just a symbol of commodity; she was an actual threat as a carrier of disease. Alan Corbain has pointed out that in the common nineteenth-century view, the prostitute "does not just symbolize moral rot; she is literally a putrid woman, as demonstrated by the odor she emits. By frequenting her, one risks the living corruption of syphilis, just as the sailor risks scurvy or the prisoner risks 'prison fever'....A second image links the prostitute less to waste or ordure than to the sewer or drain that prevents a fatal congestion and assures the elimination of excess sperm." Thus the prostitute, associated with waste and the sewer, is also identified with the corpse and the danger of infection. And, of course, all of these images were related to the general image of the diseased city, a city in need of purification, a city lacking in circulation of air and light.[28]

The city center is also the place where the image of woman with all of its repressed forces circulates: this image can be found on billboards, in illustrated magazines, in advertisements, and in the streetwalker or prostitute who flees from bourgeois morality. In the chance encounters between the *flâneur* and the prostitute, traditional notions of causality were challenged, allowing "the forces of 'exterior necessity' [to] mark the human unconscious."[29] Walter Benjamin derived his methodology or theory of shock in part from the Surrealist André Breton's nocturnal strolls through the streets of Paris, his path crossing that of many a woman. These shocking encounters or chance meetings that brought together unexpected images, things, and people generated a violent release of unconscious forces, which, in addition to causing the primal scenes of modernity mentioned above, also threatened the integrity of the subject. They were the moments when libidinal energy manifested itself, overwhelming the body's defenses and marking the subject's consciousness.[30]

Thus images found in the streets of Paris, the place of chance encounters and fleeting impressions, enabled unconscious processes to be expressed and revolutionary energies to explode. Benjamin argued that it was, above all, "the street [that] leads the strolling person into a vanished time,"[31] and the *flâneur* who was the master of this visual sphere.

> The most characteristic construction problems of the nineteenth century: train stations, exhibition halls, warehouses (according to [Siegfried] Giedion), have various collective messages in their objects. The *flâneur* finds himself drawn in by these 'frowned upon, daily,' as Giedion describes them, constructions. The appearance of the great masses in history has already been designated in them.[32]

Benjamin transcribed the Surrealists' methodology onto the historian's gaze, examining past events until they provoked an awakening. He thought that a space structured completely by images would be inaccessible to contemplation, abstraction, endless discussion, or theoretical knowledge, but would instead be one of concrete knowledge endowed with the capacity to energize action in the present.[33]

THE SUBVERSIVE ASPECTS OF FILM NOIR

We can now return to the history of the detective story and begin to examine how *film noir* attempted to represent the promises of progress and the misgivings over change that modernity inevitably wrought. Edward Dimendberg has pointed out that the *noir* cycle (1939–1959) corresponds precisely to a time of profound spatial transformations in the postwar American city.[34] Massive upheavals were created by the automobile, highway construction, suburban development, and urban redevelopment; in turn, these produced fears that the old centers of cities, which had long been associated with the essence of modernity, were being erased. These metropolitan centers were ruins threatened with death and decay, as they had been compromised by the machinations of real estate operators, strafed by bombs or dynamite, and evacuated by its middle-class citizenry for the safety of the suburbs. During this era, the link between black-and-white film and realism was at its most fragile, due to the advent of television, Technicolor, and the double feature. Many Hollywood A-rated productions were experimenting with greater realism through Technicolor and through on-location filming.[35] Realism in film also connoted a highly conventional writing style and certain ideological values. Yet the potency of human agency was no longer so clear in the postwar American metropolis, where vast urban spaces seemed to take on a dominating and crushing power of their own, where alienation and boredom were increasingly apparent, and where stereotypical preconceptions of feminine passivity might be refuted when a not-so-innocent woman was the object of a fatal attraction or became the major instigator of crime. Both agency and realism were unstable categories.[36] One response to this confusion and disorientation was the production of B-rated films: their very marginality allowed them freedom to express the anxieties and trepidations of postwar culture. To hint at revolt, to offer a more exhilarating life than bourgeois morality allowed, to wallow in pessimism and misogyny, to depict the urban malaise, to tell the story from the criminal's point of view—these were some of the themes that B-rated films explored. Many of these films now constitute what is known as the *film noir* cycle.[37]

Film noir reached its peak in 1950, when fifty-seven films of this type were produced. This number fell to a low of seven in 1958 and 1959 combined. Dimendberg believes this decline had less to do either with a growing taste for realism or with the audience's boredom with the genre's conventions, as has commonly been assumed, than it did with the ascendancy of suburban residential areas, the spreading interstate highway system, and the expanding communication networks of radio and television—for this was also the era when non-urban and travel elements or themes began to manifest themselves in American fiction.[38] Since the detective story depends on a criminal and a private eye or detective, both observing the movements of a city's inhabitants, it demands a spatially concentrated city center in order to carry out its discourse on criminality and to impose its legal authority over the urban terrain. A decentralized, fragmenting, or empty city—what Gilles Deleuze referred to as "any-space-whatever"—requires different modes of surveillance and policing, and produces effects of alienation and estrangement. Deleuze, in particular, argued that after World War II a proliferation of these "any-space-whatevers" could be seen in film sets and in exteriors such as demolished or reconstructed towns and underutilized or fallow lands, be they docklands, warehouses, or garbage dumps. "Any-space-whatever…is a perfectly singular space, which has merely lost its homogeneity, that is, the principle of its metric relations or the connections of its own parts, so that the linkages can be made in an infinite number of ways."[39] As Dimendberg describes, the *film noir* cycle exploited a temporal ordering of space, relying on work cycles, promenades, encounters, and subway and railroad time schedules as narrative devices. In contrast, "any-space-whatever" is devoid of this temporal order: it is a collection of previously unconnected, heterogeneous places, and its existence is independent of the narrative linear order that arranges the passage from one part to another. It is exemplary of a postmodernist city, not a modernist one.

One of the major elements of *film noir* is the image of the city as vital, if problematic. Thus we find dense massing of skyscrapers, dark and shadowy canyon streets, the vertical outlines of skylines, the view of the metropolis from on high, and crowded and congested thoroughfares. This is a space of modernity, a knowable, mappable terrain with identifiable monuments, favorite haunts, and protected retreats, through which the pedestrian inevitably strolls.

Yet in reality, during the *film noir* period these very places were being threatened with extinction by urban renewal programs. Kevin Lynch, in his well-known study dating from the 1950s entitled *The Image of the City*, nostalgically described the metropolis as a place of well-defined nodes, pathways, edges, landmarks, and districts, for he, too, sought to restore the smashed and disintegrating face of the postwar city to a youthful portrait of itself.[40] In *film noir* these fears of urban disfiguration and death resurface, becoming the foreboding images of the nocturnal city, places of darkened shadows that disguise the clues and diminish the detective's powers of sight. Marc Vernet claimed that "the space of night is the space in which the detective, who has everything to gain from seeing without being seen, can be seen without seeing, as the darkness conceals the gleaming surface of an eye or a weapon."[41] Rather than the city being a nineteenth-century crowd into which a criminal could suddenly disappear without leaving a trace, it became a nocturnal site where traces of crime, class distinctions, noise, dirt, and ugliness were hidden, only to reassert themselves in an uncanny play of nightmarish threats.

The city is also a locus of alienation and depravity, a dangerous and transitory place of unexpected happenings and surprise endings, a land of used-car lots and fleabag hotels where the hero is entrapped by and even complicit with evil.[42] Many *noir* films open with an aerial shot of the dark streets of the city, as if to show that the city is a sinister force that will defeat the hero. Jules Dassein's film *Naked City* (1948) opens with a distant panoramic view of Manhattan, thus making the series of objective facts defining the crime appear as just one of the thousands of stories that the city could tell in an ordinary day. The seasoned detective tells the novice, "There's your city, Halloran. Take a good look. Jean Dexter is dead. The answer must be somewhere down there."[43] As one of its screenplay writers, Malvin Wald, commented, "In the *Naked City* it is Manhattan Island and its streets and landmarks that are starred. The social body is thus, through architectural symbol, laid bare as a neutral fact, neither, so to speak, good nor bad, but something which, like the human organism itself, may catch a disease—the criminal—and this disease may elude its detectors."[44] In addition, the film ambiguously incorporates scenes of the novice detective's idyllic suburban home, which should have offered a protective spatial isolation and moral shield against the harsh realities of the city but which instead seems to threaten him as a locus of overt sexuality, domesticity, and paternal obligation. He willingly escapes from these fears of home, lured back again and again to the city by the compelling drama it presents.[45] The pleasant suburban bungalows and sunshine streets found in Hollywood prewar films have turned into *film noir*'s preference for claustrophobic interiors and for the dark alleys and empty spaces of city streets.

Edward Dimendberg posits that darkness in the postwar city bore a relation to the traumatic memories of World War II. Disguised as entertainment, the *film noir* cycle could invert these trepidations—the loss of the downtown metropolis and the horror of the war—and return them to the spectator in an aestheticized, nostalgic, and even pleasurable way.[46] Thus *film noir* is a twisted variety of the detective story, as it represents a nocturnal city that lacks any visualizeable form, a city where the detective often loses his way and the murderous can get away with their crimes. Dimendberg utilizes Ernst Bloch's theory of "non-contemporaneity" or "non-synchronous not of this time"[47] to explore the gap between the rapidly disappearing city of postwar America and its reconstruction in *film noir*. Bloch defined non-contemporaneous elements as

> a continuing influence of older circumstances and forms of production, however much they may have been crossed through, as well as of older superstructures. The *objectively* non-contemporaneous element is that which is distant from and alien to the present; it thus embraces *declining remnants* and above all an *unrefurbished* past which is not yet "resolved" in capitalist terms....Home, soil, and nation are such *objectively* raised contradictions of the traditional to the capitalist Now, in which they have been increasingly destroyed and not replaced.[48]

Bloch's montage of old and new reveals a utopian goal similar to Walter Benjamin's: he juxtaposes elements not of this time with those of the now to illuminate the order of things, to illicit a wondrous sense of seeing anew, and to shock the viewer into arranging a vision of a better future.[49] *Film noir* experiments with "non-contemporaneity" in order to explain its multi-layered interpenetration and superimposition of spaces. It builds on the ruins and remains of the historical space of the center of the city: the *film noir* hero resides in a seedy hotel with torn window shades and exposed light bulbs hanging from the ceiling, while the *femme fatale* hangs out in a two-bit motel or a room rented by the week. But rather than shock the viewer into rearranging the empty spaces of the bourgeois city into a utopian order of things to come, *film noir* offers a retreat into a privatized space, placing its hero in a detached position from which he is not responsible for the crimes he produces in and of the city. It misreads, distorts, or refuses to understand its own warnings about how the moral formulations of postwar democracy and postwar paternalism were becoming a sham.[50]

By openly criticizing the assumptions of democratic individualism and freedom as well as of capitalism's pretensions of equity, *film noir* provided the spectator with a stance that helped "to expiate our collective guilt over [World War II]."[51] Through its presentation of the detective or private eye as a socially detached, uninvolved individual—one who is incapable of establishing relationships with other human beings—*film noir* denigrated the role of agency. No one was responsible for the crimes that happened in and against the city; no one could stop the *femme fatale*. Also, by exhibiting an aesthetics of violence—a detective or private eye who was insinuatingly pervasive, intimidatingly present, and who used forceful means if necessary to extract the truth from either the innocent or the criminal—*film noir*, or so Dean MacCannell claims, "exhibited a tenderness toward fascism in the pure heart of democracy."[52] And *film noir* does not deconstruct the order of paternalism, since the father is driven to retain his bourgeois respectability, the solidarity of his family, and the appearance of impeccable morality at any cost. This obscene father-figure is thus allowed to murder and to get away with all the money, restoring the hierarchies and subjections his role traditionally encompasses.

One way that agency can be denied is by shifting the guilt onto some "other" who resides outside a moral or human order. Myths of the big city are often based on the presence of monsters—alien or man-made—but we are neither connected to nor responsible for them because these monstrous others follow laws of their own. The story of Dr. Jekyll and Mr. Hyde reflects the desire to separate the polar opposites of good and evil by assigning these characteristics to separate and distinct bodies, one that represents specialized authority and paternalistic order, and the other degenerate and deformed chaos.[53] Another example is the terrorist, whose outrageous and brutal acts of incidental warfare have always represented the fear of the other.[54] Violent films such as *Robocop* (1987) deny agency by portraying technology as reigning supreme yet out of control, and depicting late capitalism as chaotic and corrupt. In *film noir*, it is the *femme fatale* who is outside of and thus threatens the social order, and who represents the horror of a loss of authority or control.

The shifts in the form of the narrative that were encapsulated by postwar American cinema reveal other tensions as well. In *Power and Paranoia*, Dana Polan writes that the traditional assumptions of Western unity or social order were placed under stress in the 1940s and 1950s.[55] He explains that this unity was based on a closed set of values, allowing a finite array of permutations and variations. Anything aberrant or different was either discarded or somehow incorporated into an existing set, in an attempt to achieve solidarity. Thus in terms of a film narrative, the allowed forms were a sense of an ending, a victory where good prevailed, or an adventure where promises were fulfilled and plenitude inevitably achieved. Opposition, or anything that threatened this unity, had to be assimilated, reabsorbed, or sublimated. Hence even the stereotypical threatening female was reworked, so that the family fit into this schema. As a loyal follower, the female now supported the active male agent and was even dominated by him. There were, however, contradictions and cracks in this narration of solidarity, for the family and the small-town values of plain living and resourcefulness were static tropes—useful for the war effort, but blocking the forward movement of every story line. As nostalgic forms that relied on the mythology of a harmonious community life, they no longer fit with the perception of history as an unfolding drama, or with wartime reality, in which women replaced men in the factories, flew planes, and single-handedly "manned" the home front.[56]

After the war, it was necessary to bring other forces to the aid of stability and order, and this affected the writing of detective fiction. Detective stories are fascinating because the consequences of a crime are known well before the circumstances that produced them. The entire narrative structure aims to establish a linear, chronological sequence of events that in the end will explain an initial enigma. Consequently, the detective narrative intrigues the reader by telling its story backwards, from the crime to its causes. Thus it has been argued that the genre works as a self-regulatory system, with variations and permutations of its major elements although its basic structure remains the same. During World War II, similar self-regulating devices were developed for the unrelated use of laboratory science war games.[57] At the Massachusetts Institute of Technology, Norbert Wiener, the father of cybernetics, developed his prototype of the electronic predictor, designed to characterize, track, fire at, and bring down enemy aircraft. As did detective stories, the inventors of such technological defense mechanisms conceived of the enemy as a cold-blooded, machine-like opponent, a cyborgian enemy "other" that was a self-regulating, calculating, goal-driven machine. Game theory, another wartime strategy, explored the decision-making procedures of two cunning opponents who were expected to act in a rational manner over the long run yet who were willing to bluff and trick in order to obtain a victory. After the war, Wiener applied the concepts he had developed for his electronic antiaircraft predictor to the new science of "cybernetics," a word he coined in 1947 from the Greek word for steersman.[58]

It is but a short step from the conception that the enemy "other" was a cybernetic unit with feedback loops and corrective mechanisms—a kind of black box whose inner workings were not yet understood—to the theory that all of human nature was a self-regulating machine and that order and stasis in the universe could be re-established by calculating the regularities underneath the surface of flux and change. Wiener wrote:

> Strange and even repugnant as the customs of many barbarians may seem to us, they generally have a very definite homeostatic value.... It is only in the large community, where the Lords of Things as They Are protect themselves from hunger by wealth, from public opinion by privacy and anonymity, from private criticism by the laws of libel and the possession of the means of communication, that ruthlessness can reach its most sublime levels. Of all of these anti-homeostatic factors in society, the control of the means of communication is the most effective and most important....One of the lessons of the present book is that any organism is held together in this action by the possession of means for the acquisition, use, retention, and transmission of information.[59]

And in the introduction to the same book, Wiener said:

> It has long been clear to me that the modern ultra-rapid computing machine was in principle an ideal central nervous system to an apparatus for autonomic control; and that its input and output need not be in the form of numbers or diagrams but might very well be, respectively, the readings of artificial sense organs, such as photoelectric cells or thermometers, and the performance of motors or solenoids. With the aid of strain gauges or similar agencies to read the performance of these motor organs and to report, to "feed back," to the central control system as an artificial kinesthetic sense, we are already in a position to construct artificial machines of almost any degree of elaborateness of performance. Long before Nagasaki and the public awareness of the atomic bomb, it had occurred to me that

we were here in the presence of another social potentiality of
unheard-of importance for good or evil.[60]

Of course, in the 1940s, anxieties were constantly raised less anything disturb the regularities and rules of these cybernetic computing devices and thus enable the irrational and evil forces to take
command. Polan claims that during the 1940s and 1950s many scientists worked within a dialectic of victory and defeat; they constantly made an effort to represent order by moving their endeavors
from an area of threatening disarray to a place where they could
achieve "surety and security."[61] The irrational had to be transformed into the merely strange, and the disjunctive horror that severed all links between cause and effect had to be overcome. The scientist became the conveyor of logic and the advocate of progress.
Consequently, narrative as a coherent resolver of contradiction had
to discover a new form if it was to entertain and to shock in a
world where science, especially cybernetics, had become the bearer
of logic and where the fantastic now appeared in everyday life, in
the space of both the home and the city as well as in the feminine.
Desire took on an independent force instead of being held in check
by the body's constraints. And the city, rather than being a support-
ive milieu or a site of geographic certainty, achieved an ambivalent
form, becoming a place where anything could happen, where
aggressive forces lurked just beneath its well-ordered surface.

Thus Polan argues that 1940s postwar cinema can be seen as a
meditation on these inversions of social order and communal solidarity: home becomes an unstable fantasy, rejected as a source of
support or undermined by external forces. *Film noir*, in particular,
often violates the moral order that the nuclear family erects: the
hero searching for the unobtainable securities of home wanders
endlessly on the road from place to place. California, Los Angeles
in particular, is the setting for many *noir* stories; this region is
stereotypically represented as a bucolic landscape of sunshine and
plenty, but in these films it is inverted into a landscape of betrayal
where there is no refuge, no home, no retreat. For example, in *High*

Sierra (1941), Humphrey Bogart plays an ex-con who travels across the country from east to west, stopping briefly at his family farm in Indiana, desperately crossing the Mojave Desert, relentlessly hunted by the police in a frantic car chase up rugged mountain roads, where he is confronted with a "Road Closed" sign. California has no family farm, no resting spot, to offer this fugitive. It has become a land of failed hopes and false dreams.[62]

Polan also claims that in the cinema of the 1940s the woman is often presented as "the enframed world of spectacle,"[63] freed from the bounds of narration and indeed able to conflict with narrative form. She disrupts masculine control and inhibits the endeavors of men.[64] In Howard Hawks's film *The Big Sleep* (1946), for example, the woman is defined as trouble: she lies, she is a drug addict or an alcoholic, she abjures traditional female roles, she talks tough, and she kills. However, she is also able to integrate the detective into society, for though he was once an isolated figure who walked the mean streets alone, modulating his sadism and violence, she turns him into an ambivalent character, both tender and tough.[65] But the feminine and the commodity cross paths, for both are on display as part of the spectacle in which the act of showing often becomes more important than the narrative or the moral. The *femme fatale* may have acquired new roles, but she is still frozen into an image, contained within the camera that men still controlled.[66] Interestingly, in *The Big Sleep* the crimes of the daughters include pornographic photographs, for which they are being blackmailed. The camera, which usually denotes the power of truth and objective evidence, is transformed into a tool of extortion and sexual fantasy. Thus here we find the relentless commodification of everything and everyone, and the corruption of an economic system that allows women to be reduced to merchandise that can be bought, sold, and traded. The image stands for the fantastic artificiality of American culture in which the art of selling and consumer desires have won out over pure ideals. Why else do the detective and the *femme fatale* meet to plot their crime among the cans and boxes of a grocery market in the film *Double Indemnity*? Could it be to emphasize the emptiness and phoniness of the post-industrial consumer landscape that has been corrupted by false desires and vapid dreams?[67] The use of film as spectacle attempts to fight the loss of narrative form and the sense of despair over America's betrayal by consumer culture, through lulling the hero into conformity and repressed sexuality and through destroying his powers of detection. But the spectacle is also a closed circuit of pleasure, a space devoid of human agency.

Finally, let us discuss the demise of agency as it is manifest in the evacuation of the imaginary public sphere in the postwar American city. In 1949, Joseph Hudnut discussed the fact that the center of the city was being emptied of its citizens in an article entitled "The Invisible City."[68] He believed there was a poetic conspiracy against the center city: poets were among the primary critics of its clamors and indecencies, while they never stopped promoting the solace of nature, believing it to be congenial to human happiness. There were, he argued, pleasures that could be achieved only in the city: for example, its neon lights, its theaters, its art, its crowds, the comedy of its streets and shop windows, and the spectacles of its sports and recreational areas. Hudnut went beyond the realm of pleasure, however, stating that human beings desire collective life, as they need to share with one another, and as they covet the direction individual lives gain from living together in this fashion. Ideas and behaviors channeled the individual to move behind a common shield of shared values and relationships, which alone could protect the community from the hostile powers attacking it. This is what Hudnut called "the invisible city," existing beneath the streets and squares of the visible city. Similarly, in *film noir* we witness a yearning for something that is missing—a centered city, a collective totality, a shared public life. Dean MacCannell labels *noir* sensibility a false, constructed nostalgia, since he believes that the centered and nocturnal city that *noir* tried to depict never existed, and that its evocation merely functioned as "the guilty horizon of bourgeois comfort and detachment."[69]

Deleuze referred to this loss of the public sphere as the disappearance of Michel Foucault's spaces of enclosure exemplified by

the family, the factory, and the schools[70]—and by extension the
centered city, the rule of law and order, and the disruptions of the
narrative by the deceptions and artifice of the *femme fatale*. As we
have seen, the detective traditionally functions in society as a restor-
er of social order. It is his job to uncover the evidence, to construct
criminal categories of the self, and he assumes there can be no
secret irreducible to a number or a characteristic with which to classify it. Yet Joan Copjec has shown[71] that in order for the *film noir*
fiction to be possible, the clues can never make up a closed set:
there always remains one more piece of evidence to be extracted
from the crime scene in order to generate suspense and to enable
the retelling of the crime as an adventure story. Thus the space that
contains the mystery can never be completely described; it remains
partially invisible and is always breachable by the detective. Detective stories share with the science of statistics this lack of complete
closure, the use of probabilities—whether of a crime, of a social
event, or of disease. And the relationship between statistics and
the detective story involves the public sphere and the notion of a
social collectivity. But what binds together a set of individuals to
constitute a nation, a city, or a collectivity? Copjec answers this
question by demonstrating how the concept of citizenship functions. Citizens—as Hudnut so aptly described—must imagine they
belong to a closed set, whether a city or a nation, that subscribes to
a set of collective values, shared memories, and common attributes.
Yet this can be achieved only by a ruler whose authority compels or
imposes closure. Without a ruler, the set of citizens remains open,
determined only by an internal limit: the relationships of difference
or comparison that establish linkages between all the elements
within the set. Thus it is the assumption that common relationships exist that limits the set.

If in an ideal public realm, sovereign power reigns, commanding obedience and ensuring civic order, then the postwar
American city contrasts with this ideal, being a time and place
where private interests, needs, and drives arose to erase any sense
of collectivity. Copjec uses as examples the ascendancy of such

anti-urban social policies as suburban expansion, public housing, the federally-financed highway systems destroying the landscape, and regulations mandating segregation. This loss of a collective unity is also present in the *film noir* cycle, as the detective fails to establish relationships and is portrayed as an isolated character existing in places emptied of all desire: lonely rooms, two-bit hotels, and bare office spaces. He increasingly identifies with the criminal until he eventually drives himself to commit criminal acts. *Film noir* warned that this held mortal consequences for society unless some notion of community could be reintroduced. For Copjec, the voice-over in *film noir* allows for closure, as it has the role of reintroducing community and language and of framing the endless personal drives that threaten to destroy the public realm.

CHINATOWN

Now that we have heard the warnings of *film noir*—the irreconcilable destruction of the center of the city; the failure of individual agency and accountability, which allows private drives to gain ascendancy over social needs or collective desires; the aesthetic of violence; the critique of postwar democracy and capitalism—that set it apart from mainstream cultural production, let us examine the position of the neo-*noir* film *Chinatown*, and that of the neo-*noir* detectives of social reality such as Mike Davis. *Chinatown* is an allegory of the crimes perpetrated against the daughter or the city and of the impotent powers of detection, for Jake, the detective, can neither stop the crime nor punish the criminal. *Chinatown* has many *film noir* attributes, but there is a twist, as the innocent are killed and the patriarchal crimes of incest, murder, and illegal real estate transactions remain unavenged. Similarly, contemporary real estate practices in central Los Angeles go unpunished, and the third-world immigrants, the black Americans, and the homeless are continuously exploited. In both the film and in real life, the detectives or theorists acknowledge that the motives behind the crimes remain irrational, beyond explanation. But by doing so they openly reveal their impotency in allowing the space of theoretical discourse and description to be severed from the space of action and utopian hope.

Furthermore, in *Chinatown* the desire for knowledge, which is what motivates the average detective, is transformed into greedy sexual curiosity.[72] Through focusing on lurid photographs, it presents a critique of the voyeuristic gaze constructed by the cinematic apparatus. Here the sleuth, whose work is to uncover the sexual liaisons of lovers, husbands, or wives suspected of being unfaithful, cannot read the clues that are underneath his own nose. Jake's nose is severely cut and remains bandaged in almost every scene, which underscores the unsavory aspects of his nosy work as well as his faulty powers of investigation. For the entire film, both the detective and the spectator lose their ability to investigate images and representations, as both mistakenly identify what the photographs expose: they are not evidence of a sexual encounter, but rather they are evidence of a quarrel that remains overlooked as an important clue. The spectator is placed in the position of not being able to decode or trust the visual images that appear.

John Belton explains in his discussion of *Chinatown* that language always plays an important role in detective stories. A detective's powers are normally revealed in the manner in which he demonstrates control over language, especially in his witty repartee. In the opening scenes of *Double Indemnity*, for example, the bantering dialogue and double entendres not only allow the spectator to understand that the amorous relationship between the *femme fatale* and the detective is one of crime and punishment, but they also establish the sexual antagonisms that will be carried out across the film.[73] Thus the detective, on the side of rationality, is consistently given the power of language, while the *femme fatale* resorts to lies, employing language in a deceitful manner. Both the logic of the detective's reasoning and the prowess of his verbal skills enable him to hold in check the disturbing threat of the irrational.[74] But in *Chinatown*, language fails both the detective and the *femme fatale*.

Jake never displays the verbal skills that usually demonstrate the hard-boiled detective's power over his suspects; indeed, he remains relatively silent throughout the film. In addition, the woman is rendered speechless under patriarchal control, unable to articulate in words the atrocities of her existence. Evelyn, the victim, stutters every time she tries to mention her father, and even her explanation of the crime must be physically, not verbally, wrung from her. Her statement, "She's my sister…my daughter," appears incomprehensible to the audience as well as to the detective. Once Jake finally recognizes the father's crimes of incest, murder, and real estate maneuvers, he finds that the normal powers of language evade him again; he is first struck speechless, and then when he tries to use words to help Evelyn he guarantees that she will be harmed.[75]

Belton has written, "In *Chinatown*, language…and knowledge no longer meet at the crossroads, functioning together to produce knowledge of the Real, but rather fall apart in the contemplation of it."[76] The binary opposition of rational powers of detection and irrational forces of criminality dissolves. Hence the rational thinker becomes aware that knowledge has limits; it cannot comprehend the unknowable or control the unnatural. So too, the powers of language that guide Mike Davis, the neo-*noir* investigator of contemporary Los Angeles, disintegrate as he contemplates the crimes perpetrated against the city, for he is struck speechless as he recognizes that powers of agency lie elsewhere. Everything that once made the center of Los Angeles a gritty city of harsh realities and stark existence, a testing ground for the hardest *noir* detectives, has been eradicated, gentrified, or redeveloped into a sterile and barren corporate zone. In the end, we arrive at the pessimistic conclusion that crimes against the city and women are beyond comprehension, since no one is held accountable and no action appears effective in stopping the insatiable drives that have destroyed the public terrain. Jake's final words in the film are "To do as little as possible," repeating the job advice he received when he was assigned to be a detective in Chinatown. After all, Chinatown is an allegory for a place such as the contemporary city, a place where reason has no force and where violence and the irrational reign, a place where we choose to squander our energy and wealth by doing as little as possible.[77]

THE TECHNOLOGY OF VIOLENCE

Finally, let us address the inheritance of the allegory of modernity, which is the technology of violence perpetrated in and against the space of the city and the *femme fatale*. The following discussions of war, transportation technologies, and inventions in telecommunications will subsequently enable us to explore how a century of modernity has prepared us for the transference of the physical space of the city into the immaterial realm of electronic databanks, simulation models, and telecommunication networks. It will also allow us to question some of the violent effects of the ruptured time and space presently found in the metropolis, and to understand why our memory of the city is being eclipsed, our visual perception transformed, and our actual experience diminished as we move from urban space to the space of the computer screen.

WAR

In *The City of Collective Memory*, I have argued that there is a difference between collective memory and history—that memory depends on lived experiences, stories recounted, and spatial devices that prompt recall.[78] But as direct experience declines, there is a need to write these stories down and to erect a narrative form that divides the past into stages and epochs progressing towards the future. In other words, a gap in time and space must occur before history rearranges and replaces memory. Paul Virilio argues in *The Vision Machine*[79] that such a gap between memory and the perception of lived experience occurred both during and after World War I. In part, this arose because of an increased use of telecommunication devices that obliterated spatial distance and delocalized language. But it also occurred because the setting for memories was obliterated from sight, for World War I was the first war to take place in the empty wastelands of the trenches.[80]

As Virilio accounts, the battlefields of World War I had been so thoroughly decimated by explosions and aerial bombardments that any orderly background scenery necessary for recall was eradicated completely. Hence a soldier's visual memory and perception of experience were severely altered. Optical devices further altered the topographical arrangement of things in space, and telecommunications erased distances and drastically reduced the time in which messages could be relayed. And a growing dependency on focal devices such as a handgun's line of sight or a machine gun's target range, as well as aerial intelligence photographs, meant that a soldier's reliance on direct visual perception declined, for he could no longer trust his own eyes to see without prosthetic lenses.[81] Thus the telescope, the telegraph, the telephone, and ultimately the tele-photo lens and television were communication technologies that allowed the number of messages and images to increase, but they simultaneously undermined the storage of images in the brain by obliterating distances and by delocalizing signs of both language and sight. In the aftermath of World War I, these communication devices brought about a dramatic collapse in "mnemonic consolidation" and a rise of "topographical amnesia"—both still affecting perception and experience in our contemporary cities.[82]

Max Picard wrote about a similar loss after World War II, which was caused by the erasure of any stable relationship with space and time, noting:

> Through automobiles, trains, airplanes, one tries to bring all things together mechanically. One shortens space so that in space, at least, things might get closer together, so that in space everything should be gathered, if not according to its nature, then outwardly, mechanically, to a minimum. For the person who has lost inner memory and continuity, the mechanical continuity of things in the outer world

substitutes for this inner continuity. In the outer world, then, everything is forced together; all-embracing technology holds everything
together; it replaces the memory of man. Thus the individual does
not even notice that inner continuity is missing in him because
the mechanical continuity of the external functions as a matter
of course.

All things are connected in space through autos, railroads, airplanes;
the speed of outer motion has eliminated time; only space still exists.
With time no longer existing, one no longer things of permanence,
let alone an inner permanence, and inner continuity; they are not
even missed. And, yet, by the slow growth of a living thing in
nature, man is reminded of the fact that not only space but time
as well must have its part in the order of things.[83]

War in the age of electronic reproduction adds yet another spiral to
the collapse of "mnemonic consolidation" and the erasure of memory containers. In the Gulf War, for example, video- and computer-
generated imagery determined our visual experience of and attitudes towards that war, as the most potent image was simulated
from the viewpoint of a "smart bomb" as it appeared over and over
again on our television screens. Or perhaps—once it has been made
available commercially—our experience of that war will be derived
instead from the army's computer-simulated war game, "Desert
Storm," which recreates a tank battle from actual footage, enabling
the real battle to act as a feedback corrector for the simulated
imagery.[84] It has been argued that televisual imagery represses
memory, since it is not like a photograph, which can be analyzed in
depth, ripped out of the newspaper for closer scrutiny, or returned
to for re-examination. Lynne Kirby argues that "memory has an
uncertain status on television, in part because of TV's addiction to
instability and ephemera, in part because of the sound-bite conventions of news reporting and the relative absence of any archival
function on television. We hardly ever return to the past outside
television, only to unending reruns."[85] But more importantly, in

terms of the status of contemporary memory devices, those Gulf War transmissions erected an imaginary boundary line separating the impassive and immobilized spectator from the perpetrators of violent acts and the fears that these acts engender.

In post-nuclear warfare, deterrence has become the rule; deterrence means the absence or, rather, the displacement and disappearance of war, the warrior, and the battlefield. William Chaloupka says, in *Knowing Nukes,*

> Movement wipes out terrain, only to be displaced, in turn, by deterrence. The warrior has begun to be displaced (even before the advent of nuclear weapons) by techniques of barracks and training field discipline. That displacement compounds with development of the tank, then compounds again with the development of aircraft, then again with missiles. When the missile obtains a nuclear warhead, all this motion stops, in a sense. What is left, the residue, is the nothingness beckoned by nuclear war. And that goal, in turn, is quickly displaced (in a shock of horrified recognition) by the mere threat of nothingness. Teleology ends in deterrence, in the commitment to disallow the movement of events to their designed ends.[86]

Thus deterrence is yet another form of topographical amnesia, a defense against remembering and recollection. It involves the problem of how to represent nothingness, how to draw a circle around a point designated zero from which rings of disaster unfold. Zero is an ambiguous sign, for it signifies nothingness yet is the symbol for a circle drawn around an emptiness; it is the origin from which an expanding absence grows.[87] And so we might say that the city is our postmodern ground zero, impossible to represent in images no matter how often the aftermath of violence appears on televised news. As we watch the still images of the city disappear, perhaps we should recall that one of General Electric's first experiments with televised drama production was a 1928 broadcast that "simulated a guided missile attack on New York City, from the missile's point of view, a slow aerial approach ending in an explosion."[88] As do all such devices, "television plays with its own kind of doom: it does not begin with images of destruction, but with the destruction of images—a reminder that the blank screen will always be ground zero."[89]

On the other hand, we can argue that photographic coverage of World War I, with its supposed objectiveness and its documentary accuracy, produced yet another crisis of representation.[90] Tens of thousands of aerial photographs were taken during the war, enabling photography to become a significant component of military strategy and an active instrument in the construction of wartime memories. These aerial photographs provided a new relief map of the battlefield, an abstract reduction of details and facts, that appeared to have its own rational order and structure.[91]

> The war killed the natural landscape and replaced it with highly
> artificial and, within its own parameters, functional spatial arrange-
> ments. Aerial photography then, creating a metalevel artificiality,
> further abstracted from the "reality" of this artificial landscape. It
> not only eliminated smells, noises, and all other stimuli directed
> at the senses, but also projected an order onto an amorphous space
> by reducing the abundance of detail to restricted patterns of a sur-
> face texture.[92]

In order to be useful for military purposes, aerial photographs had to be deciphered and recoded in military terms. They required long-term monitoring procedures for trends to become visible; they necessitated the careful gauging of the speed of transport vehicles, projectiles, or troop movements; they forced a new spatial understanding of large-scale terrains; and they replaced the traditional focus on the warrior with technical constructions and logistics.

> Aerial photographs are symptoms of and at the same time forces
> in the process of changing the mode of perception by fusing pure
> aesthetic effects and highly functional military information. Their
> space is emptied of experience and moral content.[93]

One might also discuss the figure of woman in relation to war. The theater of war has been universally regarded in the Western world as a male preening and testing ground from which women are kept at a distance, and nearly all of the thirteen million killed and many millions crippled by World War I were men, while women were relegated to the safe if stereotypical roles of nurse, caretaker, camp follower, or entertainer. However, the first buzz-bombs dropped on civilian populations in England at the end of that war brought an image of woman as victim, which challenged her role as an unblemished symbol upholding the homeland and personifying the state for which the armies were fighting. The stasis of trench warfare as well as advances in the technologies of war, brought an end to the conventional battlefield. "This meant that war now worked to forestall representation of its aggression as spectacle. (For example, World War I photographs of the front almost invariably show either soldiers waiting in the trenches, or panoramas of a desolate no-man's-land: scenes from before or after the combat.) As only the victims or the actors in the behind-the lines war effort could be represented in action, images of war increasingly came to show women."[94] Thus the woman as victim or as a cipher of war's horrors became a key representational image of twentieth-century warfare.

TRANSPORTATION TECHNOLOGIES

It was Ernst Jünger, the author of several books written during the 1920s about his experiences in World War I, who understood that war was the "central experience of modernity" and that new technologies of warfare had changed perception.[95] In 1926 he extended this "allegory of modernity," making a connection between modernism, urbanism, and modern technology. He wrote:

> The Great War itself is a good example of the way in which the
> essence of the city has begun to take possession of the whole range

of modern life. The generation of the trenches went forth expecting a joyous war in the old style.…But just as the landscape of this battlefield proved to be no natural landscape but a technological landscape, so was the spirit that animated it, an urban spirit."[96]

And again, he observed:

We must penetrate and enter into the power of the metropolis, into the real forces of our time: the machine, the masses, and the worker. For here lies the potential energy from which will arise the nation of tomorrow: and every European people is now at work trying to harness this potential. We will try to put aside the objections of a misguided romanticism which views the machine as in conflict with culture.[97]

The metropolis enthralled Jünger not only because it contained and condensed the electrifying energy and power of new machinery— radios, trains, highways, automobiles, planes—but also because it thrust an element of danger into the boring sameness of daily life, and offered visual stimulation in the collisions and explosions that machines inevitably made when they raced out of control. For Jünger, the big city offered a new aesthetic relationship to the experience of shock and danger.[98] This new mode of perception born of the war and of fear relied on alertness, sharp perception, and vivid recall, which bestowed unusual importance on trivial things and sensory details. Aided by photographic evidence, it was also a cold, precise, and indifferent perception.[99] It effected a memory system built not on conventional spatial and temporal coordinates, but on the forward trajectories of speed and motion and on the conservatism inspired by images of poisonous wastelands, of death and annihilation. The normal sequences of past-present-future experiences were shattered in the catastrophic presence of the here and now and the dramatic simultaneity of events and times.[100]

The Futurists, Virilio claims, had foreseen this collapse of space and time that images from World War I engendered, for they "saw every vehicle or technical vector as an idea, as a vision of the universe, more than its image....[Theirs was] a new fusion-confusion of perception and object which already foreshadows video and computer operations of analogous simulations."[101] Similarly, in *Visual Thinking* Rudolph Arnheim proclaimed, "All...mobility, transportation, transmission, and communication...remove things from their natural location and interfere with their identification and efficiency."[102] When considered as a group, these discussions about topographical amnesia, about unpredictable collisions, ruptures, elisions, or deformations of visual material, enable us to understand why Dean MacCannell argues that the emblematic icon for postmodernity should be the automobile, not architecture, as has been commonly assumed. It is the automobile that not only contributes to the fragmentary nature of contemporary experience, but also expedites a failure of memory and hastens the eclipse of time by speed—losses that are characteristic of both modernity and of postmodernity. The car stands for speed, forward motion, travelling, networking, moving on...and for jam-ups, breakdowns, and accidents.[103] As war does, it collapses space and blurs time's delineation of past, present, and future.

Not surprisingly, the motorcar was also a potent symbol for the Futurist movement. It captured the manner in which modern technology changed one's perception of the world, and it emphasized creation through radical destruction. It was the perfect symbol for simultaneity, for the appearance of all objects in motion, for forward movement and constant change. It became the emblem of the Futurists in their dedicated attempt to destroy the bourgeois order. More importantly, perhaps, the automobile was an integral part of the cityscape, violently influencing the form the city would henceforth take. Speeding through the narrow streets of the modern metropolis, the car induced in the rider an intensified experience of power, exhilaration, and freedom.[104] Futurist Gino Severini claimed, "Speed has transformed our sensibility...has led to the majority of our Futurist truths...[and has] given us a new conception of space and time itself."[105] And yet another Futurist, Ardengo

Soffici, exclaimed, "External velocity, by intensifying our mental action, has modified our perception of space and time. As a result, we have the contiguousness and contemporaneity of things and events, or the simultaneity of sight and emotions."[106]

Due to its link with Fascism and its aestheticization of violence, Futurism as an art movement was largely ignored until the 1950s and 1960s when the automobile again became an everyday image of modern life and a symbol of postwar consumer society in Europe. In post-World War II America, however, the automobile was a vehicle bringing death and destruction to the core of American cities and culture. Andy Warhol's *Car Crash* art series is exemplary of the threat that technological progress posed, of the anesthetizing effect that mass production created, and of the savage assault that both mass production and alienation leveled on mind and culture. Warhol reported, "When you see a gruesome picture over and over it really doesn't have any effect."[107] And in America there were the inescapably dreadful and oppressively homogeneous suburban developments along the spreading highway systems. Ed Ruscha's photo-essays such as *26 Gas Stations* and *34 Parking Lots* capture the growing standardization that mass culture produced.[108] The freedom of mobility and the exhilaration of speed that the automobile once promised the Futurists had turned into an illusion. Instead, the open road led to the scrap heap, junkyard, used-car lot, parking lot, drive-in bank, shopping center, or gas station. The automobile and its detritus thus became recognized as powerful and destructive forces. Lewis Mumford noted in *The Highway and the City*, "In using the car to flee the metropolis...the motorist finds that he had merely transferred congestion to the highway, and had even doubled it. When he reaches his destination, he finds the countryside he has sought has disappeared: beyond him, thanks to the motorcar, lies only another suburb, just as dull as his own."[109] In spite of the Futurists' proclamations, most of the effects of highway culture have remained invisible because they have been taken for granted: no one foresaw the devastating impact that automobiles would have on cities or communities. Nor have we acknowledged the fact that the view from a car's windows is our prime experience of urban space at a time when few dare to walk the city's mean streets or explore its unmapped terrains.

Because of the dangers of downtown, eyewitness accounts of city events have declined, and vision itself is increasingly mechanized.[110] No small wonder, then, that the image of the city has dematerialized right before our eyes. With surveillance video cameras scanning and interpreting more and more parking lots, hallways, entrances, banks, supermarkets, malls, theaters, and ballparks, our everyday environments are generally usurped by technological devices that see in our place. Television in public space—so Virilio claims—is

> tirelessly on the lookout for the unexpected, the impromptu, whatever might suddenly crop up, anywhere, any day....This is the industrialization of prevention, or prediction: a sort of panic anticipation that commits the future and prolongs "the industrialization of simulation," a simulation which more often than not involves the probable breakdown of and damage to the systems in question....
> This doubling up of monitoring and surveillance clearly indicates the trend in public representation. It is a mutation that not only affects civilian life and crime, but also the military and strategic areas of defense.[111]

The overexposed city now becomes the city of concealment, revealing more and more of its crime and violence through surveillance devices but less and less of anything else. It is a city of deterrence machines that are looking, assessing, weighing every event, in order to deploy police forces and vigilantes to avert a crime, drug sale, sexual assault, burglary, illegal entry, or accident. Consequently, we find the contemporary city to be absent of community, and urban space becomes a metaphor for a disembodied, computerized cyberspace.

Surveillance machines produce data—such as the aerial photographs taken in World War I—that must be analyzed for strategical use. Some of this data creates virtual bodies in space: every time one shops with a credit card, goes to the doctor, or checks out a video or a book from a library, a virtual personal profile is created. But there is also a virtual urban space that is created through every televised looting and burning, killing and mugging, or arrest and inquest—every time a crime story is instantaneously transmitted to multiple television monitors around the world. This virtual urban space is being captured in isolated segments, narrated by narrowly defined codes, and replicated in numerous ways. Richard Dienst writes in *Still Life in Real Time* that the television "mix" structures the act of seeing in unique ways, making every change of image an occasion for potential displacement. The mix may or may not cut or connect, rupture or blend, open or close.[112] Furthermore, in the automatic time of television there occurs an outpouring of data that remains to be structured into some form of knowledge:

> Automatic time appears when an image is switched on and left running, so that it is no longer an image *of something*: it is the time of the camera's relentless stare, persisting beyond the movements of objects and scenery that pass before it. If still time slices off images and designates them as past, then automatic time opens onto an anticipated future: it is an image waiting for its event to happen.[113]

> Automatic time, the unending effusion of visuality that might have seemed closer to the steady gaze of the eye, eventually leads away from the fits and starts of perception toward an implacable and unplaceable collection of spatialized data.[114]

Life in the inferno of the postmodern city has given rise to a whole series of face-to-face equivalents or substitutions that further defines this virtual space. One newspaper has defined the "virtual downtown" as a free-floating on-line hangout in cyberspace or the Internet "with a sensibility that is lower Manhattan."[115] And students of contemporary urbanism have alerted me to the outpouring of simulated crime stories appearing on late-night television, in addition to the constant real-time coverage of the gruesome world of murder and mayhem, horrific crimes and needy victims. We all know the universalized scene of the crime: "This guy pulled a knife. Two guys jumped him." Only two cops saw "the murder as it went down" but patrol cars quickly roll up to the scene with their lights flashing. These police begin to push back the crowds and to seal off the area with yellow tape. Television crews arrive and begin to broadcast shots of twenty or more officers shooting the breeze, controlling the crowd, and waiting for the paramedics to stash the body away and for the "homicide to show up."[116] This sort of police work is simulated again and again in television crime coverage.

Melodramatic television shows such as "Cops," which follows policemen on their rounds, or "Rescue 911," which recreates events based on actual calls for help, heighten the sense of being there, and give the viewer a feeling of vicarious involvement as an "eyewitness" to the crime. These crime stories on the television screen construct the image of the city and the telling of news much the way the panoramas of the early nineteenth century did: they replicate the way things looked or happened so that the viewer can receive enjoyment from the recognition that the spectacle is a reconstruction. Perhaps there is boredom in the nightly television retelling of crimes of the city, but the viewer still wants to be thrilled by danger, even in a simulated form. The vicarious thrill of following one night in the life of cops on their beat—as "Cops" does—is carefully simulated and packaged, for the camera does not capture the moment of the crime, the emergency telephone call, or the arrival of the police. Instead, the taped and edited version of events substitutes for real city spaces and real city events. Each crime city is represented iconographically by a view of its skyscrapers, or by the identifying badges of its police force, but the city itself is seen only from the windows of a moving squad car, and usually at night. The result is a blurred and unstable image on the periphery of vision, reducing the city to a backdrop for a dramatized crime.[117] Thus television participates in the disappearance of the city by stereotyping criminals, by presenting images of nothing but dystopian cities or streets of crime, and by substituting coverage for real-time eyewitness accounts.

How, we might ask, does this affect our perception and memory of the city? Michel Foucault noted,

> Since memory is actually a very important factor in struggle...
> if one controls people's memory, one controls their dynamism.
> And one also controls their experience, their knowledge of previous struggles...[118]

The maps of the city that crime stories construct have a way of eradicating our vision of space, from which our memory of the city is formed. They displace our sense of agency, and heighten our belief that we are adrift in time and space. They are a part of the system of contemporary telecommunications, which transport us to the brave new world of cyberspace.

INVENTIONS IN TELECOMMUNICATIONS: COMPUTERS

Cyberspace's originator, William Gibson, seems to confirm the vulnerability of popular memory in his statement that "computers in my books are simply a metaphor for human memory: I'm interested in the hows and whys of memory, the ways it defines who and what we are, in how easily memory is subject to revision."[119] Yet Kathleen Biddick informs us that Gibson is never interested in a memory focused on remembering and therefore on an engaged perception or aesthetics of observation, for when his characters are in need of a historical fact they have only to access their cyberdecks.

Jacked into their simulated stimulation machines ("simstim"), they can share memories and thoughts with other simstim characters, or listen to an inhuman voice pipe figures and facts from programs or tables.[120]

> History exists in Gibson's cyberspace as facts, dates, information in dead storage....Indeed, archives once under the historical purview of the state can exist as "primitive ice" in cyberspace. Humanist history deterritorializes memory as remembering and reterritorializes it as archive. It has served as the institutional discipline of memory, marking and remarking who is remembered, what is remembered, and in what way. In deterritorializing memory, history then produces humanist memory as an object, as imprinted image locatable in its fixity, recoverable in its plenitude at the same time such history produces the space of terror as its space-off.[121]

If Britain once dreamed of an imperial archive that would enable it to control its vast and heterogeneous colonial empire by maintaining a monopoly over its stores of knowledge, then Biddick warns that cyberspace's mimicry of these tactics replicates all the repressions, oppressions, and violence that colonization engenders. She borrows from the work of Michael Taussig, who theorizes that terror is the mediator *par excellence* of colonial hegemony and its space of death—"that steaming morass of chaos, that lies on the underside of order and without which order could not exist."[122] Biddick finds that cyberspace mediates terror through narration—that we experience fear of the underworld populated by artificial intelligence machines and know torture and evil administered by misfits and deviants through words. These narrations relegate women, blacks, primitives, and misfits to the colonies where violence and death prevail.

Biddick wants us to return to the early years of computers —the postcolonial years of the 1950s—because she believes it was during this period that the computer's model of memory "encrypted and sealed over imperial histories of its design and thus foreclosed the anxiously intimate process of re-memoration and mourning needed to tell emergent histories of its fabrication."[123] The structure of both the human memory and the computer memory was thought to resemble an indexed encyclopedia, or an imperial archive under the control of the state. And so we return to the detective story's origin in the dream of an imperial archive that could keep track of, classify, order, and control all the people and places of the world.[124] Biddick reminds us that the architecture of a computer's memory was assembled, in part, out of this imaginary imperial archive that divided the globe into people who were civilized or uncivilized, who were with or without history, who had long-term or short-term memory, and who used writing or only speech.

These divisions still haunt today's computers and telecommunications. To give one example, the computer memory is a matrix for the storage of dry, abstract data and documents. Yet, as in the classical art of memory, it is recognition alone that accesses meaning, defining some pattern of thought to structure this mass of data into a systematic and usable order.[125] In other words, there exists a wide separation between documents or data and structured modes of thought, between distilled history and experienced memory. In his 1929 essay on Surrealism, Walter Benjamin tried to examine some aspects of this gap when he claimed, "The writings of this circle are not literature, but something else—demonstrations, watchwords, documents, bluffs, forgeries if you will, but at any rate not literature....The writings are concerned literally with experiences, not with theories and still less with phantasms."[126] Drawing on the Surrealists' interest in the effect a work of art might have on the viewer, in *One Way Street* Walter Benjamin made a distinction between the work of art and the document. As he described it, the work of art has a legitimate pretension to an aesthetic appreciation; a document—or a file, such as those produced by computers—can make no such claim. A work of art communicates through formal means. A document, on the other hand, communicates through its analysis of a particular subject matter. The work of art relies on a contemplative, prolonged look, while the document can be grasped instantaneously. Finally, the work of art reveals a virile, energetic force—it virtually attacks the viewer—while the document displays an innocent, irresponsible, and passive stance, most often attributed to the feminine.[127] So we find the disappearing city is documented by the hour, monitored and surveyed continuously, and its statistics and data are stored in computer files as dead storage to be manipulated by historians or controllers of popular memory. As does Benjamin's feminized document, this virtual city calls out for action and analysis but finds that its surveyors and historians most often lack the agency, responsibility, or will to intervene in the course of events. A computer operates on symbols or documents stored in its database; it can call them into memory, combine them, compare them, reorganize them, or store them over time, but the "necessary and sufficient conditions for a system to be capable of thinking" are absent.[128]

Another founding principle of computers is Foucault's warning that the purpose of surveillance is the production of suspicious behavior; as the prison produces criminality, for example, we might say our contemporary communications technology produces docile bodies whose powers of agency fail. Indeed, the computer has often been used as a metaphor of the self, even through the interior landscape of the computer is disembodied. In current interfaces with the machine, the kinesthetic body is hardly involved, as one merely touches the keyboard or moves the mouse. The computer/self distinction bears similarities to the Cartesian mind/body duality, such that thought, subjectivity, and culture are associated with the mind or the computer, and emotion, objecthood, and nature with the body or the physical self. The latter pair is thus defined as an "other" with parts that can be replaced or altered, while the former pair can be perfected by being reprogrammed or recoded.[129]

In addition, e-mail, voicemail, and telephone messages seem to be replacing person-to-person interaction. The body is becoming obsolete, a nuisance, its pains or hungers terminating interactive sessions between the computer and the mind. Since the body often malfunctions, quickly fatigues, and requires adequate supplies of food, water, and air to make it operational, to improve its performance over extended periods of time, and to enhance its longevity, it has to be redesigned.[130] Technology that once contained the body—the car, for example—now becomes a prosthetic component added onto the body, for example, as a monitor of brainwaves (EEG), muscles (EMG), heartbeat (ECG), pulse (pethysmogram), or blood flow (dopplerflow meter). Other micro-miniaturized components, such as laser lenses to probe space, exoskeletons to power the body, or robots to combat bacterial invasions, may one day be implanted in the body.[131] Through all of these devices, technology becomes a great pacifier of the body; it mediates between the body and experience, even disconnecting the former from many of its normal functions:

> DISTRAUGHT AND DISCONNECTED, THE BODY CAN ONLY RESORT TO
> INTERFACE AND SYMBIOSIS. The body may not yet surrender its
> autonomy but certainly its mobility. The body plugged into a
> machine network needs to be pacified. In fact, to function in the
> future and to truly achieve a hybrid symbiosis the body will need to
> be increasingly anesthetized.[132]

To return to the computer's effect on the city, we have to acknowledge that the structure of the public sphere is undergoing profound changes, not only as telecommunications increase personal choices over a variety of public communication systems, but also as these same technologies are consumed increasingly in privatized and domesticated forms. The Internet is perhaps the best example of the reach of the new communications web: accessed by more than two million computers, it is worldwide and open twenty-four hours a day, and it represents both a vast new marketplace for the future and a new public sphere for debate and argumentation. As one enthusiastic user relates,

> Internet is a sort of international cocktail party where you can
> talk to people from all over the world about all sorts of things that

interest you....It's informative. You need a piece of information? Post a question to the right group and you will get what you wanted and a dozen more related references. Also, sometimes information ...just comes to you.[133]

Essentially free to approximately twenty-five million people in 135 countries who have access to one of the 32,400 connected computer networks sponsored by governments and universities, it is not a service open to everyone.[134] Created in the 1970s by the United States Defense Department to facilitate the exchange of information among its workers, the Internet was also connected to research stations at universities, where students and researchers transformed it into the freewheeling global communications system of today.[135] Nevertheless, as we grow reliant on communicating through machines and on transporting objects by transmitting the necessary information across telecommunication devices, we find—to quote Mark C. Taylor and Esa Saarinen—that "the modern metropolis is being displaced by the postmodern netropolis" and "the space of the netropolis is cyberspace."[136]

In addition, this new public space for open dialog and debate is threatened with acts of regulation. The United States government is currently in the process of shifting the cost of operating and maintaining the Internet to the private sector, in a gesture that may create an extremely inequitable as well as a tightly regulated system.[137] Online services are already delimiting the range of topics available, and closing down certain "chat rooms" because of their indecent content. At the same time that cities and regions of this country are being divided into homes that have access to the "information highway" and those that do not, some districts of the city are being prepared to receive advanced communication services such as video, voice, and computer communications while others are experiencing what has been called "electronic redlining."[138] Thus the city, the region, and even the world can be grouped into information-rich or information-poor societies in the same manner as there were once societies with history and those without.

We are also witnessing the growth of a global system of mediated communications—an increasingly privatized and commercialized information society. Projecting on present trends, futurists foresee that by the turn of the twenty-first century, "five to ten corporate giants will control most of the world's important newspapers, magazines, books, broadcast stations, movies, recordings, and videocassettes."[139] This gloomy account also includes telecommunication infrastructures and data networks. The privatization of public television, school systems, research institutes, and communication networks means that market profitability becomes the sole criterion for the production of culture. Public access to these channels of telecommunication is far from guaranteed, and their content and subject matter are most often mediated or constructed by the program formats of serial soap operas, news broadcasts, or advertising messages.[140] Telecommunications are being orchestrated by interest-specific market niches at the expense of more generalized commentary, and their former collective nature is being further eroded by commercialization and corporate control.

In consequence, the city and its public sphere become increasingly virtual as we move toward interpersonal systems of communication and the "netropolis" at the expense of face-to-face communication in physical and public space. Since this virtual space has the capacity to join and yet simultaneously separate individual viewers, it produces what Jean-Paul Sartre referred to as "serial unification." Television's unifying policy, he criticized, "is negative and consequently serial. Saying what pleases everybody. But nothing pleases everybody. So you have to say nothing. On this basis, there is TV thought, TV behavior, etc., which belong to the practioinert. It is simultaneously other-directed and senseless discourse."[141] And some critics of the Internet feel the same: "Subscribers who dial up America Online find themselves in the most familiar of settings, navigating with a computer interface that is meant to look like a mall. But to some, that sense of Anytown, U.S.A., a faceless environment that reflects mass tastes, is exactly what is wrong with cyberspace."[142]

This paper was originally written for a conference entitled "Inherited Ideologies: A Re-Examination," held at the University of Pennsylvania Graduate School of Fine Arts and Annenberg Public Policy Center, 31 March–1 April 1995.

1   Rosalyn Deutsche, "*Chinatown*, Part Four? What Jake Forgets about Downtown," *Assemblage* 20 (April 1993): 32–33. Deutsche's article refers to Mike Davis's article "*Chinatown*, Part Two? The Internationalization of Downtown Los Angeles," *New Left Review* (July/August 1987): 65–86; and to Derek Gregory's article "*Chinatown*, Part Three: Soja and the Missing Spaces of Social Theory," *Strategies* 3 (1990): 40–104. But she is also indirectly commenting on the following works: Mike Davis, *The City of Quartz* (London and New York: Verso Press, 1990); Edward W. Soja, *Postmodern Geographies: The Reassertion of Space in Critical Social Theory* (New York: Verso Press, 1989); and David Harvey, *The Condition of Postmodernity* (London: Basil Blackwell, 1989).

2   Rosalyn Deutsche, "Men in Space," *Strategies* 3 (1990): 130–137; and Rosalyn Deutsche, "Boys Town," *Society and Space* 9 (1991): 5–30.

3   Sue Best, "Deconstructing Space: Anne Graham's *Installation for Walla Mulla Park* and Jeff Gibson's *Screwballs*," *Transition Issue* 42 (1993): 27–41, 66–67.

4   Deutsche, "*Chinatown*, Part Four?" 33.

5   As Joan Copjec argues, there must be a gap, a "distance between the evidence and that which the evidence establishes," that remains not visible in the evidence: the final clue that would close or solve the mystery is absent. The detective extracts this clue—always at the scene of the crime yet undetectable or invisible before his arrival—which allows him to solve the mystery. The missing clue is the woman, which makes sexual relations impossible. Joan Copjec, "The Phenomenal Nonphenomenal: Private Space in Film Noir," in *Shades of Noir*, ed. Joan Copjec (New York: Verso Press, 1993), 177–179.

6   Best, "Deconstructing Space," 36. In addition to naming Harvey and Soja as responsible for this theory, Sue Best also mentions Fredric Jameson, Michel de Certeau, Dick Hebridge, and Henri Lefebvre.

7   Plato, *Timaeus and Critias*, trans. Desmond Lee (Harmondsworth: Penguin, 1965), 69; quoted in Best, "Deconstructing Space," 29.

8   Best, "Deconstructing Space," 35.

9   In *The Production of Space* Henri Lefebvre makes these masculine encryptors accountable for the manner in which they brutally and aggressively mistreat space as a feminized body. He writes, "In abstract space, where an anaphorization occurs that transforms the body by transporting it outside itself

and into the ideal-visual realm, we also encounter a strange substitution concerning sex....The space where this substitution occurs, where nature is replaced by cold abstraction and by the absence of pleasure, is the mental space of castration...[and] the space of a metaphorization whereby the image of woman supplants the woman herself, whereby the body is fragmented, desire shattered, and life explodes into a thousand pieces. Over abstract space reigns phallic solitude and the self-destruction of desire. The representation of sex thus takes the place of sex itself, while the apologetic term 'sexuality' serves to cover up this mechanism of devaluation....Confined by the abstraction of space broken down into specialized locations, the body itself is pulverized. The body as represented by images of advertising...serves to fragment desire and doom it to anxious frustration, to the non-satisfaction of local needs. In abstract space, and wherever its influence is felt, the demise of the body has a dual character, for it is at once symbolic and concrete: concrete as a result of the aggression to which the body is subject; symbolic on account of the fragmentation of the body's living unity. This is especially true of the female body, as transformed into exchange value, into a sign of the commodity and indeed into a commodity *per se*." Henri Lefebvre, *The Production of Space*, trans. Donald Nichcolson-Smith (London: Basil Blackwell, 1991), 309–310.

10   Davis, "*Chinatown*, Part Two?"

11   Quoted in Davis, "*Chinatown*, Part Two?" 68.

12   Ernst Bloch, *The Utopian Function of Art and Literature* (Cambridge: MIT Press, 1988), 261.

13   Laura Mulvey, "The Oedipus Myth: Beyond the Riddle of the Sphinx," *Public* 2 (1989): 19–43; and Jon Thompson, *Fiction, Crime and Empire* (Urbana and Carthage: University of Illinois Press, 1993), 45–57.

14   Lawrence Rothfield, *Vital Signs: Medical Realism in Nineteenth-Century Fiction* (Princeton: Princeton University Press, 1992), 130–147.

15   Quoted in Thompson, *Fiction, Crime and Empire*, 66.

16   Quoted in Rothfield, *Vital Signs*, 142–143.

17   Michel Foucault, *The History of Sexuality*, trans. Robert Hurley (New York: Pantheon Books, 1978), 1: 45.

18   Rothfield, *Vital Signs*, 144.

19   Copjec, "The Phenomenal Nonphenomenal," 169–170.

20   Ian Hacking, "How Should We Do the History of Statistics?" in *The Foucault Effect*, ed. Graham Burchell, Colin Gordon, and Peter Miller (Chicago: Chicago University Press, 1991), 181–196.

21   Ronald. R. Thomas, "The Policing of Dreams: Nineteenth-Century Detection," *Dreams of Authority* (Ithaca: Cornell University Press, 1990), 193–253.

22   Thompson, *Fiction, Crime and Empire*, 8.

23   Christine Buci-Glucksman, "Catastrophic Utopia: The Feminine as Allegory of the Modern," in *The Making of the Modern Body*, ed. Catherine Gallagher and Thomas Laqueur (Berkeley: University of California Press, 1987), 221.

24   Ibid., 227.

25   Walter Benjamin, "Central Park," *New German Critique* 34 (Winter 1985): 43, 54; and Buci-Glucksman, "Catastrophic Utopia," 220.

26   Buci-Glucksman, "Catastrophic Utopia," 224–225.

27   Walter Benjamin, quoted in Buci-Glucksman, "Catastrophic Utopia," 222.

28   Alan Corbain, "Commercial Sexuality in Nineteenth-Century France: A System of Images and Regulations," in *The Making of the Modern Body*, ed. Catherine Gallagher and Thomas Laqueur (Berkeley: University of California Press, 1987), 210–212. Benjamin also wrote of the link between death and the feminine body: "The cherished process within baroque poetry that offers a detailed description of the beauties of the feminine body is exalted through the use of metaphor, and this in turn is secretly attached to the image of the corpse. This dismemberment of feminine beauty into its glorious parts resembles a dissection; the comparisons so frequent between the parts of the body and alabaster, snow, previous stones, or other materials most often anorganic only reinforce this sentiment." Walter Benjamin, *Paris capitale du XIXe siècle* (Paris: Les Editions du Cerf, 1993), 105.

29   Margaret Cohen, *Profane Illumination: Walter Benjamin and the Paris of Surrealist Revolution* (Berkeley: University of California Press, 1993), 135.

30   Ibid., 214. Benjamin believed that Breton "…can boast an extraordinary discovery. He was the first to perceive the revolutionary energies that appear in the 'outmoded,' in the first iron constructions, the first factory buildings, the earliest photos, the objects that have begun to be extinct, grand pianos, the dresses of five years ago, fashionable restaurants when the vogue has begun to ebb from them. The relation of these things to revolution—no one can have a more exact concept of it than these authors. No one before these visionaries and augurs perceived how destitution—not only social but architectonic, the poverty of interiors, enslaved and enslaving objects—can suddenly turn over into revolutionary nihilism." Walter Benjamin, "Surrealism," in *Reflections*, trans. Edmund Jephcott (New York: Schocken Books, 1978), 181–182.

31   Quoted in Cohen, *Profane Illumination*, 201.

32   Quoted in Edward Dimendberg, "Film Noir and Urban Space" (Ph.D. diss., University of California, Santa Cruz, 1992), 138.

33   Rainer Rochlitz, *Le désenchantement de l'art* (Paris: Gallimard, 1992), 151–155.

34   Paul Kerr, "Out of What Past? Notes on the B Film Noir," *Screen Education* 32–33 (Autumn/Winter 1979–1980); as discussed in Edward Dimendberg, "Film Noir and Urban Space," 12.

35   Ibid.

36   Thompson, *Fiction, Crime and Empire*, 36–37, 137–141.

37   Dimendberg, "Film Noir and Urban Space," 12.

38   Ibid., 253.

39   Gilles Deleuze, *Cinema! The Movement Image*, trans. Hugh Tomlinson and Barbara Habberjam (Minneapolis: University of Minnesota Press, 1986), 109; quoted in Dimendberg, "Film Noir and Urban Space," 260–261.

40   Kevin Lynch, *The Image of the City* (Cambridge: MIT Press, 1960).

41   Quoted in Dimendberg, "Film Noir and Urban Space," 57.

42   Dana Polan, *Power and Paranoia* (New York: Columbia University Press, 1986), 259.

43   Quoted in Dimendberg, "Film Noir and Urban Space," 78.

44   Ibid., 80.

45   Credit is due to Jonathan Bell for pointing out this ambivalence.

46   Dimendberg, "Film Noir and Urban Space," 64.

47   Ibid., 111–113.

48   Quoted in Dimendberg, "Film Noir and Urban Space," 112.

49   For the utopian view of Bloch's montage see Maud Levin, *Cut with a Kitchen Knife* (New Haven: Yale University Press, 1993), 29–30, 74–75.

50   Dean MacCannell, "Democracy's Turn: On Homeless Noir," in *Shades of Noir*, ed. Joan Copjec (New York: Verso Press, 1993), 279–297.

51   Ibid., 283.

52   Ibid.

53   John Hartigan, Jr., "Picturing the Underclass: Myth-Making in the Inner City," *Global City Review* 3 (Spring 1994): 9–29.

54   Enda Duffy, *The Subaltern Ulysses* (London and Minneapolis: University of Minnesota Press, 1994), 135.

55   Polan, *Power and Paranoia*, 45–99.

56   Ibid., 104–108.

57   Peter Galison, "The Ontology of the Enemy: Norbert Wiener and the Cybernetic Vision," *Critical Inquiry* 21, no. 1 (Autumn 1994): 228–266.

58   Ibid., 230–233.

59   Norbert Wiener, *Cybernetics* (1948; reprint, Cambridge: MIT Press, 1961), 161.

60   Ibid., 26–27.

61   Polan, *Power and Paranoia*, 174.

62   William Marling, "On the Relation between American Roman Noir and Film Noir," *Film Quarterly* 21, no. 3 (1993): 188–189.

63   Polan, *Power and Paranoia*, 261.

64   Ibid., 288.

65   Paul Coates, *The Gorgon's Gaze* (Cambridge: Cambridge University Press, 1991), 173–176.

66   On *The Big Sleep* see Ronald R. Thomas, "The Dream of the Empty Camera: Image, Evidence, and Authentic American Style in *American Photographs* and *Farewell, My Lovely*," *Criticism* 31, no. 3 (Summer 1994): 428, 433.

67   Marling, "On the Relation between American Roman Noir and Film Noir," 181, 191.

68   Joseph Hudnut, "The Invisible City," *Journal of the American Institute of Planners* 15 (Spring 1949): unpaginated.

69   MacCannell, "Democracy's Turn: On Homeless Noir," 279–287.

70   Gilles Deleuze, "Postscript on the Societies of Control," *October* 59 (1992): 3–7.

71   Copjec, "The Phenomenal Nonphenomenal."

72   John Belton, "Language, Oedipus, and *Chinatown*," *Modern Language Notes* 106 (1991): 933–950.

73   Ibid.

74   Ibid., 937.

75   Ibid., 944–945.

76   Ibid., 949.

77   As Los Angeles is represented by the neo-*noir* film *Chinatown*, today Paris has its literature of the *banlieue*. Its narrations are set in these new "cities," working class residential wastelands on the periphery of downtown Paris. The buildings in these areas were constructed in the 1960s and are a conglomeration of bad cement, cheap materials, bare open spaces, rusting metal railings, and walls covered with graffiti; their general appearance makes everything seem simultaneously unfinished and decrepit. These places are haunted by the remnants of humanity that the city center has either destroyed or rejected. This *banlieue* literature of the 1980s is based on the American *roman noir* and the B-grade *film noir* cycle, and just as the latter do for our society, it enables French writers to present the only sustained cultural critique of what has gone wrong in their society, assuaging their guilt and describing their regrets. The *banlieues*, where most of France's immigrant workers are assigned by the government to reside and thus where families have been squeezed into meager quarters, are the sites of recent uprisings and killings, and most of them have devolved into squalid slums. Like the neo-*noir* narrations it copies, this *banlieue* literature mediates on the poverty of experience and emptiness of feeling that arise out of these shameful sites of decaying materials and anonymous and indeterminate lives. In *Decor: Cement*, François Bon writes, "At the edges of the cities, men are interchangeable, on every landing the doors are identical, so you give in to it, because that's what chose you, that's what you were allotted, but you know very well that it could have been somebody else." Quoted in Marguerite Feitlowitz, "Le Banlieue: Life on the Edge," *Global City Review* 3 (Spring 1994): 117–133; the quotation is on page 121.

78   M. Christine Boyer, *The City of Collective Memory* (Cambridge: MIT Press, 1994).

79   Paul Virilio, *The Vision Machine*, trans. Julie Rose (Bloomington: Indiana University Press, 1994).

80   This argument relates to the classical art of memory, discussed on page 115.

81   Virilio, *The Vision Machine*, 13.

82   Ibid., 6–7.

83   Max Picard, *Hitler in Our Selves*, trans. Heinrich Hauser (Hinsdale, Illinois: Henry Regnery, 1947), 55–56; quoted in Dimendberg, "Film Noir and Urban Space," 295–296.

84   Lynne Kirby, "Death and the Photographic Body," in *Fugitive Images From Photography to Video*, ed. Patrice Petro (Bloomington: Indiana University Press, 1995), 73.

85   Ibid., 74.

86   William Chaloupka, *Knowing Nukes: The Politics and Culture of the Atom* (Minneapolis: University of Minnesota Press, 1992), 27.

87   Peter Schwenger, *Letter Bomb* (Baltimore: Johns Hopkins University Press, 1992), 25–26.

88   Richard Dienst, *Still Life in Real Time* (Durham and London: Duke University Press, 1984), 129.

89   Ibid., 130.

90   Bernd Huppauf, "Experiences of Modern Warfare and the Crisis of Representation," *New German Critique* 59 (Spring/Summer 1993): 41–76.

91   Ibid., 7.

92   Ibid., 57.

93   Ibid., 59.

94   Duffy, *The Subaltern Ulysses*, 137–148; the quotation is on page 138.

95   Anton Kaes, "The Cold Gaze: Notes on Mobilization and Modernity," *New German Critique* 59 (Spring/Summer 1993): 106.

96   Quoted in Kaes, "The Cold Gaze," 107.

97   Ibid.

98   Kaes, "The Cold Gaze," 107–108.

99   Paul Fussell, *The Great War and Modern Memory* (London and New York: Oxford University Press, Inc., 1975), 327.

100 In this confusion of experiences, the reality of the city became an illusion. As Betrand Russell recalled in the early months of war, "After seeing troop trains departing from Waterloo, I used to have strange visions of London as a place of unreality. I used in imagination to see the bridges collapse and sink, and the whole great city vanish like a morning mist. Its inhabitants began to seem like hallucinations." Quoted in Fussell, *The Great War and Modern Memory*, 326.

101   Virilio, *The Vision Machine*, 29.

102   Rudolph Arnheim, *Visual Thinking* (Berkeley: University of California Press, 1969), 142–143; quoted in Gerald Douglas Silk, "The Image and the Automobile in Modern Art" (Ph.D. diss., University of Virginia, 1976), 173.

103   Dean MacCannell, *Empty Meeting Grounds: The Tourist Papers* (London and New York: Routledge, 1992), 183–229.

104   F. T. Marinetti, "The New Religion-Morality of Speed," in *Let's Murder the Moonshine: Selected Writings* (Los Angeles: Sun and Moon Classics, 1972), 104.

105   Quoted in Silk, "The Image and the Automobile in Modern Art," 18.

106   Quoted in The Museum of Contemporary Art, *Automobile and Culture* (New York: Harry N. Abrams, Inc., 1981), 62.

107   Quoted in Silk, "The Image and the Automobile in Modern Art," 170.

108   Silk, "The Image and the Automobile in Modern Art," 196–197.

109   Quoted in Silk, "The Image and the Automobile in Modern Art," 205.

110   Virilio, *The Vision Machine*, 36, 42.

111   Ibid., 65–66.

112   Dienst, *Still Life in Real Time*, 161.

113   Ibid.

114   Ibid., 162–163.

115   Trip Gabriel, "Virtual Downtown," *New York Times*, 22 January 1995.

116   All quotations are in Richard Rayner, "Wanted: A Kinder, Gentler Cop," *New York Times Magazine* (22 January 1995). 26–28.

117   "The situation is initially established by the playing of an actual, recorded, 911 tape summoning the police to action. The first image to appear is typically that of a moving squad car with the city of location printed in text at the bottom of the screen. The film is cut, moving the eye of the camera to the back seat of the car while the 911 tape plays uninterrupted. The textual indicator at the bottom of the screen changes to indicate the time of the event and the nature of the crime as the recording of the distress call gives way to the signal of the police radio....The police arrive on the scene after the event has occurred, thus relying on the testimony of eyewitnesses to make a proper arrest. Though the real event is never captured by the camera, its authenticity is established by the assemblage of the victim's distress call, eyewitness

testimony, and police speculation…" Kimberly A. Starr, "Cops: True Tales of Crime in the Spectacle City" (paper written for Princeton University, 1994), 3.

118   Michel Foucault, "Film and Popular Memory," in *Foucault Live (Interviews 1966–84)*, ed. Sylvère Lopringer, trans. John Johnston (New York: Semiotext(e), 1989), 92.

119   From an interview, quoted in Kathleen Biddick, "Humanist History and the Haunting of Virtual Worlds: Problems of Memory and Rememoration," *Genders* 18 (1993): 48.

120   William Gibson, *Neuromancer* (New York: Ace Books, 1984), 73–74.

121   Biddick, "Humanist History," 48.

122   Michael Taussig, *Shamanism, Colonialism, and the Wild Man: A Study in Terror and Healing* (Chicago: University of Chicago Press, 1987), 4–5; the quotation is on page 4.

123   Kathleen Biddick, "Imperial Machines/Jubilee Machines: The Empire of Memory in the Sciences and Humanities," *Stanford Humanities Review Supplement* 4, no. 1 (Spring 1994): 35–38.

124   Thomas Richards, *The Imperial Archive: Knowledge and the Fantasy of Empire* (New York: Verso Press, 1993).

125   Herbert A. Simon, "Literary Criticism: A Cognitive Approach," *Stanford Humanities Review Supplement* 4, no. 1 (Spring 1994): 5.

126   Walter Benjamin, "Surrealism," in *Reflections*, trans. Edmund Jephcott (New York: Shocken Books, 1978), 179; quoted in Cohen, *Profane Illumination*, 187.

127   Walter Benjamin, "Thirteen Theses against Snobs," in *One Way Street*, trans. Edmund Jephcott and Kingsley Shorter (London: New Left Books, 1979), 65–67.

128   Simon, "Literary Criticism: A Cognitive Approach," 8.

129   Sally Pryor, "Thinking of Oneself as a Computer," *Leonardo* 24, no. 5 (1991): 585; and Stelarc, "Prosthetics, Robotics Remake Existence, *Leonardo* 24, no. 5 (1991): 591.

130   Stelarc, "Prosthetics, Robotics Remake Existence," 591.

131   Ibid., 591–595.

132   Ibid., 593.

133   Linda M. Harasim, "Global Networks: An Introduction," in *Global Networks: Computers and International Communication*, ed. Linda M. Harasim (Cambridge: MIT Press, 1993), 17.

134   Peter H. Lewis, "Getting Down to Business," *New York Times*, 19 June 1994.

135   Ashley Dunn, "Information Freeway?" *New York Times*, 4 August 1994.

136   Mark C. Taylor and Esa Saarinen, *Imagologies* (New York: Routledge, 1994), unpaginated.

137   Peter H. Lewis, "U.S. Begins Privatizing Internet's Operations," *New York Times*, 24 October 1994.

138   Steve Lohr, "Data Highway Ignoring the Poor, Study Charges," *New York Times*, 14 May 1994.

139   B. Bagdikian, "The Lords of the Global Village," *The Nation* (12 June 1989): 805; quoted in Howard Frederick, "Computer Networks and the Emergence of Global Civil Society," in *Global Networks: Computers and International Communication*, ed. Linda M. Harasim (Cambridge: MIT Press, 1993), 286.

140   Nicholas Garnhma, "The Media and the Public Sphere," in *Habermas and the Public Sphere*, ed. Craig Clahous (Cambridge: MIT Press, 1992), 359–376.

141   Jean-Paul Sartre, *Critique of Dialectical Reason*, trans. Quintin Hoare (London: Verso Press, 1991), 2: 438; quoted in Dienst, *Still Life in Real Time*, 9.

142   Gabriel, "Virtual Downtown."

CONCLUSION

T his series of essays began with an analysis of what the conflation of electronic communication technologies and the space of the city might mean. It has questioned why images of the city have been constantly evoked to represent the network of data exchange and information that has been defined as cyberspace. It has also explored how telecommunications affect visual perception, how we become engaged with the space and time of the city, and how we position ourselves as physical bodies in relation to the self-contained, simulated worlds that new electronic technologies engender. Is there a way for us to define ourselves and the space in which we dwell when the city is increasingly referenced as a space of disappearance, a space of the future but not of the present, a space of anxiety and loss?

Cyberspace is a new electronic, invisible space that allows the computer or television screen to substitute for urban space and urban experience. That our perception of space has become increasingly dependent on the simulated zone—a predigested, encoded digital box of algorithms—is evident in the manner in which the physical form of the city is displayed, in the mode in which information is formatted, and in the patterns in which televisual episodes are serially portrayed. In the disappearing city that has been fragmented into pieces, gaps, and holes and where reality is no longer used as a referent, space and time take on multiple profiles, nonlinear relations, and recursive linkages. There is an instantaneous dispersion and regrouping of fragmented bits of information and images, as telecommunications enable these to be projected and rearranged under new laws of transmission. Time shifts away from the linearity of past-present-future, becoming either a static, frozen moment that breaks time down into discrete instances, or an automatic, continuous flow, similar to a video monitor with its screen switched on and waiting for an event to happen.[1]

This book has also been an attempt to understand that cyberspace, developed and extended to facilitate the flexible flow of capital since World War II, excludes or conceals many black holes of disappearance, sites of abandonment, and positions of loss. This restrictive space contained within the invisible and immaterial electronic matrix of information flows is inherently aggressive, inevitably producing violence as an aftereffect. This can be seen in our postmodern society in the images that capture the moment of destruction (for example, the city being disfigured, buildings being blown up, or people being maimed or killed), in the weapons of violence (aerial reconnaissance photographs, or the three-dimensional simulation of enemy air space found in virtual cockpits), and in the representations of violence in film (*Blade Runner*'s dystopian images of post-nuclear-holocaust Los Angeles, or *Chinatown*'s crimes perpetrated against the daughter and the city).[2]

Increasingly in CyberCities, we fail to distinguish between experience and a reality that has been manipulated by media images; in fact, images become substitutes for direct experience. We see emerging a recursive structure divided between real time and deferred or replayed time. To use a dramatic example, in the war in Sarajevo cameras were set up at dangerous crossroads, waiting for events to happen, waiting for someone to be killed or mutilated. One reporter said, "Because the spot is treacherous, the chances are good that a few hours of patience by a cameraman will be rewarded with compelling images of a life being extinguished or incapacitated."[3] Thus the wounded in their hospital beds can watch video replays of the very moment when they were shot. They may retain painful personal memories of the incident, but when faced with constant viewings of it, their actual experience becomes increasingly disembodied, and they become outside observers of their own history.

There are similar sites in any postmodern city where places and history are being erased, where life is being sucked out and suspended in the spectacles of disappearance called "postmodern wars"—directionless, inconclusive wars in which people die "live" on television, in which the violence is directed equally towards armies and civilians, and in which the endless destruction of the city is recycled nightly on television screens across the globe. The catastrophe is that this keeps continuing; the camera and the spectators are caught in a double bind of repulsion and attraction, waiting patiently for something exciting to happen.

Let me end with an image from William Gibson, who opened his book *Neuromancer* as follows: "The sky above the port was the color of television, tuned to a dead channel."[4] Since an image always announces the death of what it represents—being a prolonged postmortem on what will inevitably depart or disappear—there is a haunting estrangement between the image and reality.[5] Do these allegories of the disappearing or invisible city represent the final and irreversible erasure of the spatial containers that once stored our icons and images, the dematerialization of the wax into which our memories were once impressed? Are cities, symbolically bombed into nothingness, the sacrificial sites of cyberspace? Or are these fears yet another fiction in what has been called our terminal identity?[6]

1   Richard Dienst, *Still Life in Real Time* (Durham and London: Duke University Press, 1984), 161.

2   W. J. T. Mitchell, *Picture Theory* (Chicago: The University of Chicago Press, 1994), 381–382.

3   Roger Cohen, "In Sarajevo, Victims of a 'Postmodern' War," *New York Times*, 21 May 1995.

4   William Gibson, *Neuromancer* (New York: Ace Books, 1984), 3.

5   Eduardo Cadava, "Words of Light: Theses on the Photography of History," in *Fugitive Images from Photography to Video*, ed. Patrice Petro (Bloomington: Indiana University Press, 1995), 223–224.

6   Scott Bukatman, *Terminal Identity: The Virtual Subject in Postmodern Science Fiction* (Durham and London: Duke University Press, 1993).

ILLUSTRATIONS

13   The human mind works by association. So why don't computers? © Apple Computer, Inc. Used with permission. All rights reserved. Apple® and the Apple logo are registered trademarks of Apple Computer, Inc.

45   Paul Citroen, *Metropolis*, 1923
     30" x 23", collage, Prentenkabinet Rijksuniversiteit te Leiden. © 1996 Paul Citroen/Licensed by VAGA, New York, NY

73   Herbert Bayer, *Lonely Metropolitan*, 1932
     © 1996 Artists Rights Society (ARS), New York/VG Bild-Kunst, Bonn

137 Artist: Melissa Grimes
     Client: Northern Telecomm

183 Lea Grundig, *La Bombe atomique*, 1948
     © 1996 Artists Rights Society (ARS), New York/VG Bild-Kunst, Bonn